The Rise of Regionalism

During the past forty years, regions have become increasingly important in Western Europe both as units of government and as sources for political mobilization.

This book examines why regional identities are stronger in some regions than in others, and why regional elites attempt to mobilize the public on a regionalist agenda at certain points in time. The author develops a model that explains change across space as well as time and provides a comprehensive discussion of the causes of regionalism. It focuses on endogenous developments in the regions and on change across time in the economic and political landscapes of the regions. Using a quantitative study of 212 Western European regions, which examines whether regionalism is related to cultural, economic and political characteristics of the regions, the book builds a model of the causes of regionalism. The issues are further explored through case studies on Scotland (UK) and Rogaland (Norway).

This book will be of interest to students and scholars of political and social sciences, especially those with an interest in regions, regionalism and regional nationalism, Scottish politics, Norwegian politics, territorial identities and territorial politics.

Rune Dahl Fitjar is Senior Research Scientist at the International Research Institute of Stavanger, Norway.

Routledge research in comparative politics

The Rise of Regionalism
Causes of regional mobilization in Western Europe

Rune Dahl Fitjar

Routledge
Taylor & Francis Group

LONDON AND NEW YORK

First published 2010
by Routledge
2 Park Square, Milton Park, Abingdon, Oxon OX14 4RN

Simultaneously published in the USA and Canada
by Routledge
270 Madison Ave, New York, NY 10016

Routledge is an imprint of the Taylor & Francis Group, an informa business

© 2010 Rune Dahl Fitjar

Typeset in Times by Wearset Ltd, Boldon, Tyne and Wear
Printed and bound in Great Britain by TJI Digital, Padstow, Cornwall

British Library Cataloguing in Publication Data
A catalogue record for this book is available from the British Library

Library of Congress Cataloging-in-Publication Data
A catalog record for this book has been requested

ISBN10: 0-415-49475-3 (hbk)
ISBN10: 0-203-87083-2 (ebk)

ISBN13: 978-0-415-49475-5 (hbk)
ISBN13: 978-0-203-87083-9 (ebk)

For Sebastian, Benedicte Aurora and Camilla

Contents

Illustrations

Figures

Tables

Preface

Arriving in London in 2002 for postgraduate studies in political science at the London School of Economics, I did not expect to be writing a thesis partly based on political developments in the region that I call home – Rogaland. At the time, Uruguayan democratization, Senegalese state-building and similarly exotic topics were more likely subjects for my PhD. However, driving from Stavanger to Oslo during a spring visit back home, my wife and I were discussing regional infrastructure and road tolls, and the conversation moved on to the topic of regions and regionalism in the Norwegian context. Realizing that this would make for a promising research topic, I wrote an MSc dissertation on the development of regionalism in Rogaland.

My theoretical perspectives were greatly influenced by the inspirational training that I had as an undergraduate at the Department of Comparative Politics at the University of Bergen, where I came to know the ideas of that great Norwegian political scientist Stein Rokkan. His work on the centre–periphery dimension in the Norwegian as well as the broader Western European context has strongly informed my understanding of states, regions and the relationship between them.

Developing this into a research proposal for a PhD at the LSE, I sought to generalize some of the findings into a broader theory that could capture the causes of variation across both time and space in Western European regionalism. In this process, I was encouraged by the approachable Erik Ringmar, who convened the MSc in Comparative Politics at the time. Both the theoretical perspectives and the empirical focus have since moved well beyond the borders of Rogaland, even if a case study of that region still forms one of the main sections of this book. However, some of the ideas that I had while studying Rogaland – the need to study regionalism in non-autonomist regions, the impact of economic growth, the focus on variation across time – have still informed my approach to regionalism and the design of this study.

When it comes to writing the thesis itself, it would certainly not have been possible to complete the project without the help of several people who have guided me along the way. Most importantly, my PhD supervisor at the LSE, Eiko Thielemann, helped me see both the bigger picture and the crucial details, keeping me on track throughout the research. His swift, thorough and useful feedback always led to improvements in my work. Michael Bruter was the project adviser, contributing his considerable methodological expertise to the design of the research. The PhD examiners, Jonathan Hopkin and Pieter van Houten, provided further input on improving the project and preparing it for publication.

Several other skilful researchers at the LSE have contributed constructive feedback from a wide variety of perspectives and assistance at various stages of the research, including David Soskice, Gwen Sasse, Abby Innes, Simon Glendinning, Rodney Barker, Sebastian Balfour, Willem Buiter, Robert Leonardi and Bill Kissane. Jouni Kuha at the Methodology Institute was a great help in designing the cross-sectional part of the research, offering clear and sensible answers to all my questions. The excellent research student community at the LSE Government Department was another great asset. Thanks in particular to the participants of the workshops in European Politics and Comparative Politics. Although I could not possibly mention all the colleagues who offered useful advice during the project, two of my fellow students were particularly essential in helping me along the way, offering both friendship and academic support. Chiara Jasson made me believe in my own abilities and the fruitfulness of the project, listening loyally to any problems I had along the way and helping me find good solutions to them. Achim Göerres was helpful in pointing out both problems and solutions in the research, teaching me a fair bit about quantitative research methods in the process. Both have also commented on several of the chapters through various stages of revisions.

While finalizing the manuscript and transforming a PhD thesis into a monograph, I have worked at the International Research Institute of Stavanger. I am grateful to several colleagues for their help in this process, as well as to the institute for providing me with the necessary resources. Kari Aarsheim, Christin Berg, Arild Farsund, Einar Leknes, Hilmar Rommetvedt and Ragnhild Wiik have all contributed their time and experience to the project. At Routledge, Lucy Dunne and Heidi Bagtazo have been a helpful editorial team.

Scientific conferences have provided access to a wider network of researchers. Thanks to participants at panels and workshops in Linköping, Bergen, Belfast, Edinburgh, Chicago, Tromsø and Stavanger, as well as at the ECPR summer school on Regions in Europe at the European University Institute, Florence. Elin Allern, Linda Berg, Andrew Davis, Howard Elcock, Anne Lise Fimreite, Ailsa Henderson, Tor Georg Jacobsen, Michael Keating, Nadia Khatib, Niels Lange, Nicola McEwen, Jörg Mathias, Gunnar Nerheim, Josefina Süssner, Per Selle, Colin Williams and many others have offered useful insights during these sessions. Parts of this book have previously been published in *Regional and Federal Studies* (2005, 15:1, 59–73) – published by Taylor & Francis Journals: www.informaworld.com; and *Scandinavian Political Studies* (2006, 29:4, 333–55) – published by Wiley Blackwell Publishers. The reviewers and editors at both journals have been highly useful in improving both my articles and the entire project.

Last, but not least, a special thank-you to my family. The support that my parents, Lillian Dahl Fitjar and Roar Fitjar, have provided in backing me all the way have been essential in making it possible for me to attempt such a big project, and they have also had the patience to read and comment on a lot of the papers that I have written. My wife, Camilla, and my son, Sebastian, kept me going throughout this project, keeping my spirits up every day for the four and a half years that we spent in London. Camilla has also helped design the charts and graphs, as well as offering feedback on my work. During the final stages of the projects, the birth of Benedicte Aurora was also a motivation to finish. All three have given me love and security, as well as inspiration and morale. This is for them.

Abbreviations

Ap	Arbeiderpartiet (Labour Party, Norway)
bn	billion
CDU	Christlich Demokratische Union Deutschlands (Christian Democratic Union of Germany)
CSU	Christlich-Soziale Union in Bayern (Christian Social Union of Bavaria)
EC	European Community
EEA	European Economic Agreement/European Economic Area
EU	European Union
FDI	foreign direct investment
FDP	Freie Demokratische Partei (Free Democratic Party, Germany)
FrP	Fremskrittspartiet (Progress Party, Norway)
GATT	General Agreement on Tariffs and Trade
GDP	gross domestic product
GDPR	gross domestic product per region
KrF	Kristelig Folkeparti (Christian People's Party, Norway)
MAR	Minorities at Risk
MP	Member of Parliament
NRK	Norsk Rikskringkasting (Norwegian Broadcasting Corporation)
NUTS	*Nomenclature des Unités Territoriales Statistiques*
pc	per capita
PDS	Partei des Demokratischen Sozialismus (Party of Democratic Socialism, Germany)
PNV	Partido Nacionalista Vasco (Basque Nationalist Party)
PP	Partido Popular (People's Party, Spain)
PPP	purchasing power parity
PSD	Suomen Sosialidemokraattinen Puolue (Finnish Social Democratic Party)
PSOE	Partido Socialista Obrero Español (Spanish Socialist Workers' Party)
SDA	Scottish Development Agency
SE	standard error
SNP	Scottish National Party

Sp	Senterpartiet (Centre Party, Norway)
SPD	Sozialdemokratische Partei Deutschlands (Social Democratic Party of Germany)
SV	Sosialistisk Venstreparti (Socialist Left Party, Norway)
VAT	value added tax
WLS	weighted least squares
WTO	World Trade Organization

1 Regions and regionalism

The twentieth century saw the victory of the nation-state over all other forms of political organization. Empires and city-states have almost receded into history. Today, the principle of national sovereignty serves as the fundamental guide of international relations. The ideology of nationalism has reached all parts of the globe, and it is seen as natural that the world should be divided into nation-states, with each nation controlling its own state – however impossible that ideal might be to achieve. This is an 'age of nationalism' (Gellner 1983). However, over the past forty years there have also been signs that this world order might be changing. While states are still the most important actors on the world stage, the pressures of globalization and international trade have reduced their capacities to control their environments. In Europe, the European Union has gradually extended its own authority, taking over many of the competencies that were traditionally the responsibilities of its member states.

As the political authority of states has been gradually dispersed to international organs, their internal homogeneity has also come under pressure. Subnational actors, such as regions, have begun to assert themselves on the international stage, with potentially severe ramifications for the economic and cultural coherence of the state. Growing spatial inequalities within states based on the success of some regions in attracting capital in the global market put pressures on national solidarity and give regions an incentive to mobilize in protection of their own interests (Bullmann 1997: 9). The effect of these historical developments has been to disperse political authority between the various layers of government to an extent not seen in Europe in the past seven centuries (Marks 1997: 20).

As a result of these developments, political scientists have become increasingly preoccupied over the past twenty years with the topics of regions and regionalism. Whereas political science, and especially the comparative politics sub-discipline, used to focus mainly on states and nations, there is today a considerable body of literature on regions, cities and other sub-state levels of government. Much of this literature concerns regionalization within the context of the European Union (EU), focusing on new institutional phenomena such as regional information offices, the Committee of the Regions, multilevel governance and the 'Europe of the regions' agenda. It is the developments towards regionalization and its consequences for nation-states and for the EU that have been at the centre of interest, while inquiries into the causes of regionalism have received comparatively less attention.

However, there is significant variation in the mobilization of regions across different parts of the continent. Regions have long held substantial autonomy in federal countries such as Germany and Austria, and the German regions have consequently also acquired a substantial role within the political system of the EU. In Belgium, Spain and parts of the United Kingdom, they have become increasingly important, gaining authority over a wide range of policy areas. However, large parts of Western Europe have held on to unitary state structures, including the Scandinavian countries, the Netherlands, Ireland, Portugal and Greece, or have regionalized power only to a limited extent, such as France. Even within states, there are substantial differences in the degree to which the populations of different regions identify with their regions, and hence in the extent to which they mobilize on a regional basis. What causes such differences between regions in their capacity to mobilize local populations? Equally, if regionalism has been growing in many parts of Europe over the past few decades, what causes the levels of regionalism to vary across time within individual regions? These are the main questions addressed in this book.

Regions and regionalism

Regionalism is a notoriously imprecise term that has been used to describe everything from decentralization of political power via economic restructuring to the mobilization of sub-national identities. Even the term 'region' itself poses frequent problems for researchers, with a wide range of definitions in use. Ahead of any meaningful discussion of the causes of regionalism, it is necessary to clarify what is meant by the terms 'region', 'regional identity' and 'regionalism' in this book.

What is a region?

There is much confusion among analysts and policymakers alike as to what constitutes a region. The definition of the term varies across state borders, and sometimes even across sectors and departments within the same state. For a student of international relations, the term refers to something else altogether. Even if one restricts oneself to sub-state regions, as in this book, the concept has at least four different meanings. One can conceive of regions as economic or cultural territories, or as units of economic planning or regional governance. The regions as defined by these concepts rarely coincide, making the matter of definition a crucial one (Loughlin 1997: 154).

Survey data illustrate the problems involved in defining a region. In a 1991 Eurobarometer survey,[1] respondents were asked what they considered to be 'their region', or the region to which they belonged. At first glance, this seems to be a natural starting-point for establishing what should be considered a region.

After all, people living in a territory should be in the best position to determine which region they live in. Just like nations, regions are imagined communities whose territories must be defined by their members (Smouts 1998; Süssner 2002). Unfortunately, there seems to be little agreement on what a region is, even among local populations. Only in fifty-eight of all the regions included in the survey did a majority of the respondents agree on any one definition of their home region. These fifty-eight regions constituted a biased subset of large regions that were concentrated in a few countries (Germany, Italy and Spain, along with a few French, Portuguese and English regions),[2] and they also exhibited stronger regional identities than the average region. Elsewhere, there was no uniformity with regard to what people identified as a region. More often than not, respondents from the same territories spread their answers evenly across a variety of units of different sizes, with a substantial proportion identifying regions smaller than the NUTS 3 level.[3] The conclusion must be that quite often people simply do not know – or at least do not agree on – what a region is.[4]

A way out of this quagmire is to focus on meso-level sub-state authorities. If one considers regionalism to be a strategy for regional political elites to augment their power vis-à-vis the central state, regional government structures must be taken as the starting-point. This is where the resources of regional political elites are to be found, and this is where their efforts at building a regional identity must begin. The two case studies covered in this book are both examples of meso-level sub-state authorities, and they are both the highest level of political unit beneath the central state in their respective countries.

Regional identity

The concept of regional identities refers to the feeling of belonging in a particular region. This is one of the many geographical and functional identities that people can use to define themselves vis-à-vis others. Political scientists have traditionally focused on national identities, and the concept of multiple identities is relatively recent in the literature. Yet people have always had more than one identity. They are men, women, young, old, working-class, students, Japanese, Europeans and Londoners. These are all objective categories, but people may identify and feel a sense of common purpose with others who share the same characteristics. Indeed, in psychology it is widely believed that people need to identify with certain sub-groups in order to establish a perception of themselves and bridge the gap between the self and the outside world (Bruter 2004: 25). Identities 'provide the feelings of self-esteem and belonging that are as essential for human survival as food in the belly' (Friedman 2000: 31).

Regional identities form part of this package, complementing other identities as well as competing with them for primacy. Yet the extent to which people identify with their region varies, and hence the levels of regional identity (i.e. the sum of regional identification among a region's inhabitants) vary across regions and time. In tune with the definition of identity, one can say that the strength of a regional identity depends on the extent to which people feel that they belong in the region and see themselves as part of a group involving all the inhabitants of the region.

In this sense, regional identity can be understood as a sense of membership of an imagined regional community. Almost all political communities are imagined, in the sense that they are not based on everyday face-to-face communication among the members. Rather, they are based on mental images in the minds of their members about the fraternity between them (Anderson, 1991: 6f.). Although Anderson discusses nations, all political communities above a certain size are imagined in this sense. Applying Anderson's terminology, a regional community is imagined in so far as people from a particular region never meet or even hear of most other people who come from that same region. It is also imagined as a community, where people feel a sense of comradeship with others from the same region, and indeed as a limited community, in so far as this regional comradeship extends only to people from the same region, and not to outsiders. However, regional communities do not necessarily imagine themselves as sovereign communities, desiring their own state. Some regional communities do desire sovereignty, whereas others form part of a wider national community that is imagined as sovereign. The desire for sovereignty is closely connected with the concept of a nation, and regional communities desiring sovereignty are indeed commonly referred to (by themselves as well as others) as stateless nations.

Imagined regional communities are created by regionalists just as imagined national communities are created by nationalists. Gellner (1983: 55) argues that nationalism 'engenders nations, and not the other way round': nationalism promotes a shared culture and a common identity among the people it defines as belonging to the nation, in effect encouraging them to imagine themselves as belonging to a national community. This is the process of nation-building. Similarly, regionalists attempt to build or strengthen the imagined regional community among inhabitants of the region through processes of region-building.

While a person's identity is essentially a subjective matter, it is unclear to what extent people can actually choose which groups to identify with. The question of choice when it comes to regional identity maps directly onto the debate between subjective and objective definitions of nationalism. Gellner (1983) distinguishes between will and culture as two conceptually distinct bases of national identity, and it seems obvious that you cannot deliberately choose your cultural background or mother tongue. If you accept will as the basis of national identity, however, you do have to make a choice as to whether or not you actually want to be part of the nation, or of the imagined community in Anderson's (1991) sense.

This is not necessarily to say that people *consciously* choose whether or not to identify with their region, or that this choice is based on rational calculations. Nor can people freely choose which region they want to identify with. For instance, a person born in Germany of German parents and who continues to live in Germany cannot easily identify himself as French. Similarly, a person who is born and bred in Bavaria does not suddenly develop a strong identification with Thuringia, unless he has some sort of connection to that region. The individual choice is restricted by a group consensus within the regional community on the criteria for membership (Henderson 2007: 54).

Regionalism

While one may identify more with some people than others, these differences do not always translate into political action. A group identity is politicized only when it affects our judgements on political issues and our decisions about how to act politically (for whom to vote, for instance). This can be used to define regionalism: it is the politicization of regional identity. Regionalists frame political issues with a basis in their regional identity, deeming the regional population to have certain common interests that they should advance as a group. This usually falls into one of two categories: promoting the economic development of the region, or preserving a cultural identity that has become threatened by cultural standardization (Rokkan and Urwin 1982: 4).

The idea that the regional population has a set of common interests leads in many cases to the conclusion that these interests could be more effectively advanced if the region were allowed more autonomy on internal matters. Regionalists therefore want to strengthen the regional layer of government by increasing the political and/or economic autonomy of the region within the national constitutional framework. They also tend to focus on the distribution of wealth and public expenditure between territories rather than between functional groups. The distribution between socio-economic groups within the region, for instance, is subordinated to the good of the region as a whole, as the various groups are considered to be cooperating for the common good.

If you may or may not be able to choose whether to have a regional identity, you do have to choose whether or not to be a regionalist. Working to promote a region entails action, and any action is the result of choice. You can, indeed you must, choose whether or not you will work to promote your region. Because it is a matter of choice, any explanation of regionalism must take into account the reasons for that choice. A cause of regionalism can be a cause only in so far as it affects the choice of whether or not to be a regionalist. It is therefore not only relevant, but completely necessary to consider the incentives for taking political action on behalf of a particular region.

Theoretical framework

Having established the definitions of the main terms, the next question is what makes regionalism and regional identities occur. Indeed, that is the main topic of this book. Several theories on why regionalism grows and declines across time, and why some regions are more regionalist than others, are presented in the next chapter. However, this section discusses the broader theoretical framework into which these theories all fit, portraying how the political mechanisms of regionalism work.

Centres and peripheries

Writing in 1377, Ibn Khaldûn (1967: 128ff.) presented an early version of the centre–periphery model. He described the *asabiyah* cycle, in which new rulers usually emerge in the peripheries of existing empires, where levels of group identity are higher than in the centre. The centre–periphery model later became one of the cornerstones of the modernization theory paradigm in the 1960s. Here, the centre was often seen as the modernizing force, bringing liberal values, democracy and capitalism to the traditional, backward societies in the periphery (Randall and Theobald 1998: 45). In the model, state-builders in the centre occupy surrounding territories and gain military control over them. These peripheries are then integrated into the administrative and economic system of the centre, as the states try to extract resources through taxation and to control trading patterns, limiting external trade and encouraging internal trade. Finally, the population in the peripheries becomes loyal to the centre through a process of cultural assimilation during the nation-building phase. This view can be found in Deutsch (1966) and in Almond and Powell (1966), for instance.

Lipset and Rokkan's (1967) ideas represent a modification of this picture, ascribing a greater role to the periphery. In their model, the centre still attempts to gain control over the periphery in the political, economic and cultural spheres through the processes of state- and nation-building. However, the peripheries try to fight this colonization by the centre and defend their own economic and cultural interests. Protests from the peripheries can focus on economic, political or cultural issues, and the structure of these protests is what shapes the cleavage structures and party systems of the states. In Lipset and Rokkan's view, the peripheries are not reactionary opponents of modernity. On the contrary, these authors see democratization and redistribution as the results of peripheral opposition to pressures from the centre. The periphery gains influence on the policy-making in the centre and a share of the spoils of economic production as a trade-off for surrendering to the political and economic dominance of the centre (Rokkan 1975: 570ff.).

In this perspective, regionalism is a natural reaction to the expansion of central authority. The peripheries react to the establishment of the state, and the dominance of its administrative and economic systems (Rokkan and Urwin 1983). The peripheries react in different ways against these efforts at colonization, and the relationships between centre and periphery are thus shaped in different ways within individual states and regions. Keating (1998: 27) sees territorial identities as being reforged during the establishment and consolidation of modern states. The patterns of territorial identity are formed by various crucial events in the history of the modern world, such as religious revival movements, local languages, literary revivals, economic developments and wars. All of these have different effects across the territories of the states, leading to internal differentiation and thus a potential for territorial mobilization (ibid.: 27).

The centre–periphery model forms a useful framework for understanding the origins of regionalism and its relations with state- and nation-building processes.

However, when it comes to growth or decline in regionalism over time, they can mainly explain why regionalism would grow during periods of fundamental expansion of the role of the state. On the other hand, changes that have occurred during shorter time periods after the end of the state-building era in Western Europe cannot be completely explained by these models. The mechanisms that make peripheries rebel against centres therefore need to be further explained, and explanations need to consider developments in the region proper as well as in the centre. The next chapter presents a number of such theories that seek to explain when and why peripheries might choose to rebel even if there is no dramatic expansion of central authority.

As an example of when fundamental changes in the role of the state have created the conditions for regionalism, the emergence of a welfare state in the late nineteenth and early twentieth centuries can provide an illustrative example. The importance of preserving distinctive local cultures and languages grew with the establishment of national education systems. Such systems tend to promote the culture of the centre, and if there are significantly different cultures in other regions, this can produce strains in the relationship between these regions and the central state. Issues of language and religion are especially crucial in this regard. The early twentieth century saw an upsurge in regionalist and nationalist movements reacting to cultural standardization. As the problem was resolved, however, the authority of the central state was restored and reinforced. The protest movements of the 1970s brought newfound legitimacy for regional and local cultures and languages, and this helped to create fertile ground for regionalist movements aimed at protecting local cultures from the expansion of the central state. Aspects of local cultures can include languages and dialects, minority religions and dissenter groups, local customs and traditions, and even a more abstract conception of a regional way of life. The crucial point is that the people in the region are aware of the factors that distinguish their culture from the central one (Vilar 1963: 75, cited in Mény 1986: 10).

Elites and masses

The discussion above talks of centres occupying and colonizing, and peripheries opposing and fighting. These are all examples of actions, which raises the question of who acts. Centres and peripheries are obviously not single entities. They are groups of people, and in the case of the peripheries these groups are organized only loosely, if at all. Thus, it is clear that peripheries cannot act. Centres are often organized as modern states, and therefore they do have mechanisms for action. Even so, this action is instigated by individuals, within centres as well as peripheries. When researchers talk about centres and peripheries acting, and about regions that act, they are therefore actually referring to individuals acting on their behalf.

These individuals are members of what are called elites. Elites can be defined as comprising people who have power within a society (Etzioni-Halevy 1993: 19). In a region, this usually includes the political leadership of the region, the upper echelons of the regional administration, as well as the most influential business executives and academics in the region. These regional elites have the potential to make rational and strategic decisions, influencing the direction of the regional political and economic development. This does not mean that masses are powerless. Indeed, much of this book focuses on the mass level. For instance, indicators of public opinion in the regions will play a crucial role in the operationalization of regionalism. The opinions of the masses are important because they determine what elites can and cannot do. This is most obviously the case when it comes to elections of the political leadership, but even between elections, elites do consider the opinions of the mass public when making decisions. If the opinions of the masses influence the actions of the elites, though, elites have an even bigger impact on the opinions of the masses (Etzioni-Halevy 1993: 24). Public opinion can therefore in many ways be seen as a reflection of the balance of power between rival elite groups.

When faced with the expansion of central authority presented in the centre–periphery theory, the elites in the periphery have two major options: resistance or cooperation. Central elites will often attempt to co-opt the peripheral elites, offering them positions and influence in the centre in return for the integration of the periphery into the centre. Alternatively, the peripheral elites can attempt to mobilize the masses in the periphery in opposition against the expansion of the centre. Both of these strategies will usually be present in any given region, as some elites ally with the centre whereas others attempt to crush this alliance. The crucial aspect for the development of regionalism is where the balance of power between these two groups is struck.

When it comes to the mobilization of the masses, elites will often seek to foment a common sense of regional identity that will ensure the continuous support and motivation of the masses in the struggle against the centre. In this way, regionalism can be used by local elites as a strategy towards their ends. They will try to promote the cultural and economic traits that distinguish the periphery from the centre, and rewrite the history of the periphery in the same way that nation-builders do. As was mentioned earlier, it is, after all, not the differentiation factors that are crucial, but rather the consciousness of these factors.[5] If the population in the periphery speaks a different language or shares an ethnicity different from that of the centre, the opposition often takes on the form of ethnic conflicts or claims to national self-determination. However, even if people living in the periphery do not claim to constitute a nation, and merely seek to protect their own cultural traditions or economic interests, the same mechanisms are still at play. Keating (1988: 8ff.) shows how nationalist and regionalist movements can be difficult to distinguish because in many ways they fulfil the same function. In his view, both are 'rational responses to the growth of the modern state and can only be understood as such' (ibid.: vii).

Explaining regionalism in this sense still leaves one major question to answer: under what circumstances will the elites in the periphery choose to ally with the centre, and under what circumstances will they ally with the masses in the periphery? Furthermore, when will they want to change allies, thereby causing an upswing in regionalism? This book argues that the outcome hinges on how dependent the region is on the central state. If the region has many resources at its disposal, it will be more likely that the elites will oppose the expansion of the centre and attempt to control these resources themselves. On the other hand, regions that are dependent on the central state will be colonized more easily.

Bottom-up perspective

Focusing on the behaviour of elites and masses within the region automatically puts the spotlight on the processes taking place within the regions themselves. It does indeed seem intuitive to study the processes within regions when seeking to explain why regionalism occurs. It would, for instance, be completely imposs-ible to explain variation between different regions without considering the devel-opments within each of them. Nonetheless, it has been fairly common in the study of regionalism for the focus to be placed elsewhere, whether on the Euro-pean Union or on the national level.

This study focuses explicitly on the developments within the regions them-selves, adopting a bottom-up perspective on regionalism. This approach enables it to explain why some regions deviate from the national norm, and why there is variation across different regions within the EU. While developments outside the regions are considered as explanatory variables, the focus remains on the extent to which the regions have been affected by these influences, and on the response that they have elicited within the regions. By focusing on the regional level itself, it is possible to get beyond generalizations about universal developments in European regions and on to a study of why some regions are mobilized and others are not, and why there are changes in the levels of regionalism across time within individual regions.

Research design

This study takes a broad perspective on regionalism. It seeks to explore whether some factors can affect regionalism regardless of context. Thus, it needs to explain why regionalism varies across both time and space. In order to achieve this, it is necessary to use a research design that makes it possible to approach the question from as many angles as possible. Therefore, this study uses a nested analysis design that combines a longitudinal and a cross-sectional analysis, and both quantitative and qualitative research methods.

Longitudinal and cross-sectional analyses

All studies in the social sciences are comparative in some sense. Either they compare across several different units (individuals, regions, states) at a fixed time-point in a cross-sectional design, or they compare within a fixed unit across an extended period of time in a longitudinal design. This is also true of studies that seek to explain regionalism. Most focus on a single region and look for an explanation of the development of regionalism in the particular historical development of that region. However, a few choose a cross-sectional design instead, explaining why regionalism is more widespread in some regions than it is in others.

The main problem with comparing either across time or across space is that some variables do not actually vary greatly across time, while others do not vary much across space. For instance, there may not be much variation in the degree to which different regions within a single state are embedded in the global economy, yet it is possible that all of these regions have experienced a massive growth in globalization across time. Conversely, the ethnicity of a region is unlikely to change dramatically across time, yet the difference in ethnic composition can be substantial even between neighbouring regions.

This study seeks explanations for variations in the levels of regionalism across both time and space. Hence, it is necessary to bridge the gap between longitudinal and cross-sectional research designs. The study is therefore composed of two parts. The first part is a cross-sectional study across 212 Western European regions, using four surveys from the 1990s and 2000s, and it examines which variables are most useful in explaining variation in the levels of regionalism across space. This model is then tested in the second part of the study, which tracks the growth of regionalism in two particular regions – Scotland and Rogaland – across forty years, analysing the extent to which the model can explain variation across time.

For the purposes of analysing hypotheses about the causes of regionalism, there are clear methodological benefits to employing this combination of cross-sectional survey data and longitudinal analysis in the operationalization of regionalism. The twinning of research designs makes it possible to test the same hypotheses using two radically different methods, which will validate each other if their conclusions correspond. The triangulation of research methods combines the in-depth knowledge that a case study produces with the universality of a large-N study, and the instant picture of a cross-sectional study with the sequential nature of a longitudinal one. The different operationalizations of regionalism will also support one another to create confidence in the reliability and validity of the measures.

Quantitative and qualitative methods

Another classic divide in the social sciences is between scholars favouring quantitative and those favouring qualitative research methods. In the field of regionalism, qualitative methods have tended to dominate, although there are some exceptions (e.g. van Houten 2003; Dardanelli 2005a; Martínez-Herrera 2005; Sorens 2005; Henderson 2007). Interviews, analyses of policy documents and historiographic accounts are most common tools for researchers in this field. One reason for this might be the lack of quantitative data available on the regional level, as most surveys are still conducted on the national level.

This study relies on both quantitative and qualitative methods in its quest for the causes of regionalism. The cross-sectional study relies exclusively on a quantitative, large-N regression analysis, but the longitudinal part of the book combines quantitative indicators with a qualitative interpretation of the causes of regionalism within each of the two case studies. This triangulation of methods is useful in furthering knowledge. In this perspective, the quantitative study is used to establish what relationships exist between the independent variables and regionalism and how strong these relationships are. These findings are carried through to the qualitative study, where the dynamics of the relationships can be examined more closely. The quantitative study establishes what to look for in the qualitative study, which can then be used to address questions such as why and how these factors influence levels of regionalism.

Nested analysis

The decision to combine cross-sectional, large-N analysis with longitudinal case studies still leaves the question of how the various strands of the analysis can be combined most fruitfully. As Lieberman (2005) argues, not all mixed strategies are productive, and there are few guides as to how methods should be mixed. Lieberman proposes a nested analysis approach, which this analysis follows to some extent. The idea behind nested analysis is that the large-N analysis should inform the approach to the case studies, with the aim of the case studies depending on the results of the large-N analysis. If the large-N analysis yields robust and satisfactory results, the aim of the case studies is to test the model developed in the large-N analysis. If the results are not robust, the case studies should aim at model-building (ibid.: 437).

However, the approach in this study deviates from Lieberman's proposals when it comes to case selection. A key aspect of Lieberman's proposal is that the selection of cases should be made on the basis of their residuals in the large-N analysis – that is, whether they are poorly or well explained by the model. There are three reasons for ignoring these suggestions in this case. First, the aim of the case studies is to assess the potential of the model in explaining variations in the levels of regionalism across time, which requires a focus on regions where things have actually changed through the period studied. The large-N analysis focuses on a single time-point and does not provide any information on the circumstances at earlier or later dates. Second, some of the data points in the large-N analysis are relatively uncertain for individual regions, making them less useful as foundations for case selection. This is particularly true for the dependent variable itself. The error terms are simply too large for it to be possible to make any solid claims about whether a particular region is on or off the regression line. Third, the theoretical foundation for selecting only cases that are well explained by the model in a model-testing exercise seems questionable, as it is hard to see how the model could be refuted under such circumstances.

Instead, the cases analysed in the longitudinal part of this book have been selected in order to maximize their variation across time on the independent variables in the model derived from the cross-sectional analysis. The large-N

analysis develops a regression model of the main predictors of regionalism across space, and this model is tested in two longitudinal studies of cases where the independent variables in the model are known or expected to vary substantially across time. The main aim of the case studies is to examine whether the development of regionalism across time conforms to the predictions that can be made on the basis of the regression model. It should be noted that the case selection aims mainly at ensuring variation within each region across time, rather than maximizing variation across the two cases. This reflects the subsequent analysis of the two cases, which also aims at explaining variation across time in each case, rather than comparing across the two cases.

Overview

This book argues that regionalism is partly based on rational calculation of the costs and benefits of mobilizing on a regional basis. The economic circumstances of a region play an important part in determining whether people will mobilize on a regional basis, and levels of regionalism can therefore vary across time as the region's economic situation changes. This is shown primarily through the relationship between economic development and regionalism, which this book demonstrates both theoretically and empirically across time and space. However, it is also reflected in the relationship between regionalism and other economic factors, such as globalization and European integration. Even the relationship between regionalism and the regional party system suggests a larger role for rationality in the explanation of regionalism than that usually afforded by theories which focus on cultural differences as the crucial explanation for regionalism.

The cross-sectional analysis explains variation in levels of regionalism across Western European regions. The study finds that a highly distinctive regional party system and a high level of economic development are the two factors most likely to lead to regionalism, along with cultural and geographical variables such as having a regional language or not bordering the national capital. European integration also appears to be positively correlated with regionalism, while the effect of globalization is less clear in the cross-sectional analysis.

The longitudinal analysis tests the model in order to examine how well it is capable of predicting variation in regionalism across time in two selected case studies, Scotland and Rogaland. The study finds a close association between economic development and regionalism across time in both case studies, leading to the conclusion that there is a causal relationship between prosperity and regionalism. None of the other variables was as strongly associated with regionalism in either case study, although European integration clearly played a part in the mobilization of Scottish regionalism (or, more appropriately, nationalism) in the 1990s.

The next chapter examines various factors that have been put forward in the existing literature as explanations of variation in the levels of regionalism across time or space. Although cultural explanations of regionalism, which have been covered thoroughly by the existing literature, are discussed in the chapter, a key aim is to get beyond these in order to examine which other variables have an effect on regionalism, in addition to culture. The chapter therefore focuses mainly on the variables covered by the new regionalism literature – that is, globalization and European integration – as well as on party systems and economic development, developing hypotheses that can be examined in the later empirical analysis. For each of these phenomena, its connection with regionalism is critically assessed, with the focus being on why and how they would affect regionalism.

The theories are then examined in the form of a cross-sectional, quantitative analysis. As part of this process, Chapter 3 develops an operational definition of regionalism that can be applied across a large number of Western European regions. The operationalization is based on the Moreno index, comparing respondents' attachment to their regions with their attachment to their states. The chapter discusses the reliability and validity of this operationalization, before presenting a range of descriptive data on the distribution of regionalism across the regions covered in the set. The data are drawn from four separate Eurobarometer surveys conducted between 1991 and 2002.

Chapter 4 continues the cross-sectional analysis by operationalizing the independent variables discussed in Chapter 2, and presenting descriptive data on each of them. The independent variables are used to develop a regression model of the causes of regionalism, revealing the effect of each of the independent variables. The model shows that levels of regionalism are significantly higher in economically developed regions with distinctive party systems and a regional language, and in regions that are closely integrated into the European Union.

The model is taken forward to a set of longitudinal case studies that examine to what extent it can also explain variations in the levels of regionalism across time. In Chapter 5, Scotland in the United Kingdom and Rogaland in Norway are presented as the two case studies, and the rationale for this decision is made clear. The chapter presents data on their development across the period from the 1960s to the 2000s, along each of the independent variables included in the regionalism model. This information can then be used to predict how regionalism will have developed over the same period, on the basis of the model. The predictions are compared to the actual development of regionalism across time in the two regions. The chapter explores a range of indicators on the levels of regionalism at various time-points for each region, attempting to accurately describe the variation across time. In the case of Scotland, data from surveys, referenda and nationalist voting contribute to a fairly precise picture of the path of regionalism across time. A quantitative content analysis of two Scottish newspapers is also conducted, yielding similar results, and this method of analysis is carried forward to the study of Rogaland, for which fewer data sources are available. The chapter concludes by comparing the actual development trajectory of regionalism with the predictions made at the beginning of the chapter. The comparison shows that economic development was particularly successful in predicting the changes across time in Scotland and Rogaland, while globalization and European integration were also broadly correlated with regionalism in the direction that the model predicted.

In Chapters 6 and 7, the specific connections between regionalism and each of the independent variables are discussed. Chapter 6 analyses the causes of nationalism in Scotland, assessing the impact of each variable on the basis of a qualitative analysis of newspaper content and election manifestos, as well as secondary literature. The aim is to probe the effect of each variable on the levels of nationalism in Scotland, assessing whether the relationships are causal and how they correspond to the theoretical accounts presented in Chapter 2. Chapter 7 analyses the causes of regionalism in Rogaland, applying a design similar to that used in the Scottish case.

Chapter 8 discusses the particular effects on petroleum in the two regions, examining whether the development of regionalism is related to their positions as petroleum capitals of their respective countries. In order to assess the generalizability of the model, the chapter briefly analyses the development of regionalism across time in some well-known cases across other major countries in Western Europe. The study finds that aspects of the model are useful in explaining most of these regionalisms, and the findings can therefore be generalized.

2   Causes of regionalism

This chapter examines different theories about the causes of regionalism and the mobilization of regional identities. The discussion starts with cultural differences between the region and the rest of the state as a key driver of regionalism, an important factor in the literature on minority nationalism. Arguing that cultural differences are more useful in explaining variations in regionalism across space than across time, the chapter goes on to discuss potential effects of some of the major processes of change in Western European regions during the second half of the twentieth century. Two of the most important such processes are those of globalization and European integration, and the literature on the effect of each on regionalism is assessed.

The impact of these two variables has been the main focus of regionalism scholars in recent years. This is understandable, as both of these developments are central to understanding processes of social and political change in Western Europe in this period, and also have a profound effect on centre–periphery relations. These two independent variables have been well developed and there are numerous empirical studies covering their various effects on the construction and development of regionalism. However, the concentration on these two phenomena has led to other factors being overlooked. This is unfortunate, as neither globalization nor European integration can provide a complete explanation of the development of regionalism. Both are macro-level developments that have had an effect across all of Western Europe, and hence are ill-equipped to explain variation across regions. In order to arrive at a fuller understanding of the causes of regionalism, it is necessary to expand one's focus and consider other explanatory variables as well. The chapter therefore goes on to discuss two factors that vary both across regions and across time: regional party system diversity and regional economic development. Each of these may have an independent effect on levels of regionalism in a region through affecting incentive structures and the perception of the region among its inhabitants.

When one inquires into the causes of regionalism, it is important to keep in mind the motivations of the actors involved. Researchers need to ask why the people living in a certain region want more political autonomy for their region. Although elites may consider political power a goal in its own right, this aim – by itself – is unlikely to convince many ordinary people of the merits of a regionalist agenda. Power is an instrument, and people want power because they want to use it for some purpose. It is not self-evident in every case what this purpose might be, nor are a region's interests necessarily best served by regional autonomy. We must therefore consider the end goals of a regionalist movement. As is mentioned in the previous chapter, these can include promoting the economic development of a region and preserving a cultural and/or national identity that has become threatened by cultural standardization (Rokkan and Urwin 1982: 4). While both of these rationales are usually found to some extent in every regionalist movement, there is a great deal of variation with regard to how much emphasis is put on each.

Culture-based explanations

The defence of cultural identity has been explored in depth in the literature on minority nationalisms and ethnic mobilization. Gellner (1983) argues that the ideology of nationalism, with its ethos of national self-determination, has become hegemonic in contemporary political debate. Accordingly, nations want to govern themselves, making the political and national communities congruent. This leaves the question of what constitutes a nation, an issue on which there has been considerable debate in the academic literature. On one side of the debate are voluntarists, arguing that nations are imagined communities bounded together by a common will (Renan 1882; Anderson 1991). According to this line of thought, a common culture may help in the construction of an imagined community (Anderson points to the territorialization of religious faith and the development of print language as key factors in causing people to imagine the existence of national communities), but it is not a necessary condition.

On the other side of the debate on nations are primordialist conceptions of nationalism, which see nations as being bound together by a common culture, be it a language, religion or ethnicity (Fichte 1845; Geertz 1963). In this view, minority cultural communities within a state – speaking a different language, or having a different faith or a different ethnicity from the majority community – by definition form minority nations, and as a consequence they desire self-government, or at least some form of institutional recognition of their nation within the broader political framework of the state.

For primordialists, regions with a distinct language, ethnicity or culture hold separate national identities. This will lead them to demand political self-determination, as they have not accepted the legitimacy of a central state dominated by a rival ethnic group. The mobilization of regions is thus construed as the battle of stateless nations for equal political rights with state-bearing nations. For voluntarists, a distinct regional culture may contribute to the construction of an imagined community, which will in turn result in the same demands for political self-determination. Thus, both perspectives lead to the conclusion that regionalism in the form of minority nationalism will be more prevalent in culturally distinctive regions. Looking at the European political landscape, this looks like a reasonable interpretation. Demands for devolution or independence have indeed been stronger in areas where most people define themselves as belonging to a stateless nation – witness for instance the dissolution of Yugoslavia, the Soviet Union and Czechoslovakia, or the regionalist movements in Spain and Belgium.

However, cultural factors alone cannot appropriately explain why there is change over time in the levels of regionalism, both in general and in specific regions. While it is clear that culture and ethnicity are by no means immutable and objectively occurring phenomena, they still do not tend to change very quickly. The maintenance of ethnic boundaries is based at least on an idea of longevity, and it does not seem credible that these ethnic and cultural differences should have suddenly appeared at some point in the early 1970s, when regionalism started becoming a widespread phenomenon in Western Europe.[1] A separate language, religion or ethnicity 'constitute[s] only a potential' for territorial mobilization (Urwin 1982: 429). In the case of minority nationalist regions, some other factors must have politicized previously dormant national identities. Furthermore, in the case of Western European regions that are indistinguishable from the rest of the state in terms of language, religion or ethnicity, yet still showed signs of regionalism in this period, factors other than culture must have been responsible.

While cultural factors are certainly important, it is necessary to consider the possibility that regionalism may be a more calculated political development. Regional political elites may try to politicize the idea of the region when the region stands to gain something from it, and regional publics may equally mobilize on a regional basis when this is beneficial for the region. In this sense, regionalism may be a political movement that is set in motion when the circumstances of the region change, with rational processes driving the politicization of regional identities.

For instance, the economic and political circumstances of a region may change profoundly over a fairly short period of time, and this can have important consequences for society. However, the economic and political causes of regionalism have not been explored to the same extent as the cultural ones, and more research is needed to explain how such factors can cause variation in regionalism across time and space. One of the major changes in economic circumstances affecting most Western European regions since the 1970s is the globalization of national economies and societies. This changes both the opportunity structures and the incentive structures for regions vis-à-vis the central state, as the next section shows.

Globalization

As technological developments have marched on, the world has gradually become smaller. Inventions such as the postal service, the radio, telegraph and telephone, television and the Internet have made it easier to communicate with people across long distances. Developments in boats, trains, cars and aviation, along with the construction of ever more roads and airports, have shortened travel times. This has made people, as well as goods and services, more mobile, and the global economy has become increasingly integrated. Arguably, the world has also become more integrated culturally, as cultural symbols and codes are increasingly shared by people across national boundaries. These changes, which can be labelled globalization, have had wide-ranging effects on social and political systems, and they have also been connected to regionalism by several authors.

Capital and labour mobility

Taken together, the developments outlined above have led to a diminishing importance for territory in economic affairs. Globalization entails the weakening of states, as they are no longer able to control the economy to the extent that they used to in the face of increasingly mobile goods, services and labour. Some have even proclaimed that states are no longer meaningful units of economic activity (Ohmae 1995). This can be seen in a number of ways: the increase in international trade, the growth of transnational companies and other international organizations, and the establishment of international economic regimes through the GATT, and later WTO, agreements, as well as the Bretton Woods institutions.

One might expect the reduced importance of territory in economic affairs to lead to the end of territory in politics as well, with a new, international political space arising to replace the existing variety of parallel national political spaces. As national borders lose their importance as boundaries for communication and trade, they are also less relevant boundaries for political debate. Public opinion and political cleavages might become international in nature, with political movements encompassing people of different nationalities.

So far, this has failed to materialize. Instead of a diminishing importance of territory, there has to some extent been a reterritorialization of economic affairs (Keating 1999a: 74; Brenner 1999a). By some accounts, territory is made even more important by globalization. Scott and Storper (2003) argue that regional economic specialization has intensified as a result of globalization, and that national economic development will be even more geographically concentrated in the future. Keating (1998: 137) points to several factors linked to territory that continue to matter to businesses. Businesses are more likely to set up industry in regions where the labour force is skilled and flexible, and where there is a high degree of technological development. The physical infrastructure also matters, and a high-quality natural and built environment can be an important pull factor, as can the presence of a network of complementary industries that can act as suppliers or buyers. Cultural and political factors in the form of public institutions, norms, values and social contexts also come into play. Even in purely intellectual activities with no transport costs, the importance of interpersonal relationships and face-to-face contact encourages geographical proximity (Leamer and Storper 2001). Thus, the sources of competitiveness are 'embedded within territorially localized production complexes [...] which provide firms with place-specific clusters of non-substitutable locational assets' (Brenner 2002: 14), such as labour, technology and infrastructure.

However, there has been a change in the nature of territorialization. Regions are emerging as new territorial economic units (Ohmae 1995; Scott 1998). Nation-states have lost the sovereign authority they once aspired to, and sub-national units have in many cases taken over some of their functions. States are no longer regarded as the all-encompassing, all-important political units (Brenner 1999b). Rather, regions and cities have assumed newfound prominence as the cores of a new regionalism that sees the region as a unified actor competing with other regions to attract inward investment and promote economic development (Le Gales and Harding 1998; Keating 1999a).

This creates an increasing demand on regional political and business elites to be proactive in the pursuit of regional economic development. The new paradigm of regional economic development is therefore radically different from old types of state-led top-down regional development policies. Today, regional development is seen as the result of efforts originating in the region proper, and regional elites have mobilized in order to generate economic development from the bottom up. This has involved a coalition between elites within regional governments, local businesses, political parties and trade unions, cutting across socio-economic cleavages to promote the interests of the region. This territorial realignment is potentially an important factor in explaining the growth of regionalism across time.

In the new regionalist model, territory has assumed the position that class used to have as the basis for political cooperation and mobilization (Mény 1986: 3). Keating (1998: 140) distinguishes between old and new paradigms of regional development based on this development. According to him, competition over the distribution of wealth within a region characterizes the old model of regional development. This has largely given way to a system of competition between regions for the wealth of the nation. Classes cooperate within the region to promote the development of the entire region, as class solidarity has given way to territorial solidarity.

Although most regions are affected by these processes to some extent, there are still substantial differences in the degree to which regions are exposed to competition from other regions, depending on the mobility of the major industries, as well as levels of exports, foreign investments and foreign immigration. Regions also differ in their awareness of this competition, as reflected in the creation or strengthening of institutions aimed at promoting the regional economy. This could affect the impact of globalization on regionalism in the region.

Glocalism

While these economic connections between globalization and regionalism have featured prominently in the regionalism literature, there are also some works in the globalization literature that consider a more cultural impact of globalization. Here, cultural consequences of globalization, such as homogenization, are considered to elicit a defensive response on the regional level, as people increasingly mobilize their local and regional identities in order to protect them from the threat of disappearance in a globally homogeneous culture.

Friedman (2000) is among the major proponents of this connection between globalization and regionalism. In his view, the world can be interpreted as a struggle between the urge to modernize and the need to belong. Friedman uses the metaphor of the Lexus, a Japanese car produced by robots, and the olive tree to describe these competing urges, noting that

> [o]live trees are important. They represent everything that roots us, anchors us, identifies us and locates us in this world – whether it be belonging to a family, a community, a tribe, a nation, a religion or, most of all, a place called home.
>
> (ibid.: 31)

As modernization in the form of technological progress has brought an increasingly global economy, our sense of belonging has come under pressure. This necessitates a response, which Friedman calls 'glocalism'. Consequently, in order to protect their culture and roots, people mobilize their regional and local identities.

Castells also sees territorial identities as essentially a defence mechanism against the pressures of globalization, which leaves 'people with no other choice than either to surrender or to react on the basis of the most immediate source of self-recognition and autonomous organization: their locality' (1997: 61). In his view, the effect of globalization is mainly to individualize, or even atomize, society, as local networks are increasingly eroded. This individuality makes some people feel insecure, and collective identities represent a 'defensive reaction against the impositions of global disorder and uncontrollable, fast-paced change' (ibid.: 64).

European integration

While globalization has affected every continent of the world, a parallel process of economic, cultural and, indeed, political integration has been unique to Europe. Since the late 1950s, European integration has gradually become deeper, extending into new policy areas and territories. From the Treaty of Rome in 1957 to the Maastricht Treaty of 1992 and beyond, European integration has moved from the technical integration of a limited number of industries across six countries to a full-scale political union between twenty-seven countries, with a democratically elected Parliament, an integrated market and supranational jurisdiction.

The idea that European integration would have an impact on regionalism is partly connected to the globalization argument, as the EU economy may be considered a concentrated microcosm of the global world economy. Internationalization of economic activities, as measured for instance by the volume of international trade, has been stronger between the EU member states than almost anywhere else in the world, and national markets have lost importance with the development of the common market. However, regionalism is also partly conceived as the result of a conscious political effort to strengthen the regions, with supranational institutions – notably the European Commission – encouraging regions to mobilize in order to put pressure on the states from above and below (Bullmann 1997; Rokkan and Urwin 1982).

In terms of the centre–periphery model discussed in Chapter 1, this can be interpreted as pressures from a new European centre in Brussels, turning the national capitals into European peripheries. This change of roles for the historical centres has left them vulnerable to pressures from below. As the states lose their extractive, distributive and homogenizing capacities, regions gain more room for manoeuvre. They now have the opportunity to redefine their economical and cultural position vis-à-vis the centre. Businesses in the periphery can choose to trade across borders instead of with the national centre. Identities become more fluent as people shift between a national, European and regional identity. Through contact with people from neighbouring states, Europeans may learn that the cultural cleavages are not as large as they had previously thought, and may even find more in common with people from neighbouring regions in other states than with people from other regions in the same state. In this way, regional identities may be strengthened by the growing integration between European states.

Trade and the single market

In the economic sphere, the EU contributes to regionalism through providing a particular set of institutions, most notably the single market, that may serve as an alternative to the institutions of the nation-state and decrease peripheral regions' dependence on the national centre. The states have lost control over their internal markets as a result of the integration into a single European market. Now the resources in a state are no longer necessarily controlled from the centre, nor do the borders of the state constitute natural boundaries for economic activity. Instead, goods, services, labour and capital move freely across borders throughout the European Economic Area.

This is particularly important for regions where secession is a potential strategy. The single market can reduce the costs of secession for regions, as the EU would provide continued access to markets across the European Economic Area. This can reduce the fears of regional businesses that often produce for markets elsewhere in the state. However, reducing the costs of secession is likely to have an impact even in regions where it is not considered a valid option. By reducing the dependence of regions upon their respective states, European integration has improved the bargaining power of regional elites, thus making it more likely that regionalism will grow.

Alesina *et al.* (2000) argue that the size of the political unit no longer matters when restrictions to trade are removed. Smaller economies can more easily succeed in an open economy, where the size of the domestic market is irrelevant as producers have access to large external markets anyway. This makes secession a more viable option for regions. Indeed, as world markets have become increasingly open, the number of states in the world has also grown correspondingly, and hence the average state has become smaller. Working from the same theoretical framework, Sorens (2004) demonstrates a connection between globalization and support for secessionist political parties. While global markets are still far from open, the EU does present the same opportunities to regions within its boundaries, as the size of the economy makes little difference when there are no restrictions to trade within the EU.

This is reinforced by the direct support that the EU provides for some peripheral regions through structural funds, further decreasing their dependence on the state. Regional policies in the EU take the form of subsidies for poorer regions, known as structural funds, through which the regions can gain direct access to EU funding. This provides regional governments with an independent resource base and an incentive to mobilize in order to improve the region's capacity to manage the funds successfully.

Multilevel governance

Politically, authority is also sifting away from the national capitals and towards the decision-making organs in Brussels. Within Brussels, it is the supranational organs, representing the Union as a whole, that are securing an ever-stronger position. These include the Commission, the Parliament, the European Court of Justice and the European Central Bank (Hix 1999: 327ff.). In turn, these supranational institutions – notably the Commission – have been encouraging regions to mobilize, assisted by other Europhile political forces. Historically, regionalist and European federalist ideologies have had much in common. Many regionalists were European federalists, and many federalists were regionalists, united by a common opposition to the authority of the traditional nation-state (Loughlin 1996: 142).

Accordingly, supranational and regional institutions have been important allies within the EU. Supra- and sub-state political elites have reinforced each other and put pressure on the states to delegate authority upwards and downwards in the political system (Rokkan and Urwin 1982). Pressures on the nation-states from above have restricted their capacities to manage regional disparities within their borders. Regional political elites have exploited this situation to establish themselves as actors in their own right on the European stage (Bullmann 1997: 10). Through the creation of the Committee of the Regions and the establishment of numerous regional information offices, regional elites have emerged as important policy-influencing forces in the EU. This development has been encouraged by supranational institutions such as the Commission, eager to promote integration through reducing the influence of the non-federal organs (Loughlin 1996: 154).

The Commission also has another, more functional, reason to support the regions. The Commission is an institution of limited resources and wide jurisdiction. The main source of information about local issues is therefore the member states, and this creates a risk of bias in the information that Commissioners receive. The regional information offices have therefore been welcomed as alternative sources of information, providing a different perspective from the member states. This increases the independence and the political weight of the Commission, and reduces its dependence on the member states (Marks *et al.* 1996: 186f.). This has important consequences for regions, and the opportunities for para-diplomatic activities have brought a new international dimension to regionalism (Keating 1999b: 14).

The development of an institutional culture within the EU has also had a diffusion effect on countries outside the union. The requirements for a regional level of government in all member countries, along with the ideology of a Europe of the Regions, created powerful pressures for regionalization in the efforts to 'Europeanize' Eastern Europe. This also gave regional movements legitimacy to push forward with their claims (Wolczuk 2002: 203f.). Bukve (2008) puts forward a similar argument in explaining regional reform attempts in Norway. Focusing on the influence of the EU in terms of ideas, he argues that regionalization became a hegemonic idea in Europe during the 1990s, pushing all the Nordic countries to attempt reforms in order to gain legitimacy. He frames Nordic regional reforms as a European idea looking for a Nordic problem to solve.

European identity

One major asset for the states in relation to sub-state regions is the symbols of nationalism. An important ambition of the European project has been to counteract the effects of nation-building in the member states by creating an overarching European identity. This has seen the introduction of the European flag, a European hymn and a common European currency. By challenging national identities, the EU aims to reduce the resilience of nation-states. The EU institutions have been instrumental in creating a mass European identity over the past thirty years. In particular, the Schengen area and the euro currency have recently contributed to the construction of a common European identity, but the introduction of common European symbols has also had an impact on popular identification. Although citizens mainly hold a civic conception of European identity, there is also an element of cultural identification with Europe (Bruter 2005: 166ff.).

This may cause problems for national solidarity in the form of increasing tendencies of regions to focus on their own economic development as opposed to that of the entire nation. It may also cause increasing cultural differences within the nation-states, which may reinforce the tendencies towards regionalism. Increased geographical mobility has also brought people of different nationalities together, thereby helping to break down the barriers between them.

While there is a strong case to be made for the impact of both globalization and European integration on the rise of regionalism in Western Europe since the 1970s, both of these processes are developments on the macro level that should have an effect on all European regions. While differences across regions in terms of cultural diversity might affect the ability of these phenomena to fuel regionalism, another explanation for variation in levels of regionalism across both time and space might be political or economic processes going on within the regions themselves. Thus far, the literature on regionalism has paid comparatively less attention to such internal processes within regions. This book seeks to correct this through considering the impact of regional disparities in terms of political party preferences and economic development.

Party systems

Political parties and the competition between them have been a popular focus for political scientists working in a number of different areas, particularly within the various strands of new institutionalism. The dynamics of party competition can also be used to explain mobilization of regionalism, above all in regions where the regional party system differs markedly from the national party system. In such regions, conflicts between the regional and national governments can serve as a basis for regional mobilization, and diverging political preferences might be a powerful incentive for desiring regionalization of power.

The terms 'regional party system' and 'regional voting' refer to the system of party competition within a region, whether the competition takes place in the context of regional or national elections. However, the mechanisms through which regional voting is likely to affect regionalism are different in the context of regional as distinct from national elections, and the discussion therefore needs to distinguish between these two types of election.

Regional elections

From the perspective of individual parties, regional voting can take two different forms. Parties can be either more or less successful in a particular region than in the country as a whole. However, this usually becomes important only when the variation is large enough to produce a different majority or a different governing coalition at the regional level as compared with that on the national level. In most countries with regional governments, some regions are governed by a national opposition party. This can lead to conflict between the regional and national government, encouraging the mobilization of regionalism.

National opposition parties that are in office at the regional level have strong incentives to support the transfer of powers to the regional level in order to increase their power. These incentives grow with the security of the party's position in the region and decrease with the strength of its position at the national level. If the minority party in a two-party system wins a majority in a particular region in every single election and loses all the elections at the national level by a clear margin, regionalization of power might be the only way for it to gain political influence. Such a party would have strong incentives to attempt to mobilize the regional public in favour of devolution. To the extent that regional political elites, in this case the regional government party, manage to influence the electorate through promoting their political programme or setting the agenda for political discussion, it is likely that these attempts will encourage a growth of regionalism in the region.

Developments in several democracies in Western Europe during the 1980s and 1990s support the hypothesis that opposition parties tend to favour regionalization of power. Hopkin (2003: 229) notes that Italy and Spain in the 1970s, France in the 1980s and the United Kingdom in the 1980s and 1990s are examples of countries where national opposition parties have supported devolution, and later implemented it when they came into power. On a similar note, Ashford (1982: 2) claims that 'urging structural change is most often the argument of oppositions', while governing parties rarely want to risk upsetting the party organization through territorial restructuring. Even traditionally centralist parties can be compelled to support regionalization when they dominate regional politics with little prospect of winning power at the central level, as witnessed for instance in the case of the Galician regional branch of the Spanish Partido Popular in the 1980s (Schrijver 2005: 282).

Regional government by national opposition parties is also amenable to blame games. Regional politicians can reap rewards for their party at both the regional and the national level through blaming the national government for any failures of regional policy or any grievances that the electorate may have. This might be labelled 'vertical diffusion of responsibility' (McGraw 1990: 121). During the welfare state retrenchment of the 1980s and 1990s, blame avoidance strategies were crucial in the face of the high political costs associated with cutbacks in welfare (Pierson 1996). If the regional government convinces the electorate that the national government is actually at fault, resentment towards the central state may start to grow, and people will be more likely to support regionalization of power.

National elections

As opposed to regional elections, the effect of regional voting in national elections is mainly related to the parties that win a lower share of the regional vote than their countrywide share. Specifically, regionalism can be affected by the lack of support for large national parties that have spent a lot of time in office. If the party governing the central state is unpopular in a particular region, opposition towards it might encourage cynicism and disaffection with the political system, as voters feel that they are not represented by the central government. This is particularly likely if the party stays in government for an extended period of time.

Opposition towards a political party that is dominant at the central level might also create incentives to regionalize political power. If the population of a territory consistently holds diverging political preferences as compared with those of the majority central state population, regionalization of power might be the only way in which these people can implement their preferred policies. From a rational voter perspective, one might say that the most compelling argument for wanting to devolve powers to a regional government is if the regional government would pursue a policy programme that was closer to the voter's preferences than that of a national government. If there were no difference between the policies of the regional and national governments, devolution of power would be pointless from a rationalist perspective, as the output would remain the same (Alesina and Spolaore 1997; Bolton and Roland 1997). Devolution would then be purely a question of economic efficiency.

Regional and national parties

From a territorial perspective, parties competing in a regional party system can be classified into two categories: regional and national parties. While national parties claim to represent the entire population of the state, regional parties associate themselves with a territorially defined sub-group of the population. Although it is not a defining property, regional parties tend to propose candidates for elections only in the region or regions with which they are associated, while national parties compete in elections across most or all of the state. Regional party systems can involve competition between various regional parties, between regional and national parties, or between various national parties.

By their very nature, regional parties represent the politicization of the regional level. They are necessarily based on a belief that the inhabitants of the region share certain common interests that benefit from being organized into a party political organization.[2] As such, regional parties are themselves symptoms of regionalism, at least among their supporters, and the level of support for regional parties could be seen as an indication of the level of regionalism in the region. Regional parties themselves obviously try to persuade more people to become regionalist in order to improve their own electoral appeal, and to the extent that they are successful, they could and should be seen as causes of regionalism. However, there would be no market for a regional party if there were not at least some sense of common interests or common purpose in the regional population a priori, and an increase in regionalism due to an external cause would be likely to improve the appeal of the regional party without the party in itself acting as the cause of regionalism. In this book, the support for regional parties is therefore mainly treated as an indication of levels of regionalism, rather than as a cause thereof.

While the existence of regional parties is mainly an indication of regionalism, the direction of causality is reversed when it comes to the relationship between national parties and regionalism. For the reasons outlined in the preceding two sections, it is useful to see variations in the support for national parties across regions as factors that can cause regionalism. Conversely, the support for national parties in a region is less affected by regionalism than by a wide range of other factors. Individual characteristics that structure people's vote, such as income, education, occupation and age, are unevenly distributed across different regions, and this accounts for a large proportion of the variation across regions in the support for political parties. Indeed, some studies have even indicated that the variation across regions is fully explained by the distribution of social and economic characteristics, and that the regions themselves do not matter as such (McAllister and Studlar 1992: 175). However, later studies have revealed that voters do tend to evaluate how government policies affect their regional economies, even beyond considering the effects on their personal economies (Pattie and Johnston 1995).

Still, regionalism does appear to play a minor part in explaining regional voting patterns in most regions, compared to factors such as average levels of income, the proportion of people working in different sectors of the economy, and religion. Regional parties obviously influence regional vote distinctiveness in so far as their very presence causes the voting patterns to diverge from the national voting pattern. However, most regions do not have any significant regional parties, and other mechanisms explain voting patterns in these regions. Hearl *et al.* (1996) suggest that unemployment and employment in agriculture are crucial factors in explaining regional vote distinctiveness across most countries in Western Europe. As most regional party systems are made up predominantly of national parties, this variable is treated mainly as a potential explanatory variable in relation to regionalism in this study.

Having established the theoretical basis for why diverging regional party systems might encourage the development of regionalism, this discussion now moves on to consider the effects of divergence in regional economies. While regional economies may diverge in a number of ways, this book mainly deals with differences in economic development both across regions and within regions across time.

Economic development

The internal colonialism school is responsible for bringing the relationship between economic development and regional identities into focus in the regional sciences. Notably, Lafont's (1967) work on the regionalist revolution in France introduced the notion of a colonial relationship between centre and periphery within the metropolitan state. He portrays this relationship as one of exploitation, and goes on to establish a theory of regional mobilization that has much in common with Marxist revolutionary theory. The theory is based on the proposition that the centre and the peripheries have different roles in the national economy. Economic power is based in the centre, and the role of the peripheries is essentially to provide the metropolis with raw materials. This leads to national differentiation, as the peripheries will usually specialize in only a few primary commodities or raw materials (Hechter 1975: 30). Because of the exploitative nature of the relationship between centre and periphery, they will never integrate economically or culturally, and the discriminated-against workers in the periphery will instead develop a sense of solidarity based on their shared position in the national economy. This paves the way for the development of a common identity in opposition to the powers that be in the centre, and the masses in the peripheries will revolt against the centre through revolution. This rebellion will be strongest in the most economically deprived regions, where the grievances are most acute, and the theory therefore proposes that regionalism will be stronger in poorer regions.

The internal colonialism argument can be seen as an application of the Frankian dependency theory paradigm (Frank 1967) to domestic politics. Hechter (1975: 31) is explicit in establishing this theoretical connection. He claims that the colonial type of dependent development is not found only in overseas colonies. The relationship between centre and periphery within a state works in the same way. The peripheries are dominated by the metropolitan economy, and their function is essentially to provide the metropolis with raw materials. This leads the peripheries to specialize in only a few primary commodities or raw materials (ibid.: 30). Given the similarities of their economic and political positions, Hechter argues that it is not unreasonable to expect the same social and political developments to take place in overseas and internal colonies. As the colonies in the Americas and Africa rebelled against the metropolis to claim independence, Hechter expects the same to happen in the internal colonies. The increased contact between the two will only lead to 'a malintegration established on terms increasingly regarded as unjust and illegitimate' (ibid.: 34). This creates fertile space for the growth of regionalist movements in the peripheries.

However, as Keating (1988: 12) points out, there is little empirical evidence that regionalism is actually more common in poor regions. On the contrary, rich regions tend to exhibit the stronger regionalist tendencies. There are also some theoretical weaknesses that hurt the argument of the writers in this school. One major problem is that a one-dimensional vilification of the centre as exploiter of the peripheries is far too simplistic. The peripheries gain as well as lose from their relationship with national centres, and although the centres may extract resources from the peripheries, they also aid their economies in many ways. The idea of a single economic centre where all meaningful economic activity takes place is also out of touch with the polycephalic reality of many modern states, as economic production is often spread across the territory, and does not necessarily coincide with the political centres.

Indeed, the dispersion of production and the associated emergence of prosperous peripheral regions in many countries suggest that researchers should consider exactly the opposite relationship between regionalism and economic growth to that forwarded by the internal colonialists. This is partly related to the strength of their bargaining positions. Economically successful regions are less dependent on the central state and better equipped to succeed on their own. However, in addition to the direct fiscal incentives, richer regions are also likely to desire a degree of political power that matches their economic importance within the state, which can be another incentive for politicizing the region. A sense of economic power can even boost a sense of self-esteem that can justify such demands in the minds of the public.

Fiscal incentives

Most obviously, there is a direct fiscal incentive to demand economic and political decentralization. Control over economic activities is one of the most important features of the central state. Indeed, one of the defining characteristics of a modern state is its monopoly of tax collection (Schumpeter 1961). Tax collection means that economic capital is extracted from the territory and redistributed among all the regions in a state. Whereas relatively poor regions benefit from transfers from the central state, the richer regions lose from this arrangement. This is likely to become a source of frustration in these regions, as they feel that they are paying heavily and getting little in return. Regional elites can play a role in developing a discourse that convinces the regional public that their standard of living would be better if they did not have to fund the poorer regions of the state, and this can lead to demands for keeping more of the wealth locally. Acquiring regional control over tax collection would entail greater economic wealth for these regions.

This perspective has been developed into a rational choice model of regional policies by Persson and Tabellini (2000), who argue that the economic calculations of the median voter in the region are crucial to whether regionalism will develop or not. These calculations need to consider the costs of transfers to other regions in terms of taxes, but also the benefits from public expenditure in the region itself. A region that is more prosperous than the national average might still benefit from receiving a higher share of government expenditure than other regions, and thus have no fiscal incentives to desire greater autonomy. A third factor that needs to be considered is the potential cost of setting up new regional institutions, which would add to the tax burden of the median voter. Finally, the relative distribution of resources at the regional and state levels matters. If resources are distributed more evenly in the region than in the state, the regional median voter is likely to be richer than the national median voter, and he or she would therefore be expected to favour a lower tax rate. These differences in political preferences can be a powerful incentive for desiring more political autonomy (Persson and Tabellini 2000: 132ff.).

A similar model is presented by Bolton and Roland (1997), who place more emphasis on the income distribution factor. They argue that different preferences over redistribution of resources are the foundation of decisions to separate. These can be traced back to differences in the distribution of income across the regions. An implication of this is that poorer regions might also desire political autonomy if it would lead to a different political leadership with different redistributionary policies. Similarly, Bookman (1993: 115) argues that grievances over the input/output balance can be a prime cause of regionalism in any region, rich or poor. While rich regions can claim that they are contributing too much, as outlined above, poor regions can blame their lack of development on the scarcity of public investments in the region. Indeed, he finds that economic considerations play a part in most of the thirty-seven secessionist regions that he studies. However, Dion (1996) argues that while economic growth improves public confidence in secession, it also reduces grievances against the current political situation. The public may fear that changes in the political status of the region will have negative effects on the economy.

Gold (2003: 7) suggests that the increased competition between regions brought about by globalization provides a further incentive for regionalism in prosperous regions. In the battle to remain competitive and attract businesses, wealthy regions can no longer afford to subsidize poorer regions. If they were free of the responsibility of subsidizing the poorer regions, they could redirect public funds to projects that would make them more competitive. This makes the option of increased autonomy or secession even more attractive. Zürn and Lange (1999: 5) make a similar point, coining the term 'welfare regionalism' to describe this mechanism.

Economic centrality, political peripherality

There is also a psychological effect of relative economic growth. When the periphery becomes economically more powerful than the centre, it may not be content to remain a periphery. This may lead prosperous peripheries to demand a more central position in political and cultural affairs, matching their economic power. These regions are also in a position to put power behind their demands, as they are less dependent on the central state and better equipped to succeed on their own (Treisman 1997: 220). Urwin (1982: 430) makes the point that 'superior or improving economic regions with a real or potential economic weight that more demonstratively can support independence and/or counter-balance the political resources of the centre' pose the greatest threat to the centre. Similarly, Rokkan (1970: 120) argues that 'conflict between the capital and areas of growth in the provinces' poses a potential for territorial resistance in the nation-building process, and that 'there will be unavoidable tension between the culturally and economically advanced areas and the backward periphery'.

Making a similar point, Gourevitch (1979) notes that peripheral nationalism occurs when the political capital is in economic decline. He focuses on whether the political leadership and economic centre of a country coincide, arguing that politically peripheral economic centres would develop nationalist movements if they had 'ethnic potential' in the form of a distinct language, institutions or historical traditions (see also Laitin 1991: 144). From a more recent perspective, regions vying for political power in the EU are classified as having 'a consciousness rooted in affluence, not in cultural identity' (Harvie 1994: 66). This applies for instance to Baden-Württemberg and Rhône-Alpes – two of the self-proclaimed 'Four Motors for Europe'.

Conclusion

This discussion has suggested five key variables that may have an effect on the development of regionalism. Figure 2.1 presents a schematic overview of the model. One of the variables, cultural distinctiveness, is expected to vary mostly

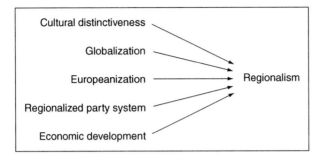

Figure 2.1 A model of regionalism.

across regions, while two others, globalization and European integration, are expected to vary mostly across time. The final two variables, party system distinctiveness and economic development, can be expected to vary both across regions and across time.

Each of these factors changes either the opportunity structures for peripheral regions or the incentives to mobilize on a regionalist agenda. Some of the factors even affect capital regions, which also find themselves competing with other regions in the global economy or participating in EU policymaking. Regional elites play an important role in interpreting the changed opportunities and incentives for regionalism and conveying these changes to the mass public. In many cases, regional governments form this function, but opposition political parties, business interests, trade unions and the media may also pursue regionalist politics that they aim to garner support for.

The following chapters will attempt to operationalize these theories on regionalism and examine the effects of each of the variables on regionalism in Western Europe. A quantitative analysis in Chapter 4 will focus on the extent to which each of these variables can explain the variation in levels of regionalism across different European regions. Subsequently, a longitudinal analysis of how regionalism has changed across time in two particular regions, Scotland and Rogaland, will examine the extent to which they can explain variation across time.

3   Regionalism in Western Europe

The fundamental question in the development of a research design is how the theories discussed in Chapter 2 can be tested. In approaching this question, it is crucial to find a way to measure levels of regionalism within different regions. After all, it is impossible to explain why regionalism is more widespread in some areas than in others without knowing which regions do actually manage to mobilize their populations. Equally, it is impossible to explain why regionalism grows or decreases over time without knowing at what times regionalism is strong or weak. So far, most studies of regionalism have analysed developments in individual regions, resulting in theories that are suited to explaining these cases, but not necessarily others. Larger cross-sectional studies have mainly been based on qualitative data. Therefore, little work has been done on the question of how regionalism should be measured, and data on the phenomenon are sparse. Without data and a method for testing the theories, we cannot determine whether the findings are generalizable and reliable. For the field to progress, it needs theories that seek to explain the varying degrees of regionalism across different regions, as well as over time.

This chapter develops an operational measure of regionalism that can be applied across a large number of European regions, and it proceeds to use the Eurobarometer survey series to create a data set showing the distribution of regionalism across Western European countries. The measure is based on a set of questions covering popular feelings of attachment towards regions and countries. Once the reliability and validity of the measure have been established, the chapter presents some descriptive data on estimated levels of regionalism in a selection of European regions for illustrative purposes.

Defining the unit

The introduction to this book raises the question of defining the concept of a region, and it proposed dealing mainly with sub-state administrative units. When it comes to a cross-sectional quantitative analysis of regions in different countries, there are even further complications. Even focusing on political regions leaves a heterogeneous bunch of units. Among the European Union member states, there are hardly two states that have identical meso-level administration structures. The variations span from textbook federal structures in Germany and Austria, via the complex asymmetrical federal, quasi-federal or regionalized systems of Belgium, Spain and Italy to a variety of regional government structures in unitary states. These range from multilayered systems such as the nations and counties of the United Kingdom, and the *régions* and *départements* in France, to the simpler Swedish and Dutch systems. Other states, such as Luxembourg, are too small to be subdivided into regions. In terms of size, regions range from almost 18 million inhabitants in North Rhine-Westphalia (more than many EU member states) to only 26,000 in tiny Leitrim County, Ireland.

The NUTS scheme does offer a system for classifying these regions. However, it groups together regions that have completely different functions, in some cases manufacturing artificial regions for the purposes of statistical comparison. The NUTS 2 level is most useful, as it includes the meso-level regional authorities in most countries. In France, the Netherlands, Italy, Spain, Portugal and Norway, the main units of regional governance are included on the NUTS 2 level. However, the German *Länder* are NUTS 1 regions, and countries such as Ireland, Denmark and parts of the United Kingdom still had artificially created regions on the NUTS 2 level. As is mentioned in Chapter 1, this analysis defines regions according to regional government structures, using NUTS 2 regions in most cases and NUTS 1 regions in the case of Germany.[1] Denmark, Luxembourg and Ireland were excluded from the analysis because the data set used did not subdivide responses in these countries into meaningful regions.

Surveying regionalism

As is mentioned in Chapter 1, most previous studies have taken a qualitative approach to the study of regionalism. As a result, much is known about the political dynamics of regionalist movements in individual regions. The literature can explain how these movements develop, what their political aims are, and what kind of institutions they usually set up, and why. However, when it comes to explaining the differences between regions where such movements are prominent and regions where they are not, there is still much work to be done. Existing studies can explain why regionalism has developed in particular regions, but they tend not to be able to produce general analyses of why regionalism is more prominent in some regions than in others. In order to achieve this, a more quantitative approach is needed.

While the majority of studies have used qualitative data, there are some quantitative analyses of Western European regionalism. For instance, van Houten (2003) presents a cross-sectional study of demands for regional autonomy in Europe in which he covers eighty-three regions in six countries. This study focuses on the demands of political elites, developing an index on the basis of two dimensions: first, whether the political actors who demand autonomy form an opposition within the region or whether they are part of the regional government; and second, the level of political autonomy that these actors demand, focusing on whether they seek only spending powers, or taxing powers as well.

In this way, regions where there are demands for autonomy can be classified on a scale from 1 to 3.

This is a useful indicator when it comes to distinguishing between varying levels of regionalism in regions where there are demands for political autonomy. However, most regions in Western Europe do not have political elites demanding autonomy, and the majority of the regions would therefore score zero on this measure. Even though there is likely to be substantial variation in levels of regionalism across regions where no important political actors are demanding autonomy, the indicator has no potential to measure such variation. Consequently, it is not able to provide information on the full variation in regionalism at the lower end of the spectrum.

In another study, Gordin (2001) focuses on the support for regionalist political parties in his analysis of twelve ethno-regionalist parties, applying a Boolean analysis. However, as the small number of units in this study indicates, such parties are present only in a limited number of regions, and it is therefore not possible to study regionalism on a broader scale with this indicator. Brancati (2008) uses a similar dependent variable, but she increases the number of observations through using individual elections as the units in her analysis. In this way, she is able to analyse the variation in voting for regional parties across a large number of elections in thirty-seven countries, twelve of which are in Western Europe.

Similarly, Sorens (2004) studies secessionist party vote share in fifteen regions (thirteen of which are in Western Europe) across 123 elections. The aim of his study is to examine the factors behind longitudinal variation in support for secessionist parties, rather than to explain secessionism as such, and he therefore limits his analysis to regions that have had secessionist parties across a twenty-year time frame. In a later study, Sorens (2005) extends his analysis to cover all regions in what he defines as well-established democracies with significant regional differentiation, while keeping the same indicator for his dependent variable. This leaves 431 regions, most of which do not have any secessionist parties.

While the above-mentioned authors present reliable models that explain variation in the support for regional, ethno-regionalist and secessionist parties, there are still problems with using these indicators as measures of regionalism. Regionalist mobilization takes different forms across regions and only rarely involves the construction of regionalist political parties. Instead of forming a political party, regionalists may mobilize through regional branches of the national parties, or even outside party politics. Furthermore, the regionalist parties themselves are not directly comparable across different regions. Their political profiles vary across several dimensions, from extremists to moderates, left-wingers to right-wingers, and catch-all parties to fringe groups. As a consequence, there may be substantial variations in the extent to which they attract non-regionalist voters. Similarly, regionalists may vote for non-regionalist parties in varying numbers depending on the profiles of the other parties in the political system as well as of the regionalist parties themselves.

There are several other quantitative studies of various aspects of secessionism and territorial conflict. Many of these are related to the Minorities at Risk (MAR) project. MAR indicators on anti-regime rebellion and intercommunal conflict have been used in several studies (Gurr 1993; Brancati 2006; Saxton and Benson 2006), and they can be interpreted as indicators of regionalist conflicts to the extent that the movements are geographically concentrated. The indicators of group collective interests, which measure grievances over a range of political, economic and cultural issues among ethnic groups, have also been used in some studies (Fox 1999, 2001).

However, it would be highly problematic to use these indicators in a study of regionalism in Western Europe, where violent conflicts over territorial politics have been fairly rare and the vast majority of regionalist movements use peaceful, democratic means. Furthermore, it is not necessarily the case that levels of regionalism are higher in the regions that have the most violent regionalist movements. The Minority at Risk data set therefore does not seem particularly useful for studying regionalism in Western Europe.

In order to overcome the limitations of existing quantitative indicators, it would be desirable to develop an operationalization of regionalism that allowed for variation within the large group of regions with lower levels of regionalism. Survey data present an opportunity to achieve this, and also have the benefit that they can capture attitudes towards regionalism at the mass level directly.

There are some studies that measure regionalism on the basis of survey data. Most of these have been based on surveys conducted in individual regions, and their approaches are discussed in the text that follows. However, the Eurobarometer series have included questions on regional identities at irregular intervals, presenting an opportunity to study variations in regionalism across a large number of regions. Between 1980 and 2003, four Eurobarometer surveys asked such questions, and this chapter will use data from all of these surveys in order to develop a measure of regionalism. The four studies were conducted in 1991, 1995, 2000 and 2002. The chapter will combine data from all four surveys into an average measure of regionalism across the period. This means that it will not be possible to trace the evolution of regionalism across time at this stage of the analysis, but this approach will maximize the number of respondents from each region (and hence minimize the error term), which will strengthen the comparison across regions.

This still leaves the question of how to operationalize regionalism with the use of survey data. Existing surveys present two main possibilities, namely looking at absolute levels of regional identity, or at levels of regional identity relative to state identity. The following section discusses the merits of each of these approaches.

The Moreno question

In the search for a viable operational definition of regionalism, existing studies are a natural first port of call. There are several surveys that seek to measure levels of regionalism in individual regions, mostly where there are strong demands for political autonomy. The most popular instrument in this line of research is the so-called Moreno question, which is a bipolar scale asking respondents to compare their attachment to the regional community with their attachment to the state community. Respondents are given five answer options, for instance (in the case of Catalonia):

1   Catalan, not Spanish
2   More Catalan than Spanish
3   Equally Catalan and Spanish
4   More Spanish than Catalan
5   Spanish, not Catalan.

The instrument is named after Luis Moreno, who popularized it during work on his doctoral dissertation on Scottish and Catalan nationalism (Moreno 1986). However, Moreno (2006) himself credits Linz (1973) with originally designing the question in his work on peripheral nationalisms in Spain. The Moreno question has remained popular in studies of Scottish identity, for instance by Brown *et al.* (1998), who created a time series from 1986 to 1997 by combining four different surveys, all of which included the Moreno question. Similarly, De Winter and Frognier (1999) used the Moreno question in their study of Walloon regional identity from 1975 to 1996. In Spain, the Centro de Estudios de la Realidad Social carried out monthly national surveys between 1991 and 1995, which are used by Moreno *et al.* (1998) in their study of Catalan regionalism, as well as in Máiz and Losada's (2000) study of Galician regionalism from 1984 to 1992.

The Moreno question remains the most popular measure of regionalism for individual regions, but, unfortunately, surveys that include it have been carried out in only a few regions. There are therefore few studies that attempt to use the Moreno question in a cross-sectional design. The above-mentioned study by Moreno *et al.* (1998) does compare Catalonia with other Spanish regions, but it does not stretch beyond the national context. Martínez-Herrera (2005) covers five regions in three different countries, but he uses the Moreno question exclusively to compare the developments across time within each of these five regions and does not compare across the regions. It is therefore necessary to consider which questions are posed on a larger cross-sectional scale, and how these might be used in the study of regionalism.

Eurobarometer

As is mentioned above, Eurobarometer has carried out several surveys in which regional identities have been explored. As opposed to the bipolar Moreno question, which asks for relative attachment, Eurobarometer surveys ask respondents to rate their attachment to their region, as well as their town or village, country, the EU and Europe, on an absolute level. Respondents are asked 'how attached do you feel to…?' for each of these geographical levels, with the answer options being 'very attached', 'fairly attached', 'not very attached' and 'not at all attached'. Compared with the Moreno question, the benefit of the Eurobarometer series is that it covers all regions within the European Union,[2] and it therefore allows for the construction of a much larger data set.

Marks (1999: 73) develops an index on the basis of these alternatives, coding them with values from 1 to 4. Subsequently, he uses the averages as measures of the levels of regional identity, comparing these with levels of local, national and European identity. For these purposes, this approach works well. Converting regions into the unit of analysis and treating the responses of people living in the region as a measure of the degree of regionalism might therefore be a way of studying variations across regions.

However, Marks's operationalization runs into problems because the quantification of attachment levels is highly subjective, and people are therefore not likely to agree on where to draw the difference between 'very attached' and 'fairly attached'. This has the result that some people state that they are very attached to all sorts of geographical units, whereas others do not consider themselves to be attached to anything at all. Indeed, studying the relationship between 'attachment to region' and 'attachment to country', there is a strong and significant positive correlation between them – a point picked up by both Bruter (2001) and Marks (1999: 74) himself, among others.

Furthermore, there is a great deal of variation across different countries and regions with regard to how likely people are to quantify a given attachment as very high or fairly high. Table 3.1 shows the scores at the statewide level[3] in the 1991 Eurobarometer survey, which Marks (1999) uses. This study covered the eleven European Community member states at the time, as well as Norway. The

Table 3.1 Regionalism index scores for surveyed countries in 1991

Marks (1999)		*Moreno index*	
Greece	3.8	East Germany	31.8
Spain	3.7	Belgium	28.5
Portugal	3.7	West Germany	28.3
East Germany	3.6	Spain	19.2
West Germany	3.6	Netherlands	16.4
Ireland	3.6	Great Britain	16.1
Denmark	3.6	France	15.3
Great Britain	3.4	Italy	15.1
Italy	3.4	Portugal	13.9
France	3.3	Norway	13.2
Belgium	3.2	Luxembourg	12.9
Netherlands	3.0	Denmark	8.5
		Ireland	8.3
		Greece	8.2
Average	3.5	Average	16.8
St. deviation	0.2	St. deviation	7.6

Sources: Eurobarometer 36.0 and Marks (1999).

first column in the table shows the average scores on Marks's index. The Southern European countries come out on top on the index, whereas Belgium and the Netherlands are the lowest-ranked countries. These findings seem counterintuitive. Belgium has some of the most prominent regionalist movements in Europe, with consistent pressures for autonomy and successful regionalist political parties. Meanwhile, demands for regional autonomy are hardly widespread in Greece and Portugal (except for the islands of Madeira and the Azores), even though the regions hardly have any power at all in these countries at present. The reason for this outcome is that there seems to be a tendency towards stronger levels of attachment to geographical entities in general among Southern Europeans, whereas the Belgians and Dutch are less likely to quantify their attachment very highly.

Best of both worlds

The optimal solution would therefore be to combine the validity of the Moreno question with the data availability of the Eurobarometer series. This can be done by recoding the responses for the questions on respondents' attachment to their regions and to their countries into a single variable covering their relative attachment to their region vis-à-vis their country. Here, a regionalist is considered to be someone who is more strongly attached to his or her region than to his or her country. Respondents who state that they have a higher level of attachment with their region than with their country are classified as primarily regional identifiers,[4] and the proportion of primarily regional identifiers within a region can be used as the operational definition of the level of regionalism in that region. For now, this measure will be referred to as the Moreno index.

Henderson (2007: 126f.) applies a similar methodology in her study of Quebecois nationalism, recoding self-reported attachment ratings to Quebec and Canada on a 0–100 point scale into a measure approximating the Moreno scale. She argues that what distinguishes Quebecois from other Canadians is not so much a stronger attachment to the region (or sub-state nation) as a weaker attachment to the state. Considering the unexpected results on the pure attachment question presented above, this may well also be the case in other regions with high levels of regionalism, making it important to take levels of attachment towards the state into account in the cross-regional analysis. When one compares these results with surveys that actually ask the Moreno question, the main difference is that fewer respondents state an exclusive attachment to either the state or regional level, and a higher proportion state an equal identity.

Berg (2007) takes a slightly different approach in her study of multilevel identities, although still applying the basic idea of comparing attachment scores across territorial levels. She classifies respondents according to the level, form and strength of their attachment, developing a six-category scale running from 'unattached' to 'equally attached to all territorial levels'. The category 'primarily sub-national' includes respondents who report a stronger attachment to *either* their town/village or region than to the state or supranational level. While this is appropriate in a study of identities towards multiple levels of government, the present study focuses specifically on the regional level and its relationship to the state. Therefore, the Moreno index as presented above will be applied.

The last column in Table 3.1 shows how the states included in the Eurobarometer survey rank on the Moreno index. Intuitively, these rankings conform more closely to what we would expect to see than does Marks's index. The Moreno index suggests that regionalism is most widespread in Germany, Belgium and Spain, which is also where some of the most frequently studied regionalisms in Europe can be found. In Belgium and Spain, there are consistent demands from the regional level for more autonomy, whereas the German regions have been proactive in promoting the regional level in the EU. On this index, regionalism is least important in Greece, Denmark and Ireland. These are all small countries in terms of area, where local governments have been more important than regions, and none of these countries has any prominent regionalist movements or political parties. The findings on the Moreno index therefore seem to broadly match the distribution of regionalist demands across Europe. On this basis, we can conclude that the Moreno index appears to be the most appropriate measure of regionalism, and this measure will henceforth be referred to as the 'regionalism index'.

Assessment of the indicator

While the data presented in Table 3.1 provide some indication of the reliability and validity of the regionalism index measure, this section conducts a more stringent examination of the indicator. Statistical tests of the reliability and validity of the index can determine more objectively whether it is an appropriate measure that can be carried forward into the regression analysis stage of the study. In addition to using the 1991 Eurobarometer survey, the data set will now be extended with the surveys from 1995, 2000 and 2002, as discussed earlier.

The reliability of the regionalism index can be examined by testing whether the estimates for individual regions are stable across time. Although some variation in the levels of regionalism should be expected across the eleven years covered by the four surveys, the estimates should still remain broadly similar across time if the index is reliable. The four surveys can thus be combined to conduct a test–retest of the reliability of the regionalism index. Running a weighted reliability analysis of the four items on the regions covered by all four surveys returns a Cronbach's alpha[5] of 0.85, which is high, especially considering that it is likely that this test would underestimate the reliability of the index, given the long time intervals between the surveys, as well as the fact that the respondents are different in each survey. The regionalism index is therefore a reliable indicator.

While it is crucial that the regionalism index is a reliable measure, it is equally important that it is a valid measure – that is, that it actually measures regionalism. The connection between the regionalism index and the concept of regionalism can be examined both theoretically and through an empirical test known as the construct validity test. The operationalization of the theoretical variable 'regionalism' is based on the notion that regionalism is closely related to a preference for regional identification vis-à-vis state identification. People who identify more closely with the region than with the state are likely to favour vesting more power in the regional level of government than in the central level, as they regard the regional public as a more appropriate *demos*. This assumption is based on two ideas: first, that a democracy requires agreement on the definition of the *demos* (Linz and Stepan 1996: 26), or on the body of people who make decisions and for whom decisions are made; and second, that the contemporary definition of the *demos* tends to be based on a sense of community or common identity (Gellner 1983).

When the people of a region regard the statewide *demos* as inappropriate for deciding over a policy area that affects the region, they will want to redefine the *demos* in order to make it congruent with the regional public.[6] The regional public is then regarded as the community that is affected by the decisions made. On the contrary, if people do not feel any sense of identity towards the regional level, it is unlikely that they will favour devolving power to the regions, as there would not be any reason why the various regions within a state could not be governed by the same national *demos*. In this perspective, the people of all regions are regarded as belonging to the same community.

Figure 3.1 presents the measurement model underlying the operationalization of regionalism. The figure shows that the operationalization is based on a formative measurement model, where the operational variable is predicted to influence the theoretical variable – that is, regional identities are expected to influence the desire for regional autonomy.

If we now return to the definition of regionalism presented in Chapter 1, this operationalization assumes that there is a strong and consistent relationship between regional identities and regionalism across different regions. On the other hand, the indicator is not able to capture variation in the politicization of identities across different regions. It is therefore necessary to assume that regional identities are politicized in roughly equal proportions to their size. This assumption can be tested through the use of a construct validity test,[7] which examines the relationship between the indicator and a variable that is closely related to politicized regionalism. In this case, desire for regional autonomy can be expected to be correlated with actual regional autonomy. A central demand of

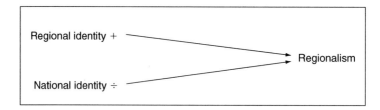

Figure 3.1 Measurement model.

many regionalist campaigns is the strengthening of political institutions, for instance through devolution. Some such campaigns have indeed been successful as well, as witnessed by the development of regional institutions in Belgium, Spain and the United Kingdom, for instance.

The theoretical discussion presented regionalism as a phenomenon occupying the political space between regional identities and regional political institutions. Regionalism is based on regional identities, and it tends to lead to demands for strengthening the regional institutions. If the construct validity test shows a strong correlation between regional identities and regional political institutions, it is reasonable to assume that this captures the processes of regionalism that take place between the formation of identity and the success of the political campaign. If so, the index would be a useful indicator of regionalism.

In order to be able to examine this relationship, one must also operationalize the theoretical variable 'regional political institutions'. This requires a measure of the strength of regional political institutions. Hooghe and Marks (2001: 193f.) provide the most thorough effort so far to construct an index of regional institutions.[8] Their index is a variation on Lane and Ersson's (1994) index of territorial autonomy, which has been popular among scholars. Hooghe and Marks have built their index around four general themes: constitutional federalism, special territorial autonomy, role of regions in central government, and regional elections. This seems like a useful way to conceptualize the institutional strength of regional governments. However, as their index refers to levels of regional governance in states, a few modifications are needed.

When the units of measurement are regions instead of states, the constitutional federalism and special territorial autonomy dimensions can be combined into a single dimension measuring the formal powers of the regional institutions. In states where some regions have special powers, these regions will simply score higher on the dimension than other regions in the same state. The dimension combining these two aspects of Hooghe and Marks's index will be labelled 'autonomy' below. As this index is intended to measure the strength of regional institutions as opposed to territorial autonomy, the power-sharing dimension in Hooghe and Marks's index is also dropped. The index thus focuses on the extent to which regions govern themselves, and does not consider their power at the central level. Apart from this, the criteria on the index are identical to those of Hooghe and Marks (2001), with one point awarded for each of the following properties:

- Autonomy:
  - The existence of a functioning regional tier of government.
  - Extensive authoritative competencies, including control over two or more of the following: taxation, police, education policy (including tertiary education), cultural policy, transport and communications policy, economic development policy, local government and determination of regional political institutions (e.g. administrative hiring, budget process, timing of regional elections).

- Specific regional competencies that are constitutionally guaranteed.
- A federal state in which constitutional change is co-decided by the central state and regions.
- Elections:
  - The region has an elected assembly.
  - The regional assembly is directly elected.

Table 3.2 shows how the regions in the data set score on the index of regional political institutions. The scores diverge somewhat from those provided by Hooghe and Marks (2001), not least because individual regions are units. This means that in the case of the United Kingdom, for instance, the Scottish and Welsh regions score higher, while the English regions are awarded a lower score. Also, Hooghe and Marks do not count the Swedish *län* and the Finnish *maakunnat* as regions, classifying them instead as local governments. However, they constitute a meso level of government above the municipality level and therefore fall within the definition of regionalism applied in this book. Hooghe and Marks argue that they have too few inhabitants to be classified as regions,

Table 3.2 Index of regional political institutions

	Autonomy	Elections	Total
Austria	4	2	6
Belgium before 1989	2	2	4
Belgium 1989–93	3	2	5
Belgium 1993 to present	4	2	6
Finland before 1994	0	0	0
Finland 1994 to present	1	1	2
Kainuu 2005 to present	1	2	3
Åland	4	2	6
France 1972–86	1	0	1
France 1986 to present	2	2	4
Germany	4	2	6
Greece before 1994	0	0	0
Greece 1994 to present	1	0	1
Italy – historic regions	3	2	5
Italy – rest 1976–96	2	2	4
Italy – rest 1996 to present	3	2	5
Netherlands	1	2	3
Norway	1	2	3
Portugal	1	0	1
Madeira and Azores	3	2	5
Spain – historical nationalities	4	2	6
Spain – rest	3	2	5
Sweden	1	2	3
England	0–1	0	0–1
Scotland, Wales before 1999	1	0	1
Scotland, Wales 1999 to present	3	2	5

but this is mainly due to the fact that Sweden and Finland are small countries. One does not exclude countries from comparative analysis solely on the basis that they are small, and therefore one should not exclude small regions either. Furthermore, the Nordic regions are among Europe's largest in area – another indication that they should not be classified as local governments. Both the *län* and the *maakunnat* were classified as regions by Hooghe *et al.* (2008).

The construct validity of the regionalism index can then be examined by looking at the relationship between regionalism and political institutions. Figure 3.2 presents the rationale behind this validity test.

An analysis of the correlation between the regionalism index scores and the regional institutions index scores shows that there is indeed a strong connection between these two indices. The correlation between the weighted average regionalism index scores across the four surveys and the regional institution scores for 2000 has a Pearson's R of 0.60. This is significant at the 99 per cent confidence level.[9] The reasonably strong correlation between the indices measuring regionalism and regional institutions conforms to the theoretical expectations of a causal relationship between regionalism and political institutions. This suggests that both indices are valid measures of the underlying theoretical concepts that they relate to, and the regionalism index can therefore be taken to be an appropriate measure of regionalism in the analysis that follows.

Caveat

The validity test has made the assumption that regional institutions are mainly an effect of regionalism. However, there are some theoretical reasons to consider regional institutions to be a cause of regionalism rather than a consequence thereof. One might expect regional political institutions to have a positive effect on the development of regionalism. It is easier to mobilize when there is a strong institution that can promote regionalism as well as serve as a basis for it. In regions with strong political institutions, it will also be much easier for regionalist

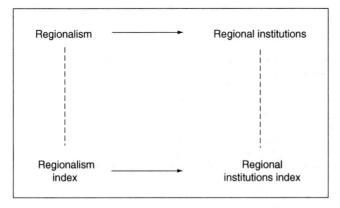

Figure 3.2 Construct validity test.

elites to spread their message to the general population. This is particularly obvious in cases where the regional authorities control education policy, but there are also plenty of opportunities for regional institutions to celebrate regional culture and heritage through festivities and events of a more voluntary nature. The relationship between regionalism and regional institutions thus poses something of a chicken-and-egg conundrum. If institutions might indeed be a cause of regionalism, it is necessary to consider the possibility of including them in the regression model. However, given the strong theoretical reasons to consider them a consequence of regionalism instead, institutions could probably more usefully be seen as manifestations of past levels of regionalism. Including them in the model would in this case in effect be paramount to regressing regionalism onto itself, or at least to using regionalism in the past to explain regionalism in the present, which would not be very interesting.

It is possible to draw further information from the longitudinal variation on the institutions dimension. If institutions were indeed a reflection of regionalism, the strength of the institutions might be expected to fall more into line with the levels of regionalism with time. Table 3.3 varies the time of measurement of both the institutions index and the weighted regionalism index, examining how the correlations between the two develop across time. The analysis includes only regions for which there are data for all time-points. The data suggest that the distribution of institutions seem to be becoming more similar to the distribution of regionalism across time, as the correlations generally tend to become stronger as time passes on the institutions variable. On the other hand, there is no clear indication of the correlations becoming stronger as the time of measurement is varied on the regionalism index.

On the balance of evidence, this suggests that regionalism has a strong effect on the establishment of political institutions. If political institutions were to be included as an independent variable in the regression model, there would therefore be a high risk of picking up feedback effects – in effect, using the institutionalization of past levels of regionalism to explain present levels of regionalism. Strong political institutions will therefore be considered an effect of regionalism – rather than a cause thereof – and hence not included in the later regression model.

Table 3.3 Correlation matrix for regionalism and political institutions

	Reg. 1991	*Reg. 1995*	*Reg. 2000*	*Reg. 2002*
Institutions 1985	0.24*	0.36*	0.19*	0.36*
Institutions 1990	0.55*	0.57*	0.42*	0.55*
Institutions 1995	0.55*	0.59*	0.42*	0.55*
Institutions 2000	0.53*	0.60*	0.42*	0.56*

Notes
Measure: Pearson's R.
$n = 145$.
* $p < 0.05$.

Distribution on the regionalism index

The average regionalism index scores across all the four Eurobarometer surveys[10] analysed are shown for individual regions in Appendix A. A preliminary look at the data shows that the average region has an index score of 15.5, with a standard deviation of 7.8. The average scores across all four surveys vary from more than 45 per cent, primarily regional identifiers in the Basque Country, to only 3.3 per cent in Northern Savonia (Finland).

The distribution on the index is skewed to the right, with a high proportion of regions having relatively low levels of regionalism, and a few outliers exhibiting high levels. The skewness statistic for the average across the four surveys is 0.77, with a standard error of 0.17. Hence, the distribution is significantly skewed. Figure 3.3 shows the distribution of the regions on the average regionalism index.

The skewness suggests that the regionalism index follows a non-normal distribution, which might create problems for the least-squares regression analysis. Better results might be obtained by analysing the base-e logarithms of the index, assuming that it follows a log-normal distribution. The distribution of the logarithms is now skewed to the left, but it is less skewed than the index itself. The logged regionalism index has a skewness statistic of −0.38, with a standard error of 0.17. Hence, the logarithmic transformation of the index will be taken as the dependent variable in the regression analysis in Chapter 4.

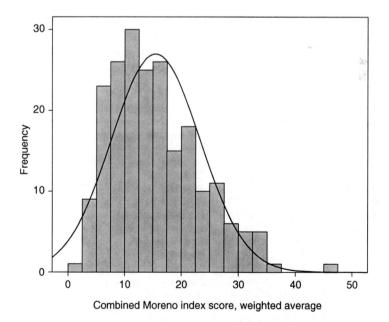

Figure 3.3 Frequency distribution on the regionalism index.

Levels of regionalism in some European regions

Now that the reliability and validity of the index have been established, some of the data derived from the Eurobarometer survey series regarding the distribution of regionalism across Western Europe can be presented. Table 3.4 shows the ten regions with the most extreme average values on either end of the scale. The list of the most regionalist regions contains several of the most frequently studied regionalisms in Western Europe, with the Basque Country, Catalonia, one Scottish and two Flemish regions all featuring in the top five. The top ten list further includes three German regions and two peripheral island regions in the Atlantic: the Canaries and the Azores. The list of the least regionalist regions includes only regions from Spain, Greece and Finland, and it is dominated by areas close to the capitals of these three countries, although the lowest-ranking region on the measure, Northern Savonia, lies in the eastern central part of Finland, close to the Russian border.

Spain appears to be the country with the highest degree of internal variation when it comes to regionalism. Three Spanish regions rank among the top seven, while five rank among the bottom ten regions on the index. The latter category includes the Castilian heartland, as well as two predominantly Castilian regions that border areas with higher levels of regionalism. This reveals the internal tensions within the Spanish state, where the dominant Castilian-speaking group seems to have become increasingly loyal to the state in response to pressures from non-Castilian areas for devolution or secession. The two highest-ranking Spanish regions, the Basque Country and Catalonia, have consistently demanded increased political autonomy and recognition of their special status since the creation of the Spanish state, and their regionalist campaigns are widely regarded by the Castilian population as threats to the integrity of the state.

The list of the most extreme cases throws up some categories of regions that might warrant a closer look. Several of the regions in the top ten are character-

Table 3.4 Highest- and lowest-ranking regions on the regionalism index

The ten most regionalist regions			The ten least regionalist regions		
Basque Country	45.4	(±6.6)	Northern Savonia	3.3	(±2.9)
West Flanders	35.8	(±4.4)	Epirus	3.4	(±2.7)
Highlands & Islands	34.2	(±15.1)	Tavastia	3.7	(±4.1)
Catalonia	34.1	(±3.7)	Madrid	4.0	(±1.7)
East Flanders	34.1	(±4.0)	Castile-La Mancha	4.1	(±2.9)
Mecklenburg-W.P.	34.1	(±4.3)	Attika/Centr. Greece	4.1	(±1.0)
Canary Islands	33.6	(±7.6)	Castile and León	4.9	(±2.6)
Berlin	31.4	(±4.1)	Satakunta	4.9	(±3.5)
Azores	31.2	(±9.4)	Cantabria	5.5	(±6.0)
Saarland	30.9	(±10.1)	Murcia	5.7	(±4.4)

Notes
Figures in parentheses denote 95% confidence intervals for the proportions.
Based on average scores across all the four surveys, excluding regions with two scores or less.

ized by linguistic differences with the rest of the state, and it might be interesting to examine other regions that are in the same situation. It might also be interesting to compare the Canary Islands and the Azores with other island regions in Europe to examine whether islands differ from other regions with regard to regionalism. Finally, the appearance of capitals in both the top and bottom ten of the distribution merits a closer look at regionalism in European capital regions. The following sections present the distributions on the regionalism index within each of these categories.

Linguistic minorities

Table 3.5 presents a list of regions with significant minority languages. In this context, this means that either a majority of the regional population speaks a different language from the majority language in the state, or that there is a completely indigenous language in the region. This leaves twenty regions with significant minority languages covered by this study. It is interesting to note that sixteen of these have index scores above the series average of 15.5. The Basque Country and Catalonia are still in a league of their own when it comes to regionalist sentiments, but a large number of these linguistic minority regions score above 20 on the index.

Among the regions featuring in the top half of this list are some of the less well known nationalisms in Europe, such as those found in Brittany and Trentino Alto Adige (South Tyrol). The regionalism index scores are higher in both

Table 3.5 Regions with significant minority languages

Basque Country	45.4	(±6.6)
Catalonia	34.1	(±3.7)
Flanders*	29.7	(±1.9)
Balearic Islands	27.8	(±10.4)
Finnmark	27.3	(±26.3)
Scotland*	26.5	(±4.3)
Trentino Alto Adige	26.3	(±11.4)
Brittany	24.0	(±5.9)
Wales*	23.7	(±5.8)
Galicia	21.5	(±4.8)
Aquitaine	20.5	(±5.7)
Norrbotten	20.0	(±14.1)
Wallonia*	19.7	(±2.1)
Friesland	18.7	(±4.9)
Sardinia	18.7	(±7.4)
Languedoc-Roussillon	16.1	(±5.7)
Valencia	14.3	(±3.5)
Friuli-Venezia Giulia	13.5	(±6.8)
Ostrobothnia	12.2	(±6.5)
North Karelia	9.7	(±5.7)

Note
* Weighted average for all sub-regions within Flanders, Wallonia, Scotland and Wales.

these regions than in places such as Wales and Wallonia, although the differences are not statistically significant. Even a region such as Scotland, well known for its autonomist tendencies, only just manages to eclipse Brittany and Trentino Alto Adige on this measure. This may be indicative of a regional identity that has not been politicized to the same extent as in comparable regions, or it may be that regionalism is a more important phenomenon in these regions than is suggested by the lack of focus on them in the literature. Compared to Wales, around 3 percentage points more of Scots claim a primary regional attachment, although the difference between these two regions is also not statistically significant.

It is also interesting to note the differences between the various regions within the Catalan language group. The traditional heartland of Catalonia is close to the top of the list, along with the Balearic Islands. However, regionalism does not appear to be as strong in the northern and southern peripheries of the Catalan Countries. Valencia scores below the series average on the index, and its population appears to identify more closely with the Spanish state, despite attempts to extend political autonomy and secure the independent status of the Valencian dialect of Catalan. Across the border, Languedoc-Roussillon also appears to be fairly well integrated into the French state, although these data do not reveal whether this also holds for the Catalan-speaking minority in the region. The same is true for Sardinia, where Catalan-speakers also make up only a small minority of the population.

In Northern Europe, regional languages appear to be less of a factor for regionalist mobilization. The two Finnish regions of Ostrobothnia and North Karelia have the lowest score of all the regions with minority languages in this study, and both have levels of regionalism that are lower than the series average. On the other hand, the northernmost regions in Norway and Sweden, which both have a minority Sami-speaking population, score substantially higher on the regionalism index. Finnmark in Norway is the fourth highest-scoring region in this sub-set, while Swedish Norrbotten also scores above the series average. However, for both of these regions the data are based on a very small number of respondents, and the estimates are therefore highly insecure.

Islands

Islands can be quite different from other peripheral regions. Because of the more complicated communication with the mainland, and possibly the different way of life that islands encourage, it is easy to see how islands can develop separate identities. It is also easy to distinguish the borders of island regions, making it obvious for everybody where the region ends. Table 3.6 presents the regionalism index scores for the regions in Europe that consist exclusively of islands or groups of islands.

There is a great deal of variation between the island regions of Western Europe. The more remote islands in the Atlantic tend to score fairly highly on the regionalism index, with the Canaries and the Azores both among the top ten

Table 3.6 Island regions

Canaries	33.6	(±7.6)
Azores	31.2	(±9.4)
Balearics	27.8	(±10.4)
Sardinia	18.7	(±7.4)
Sicily	17.8	(±4.1)
Madeira	17.0	(±7.4)
Gotland	10.0	(±16.3)
Crete	7.4	(±3.5)
Eastern Aegean Islands	6.6	(±4.1)

regionalist regions in the study. In both of these regions, more than three in ten respondents claim to identify more closely with their region than with Spain and Portugal, respectively. On the other hand, Madeira scores more modestly, rising barely above the mean, with 17 per cent primarily regional identifiers. Allegiance to the Portuguese state seems to be much higher there than in the more distant Azores.

Between the two Portuguese island regions in the Atlantic on the ranking are the three island regions in the Western Mediterranean. Among these, the Balearics seem by far the most regionalist on the basis of these data, with more than one in four respondents claiming to identify more closely with the islands than with the Spanish state. On the other hand, the Italian island regions of Sardinia and Sicily do not score much above the average for the set, despite the fact that both regions have some political autonomy.

At the other end of the spectrum, the two Greek island regions of Crete and the Eastern Aegean Islands score well below the average on the regionalism index. In both of these regions, well under one in ten respondents claim to identify predominantly with the islands vis-à-vis the Greek state, and Greek national identity thus seems to have a fairly strong foothold on the islands as well. This might be due to the content of Greek national identity, which is certainly partly based on myths and imagery from the islands. Arguably, islands form a more important part both economically and politically of the Greek state than any of the other states in this study. It is therefore perhaps not surprising that the Greek islands differ from the rest of the set with regard to regionalism. The Swedish island region of Gotland also scores below the average on the index, although again the estimate for this region is highly insecure, given the low number of respondents.

National capitals

Contrary to the historic regionalisms considered above, national capitals are usually regarded as having low levels of regionalism. In the classic centre–periphery theories discussed in Chapter 1, capitals are seen as conquerors of the other regions within the state and could be expected to remain loyal to their own creation. In centralist states, capitals also benefit economically from being

Table 3.7 National capitals

Berlin	30.1	(±4.1)
Brussels	17.3	(±3.5)
North Holland (Amsterdam)	15.5	(±2.8)
London	15.1	(±3.2)
Vienna	12.8	(±2.8)
Île de France (Paris)	12.5	(±2.4)
Lazio (Rome)	10.5	(±3.2)
Lisbon	9.8	(±1.6)
Uusimaa (Helsinki)	9.6	(±2.1)
Attika/Central Greece (Athens)	4.1	(±1.0)
Madrid	4.0	(±1.7)

political centres, and one would therefore not expect them to favour decentralization of power. Levels of regionalism in national capitals can thus say something about the extent to which the centre–periphery paradigm holds for people living in the centre across different countries in Europe. Table 3.7 presents a list of the average levels of regionalism in the ten national capitals for which I have data for at least two time-points.

As the table shows, nine of the eleven capitals score below the series average on the regionalism index, the exceptions being federal Berlin and Brussels. Berlin is an extreme outlier in this set, but the German capital has also had quite a distinct history in the post-Second World War period. Under communism, West Berlin was isolated from both East and West Germany, and it seems that a distinct Berliner identity developed during this period and remains alive today. To a much less extreme extent, Brussels presents a similar story of being an enclave, isolated through geography from Wallonia and through language from Flanders.

Both Berlin and Brussels are capitals of decentralized countries, and a good deal of political power is situated outside these capitals. The latter is also true for Amsterdam, which ranks third in this set. While the Netherlands is a unitary state, the distribution of political power between Amsterdam and The Hague means that Amsterdam does not benefit from all of the advantages of being a capital city. Competition between various cities for primacy might also contribute to the development of regionalism in Berlin and Amsterdam, suggesting that there might be a difference between monocephalic and polycephalic states in this regard. However, Rome does not score particularly highly on the index, despite being the capital of a polycephalic country, and similarly, Vienna does not score very highly despite being the capital of a federal state.

The rest of the capitals cluster in the bottom half of the Western European regions, with the Greek and Spanish capitals distinguishing themselves as extreme outliers in the bottom of the set. Madrid is the most state-nationalist of the capitals, possibly as a reaction to the high levels of regionalism in other parts of the country, and together with Athens it makes up the bottom end of the list.

Conclusion

By combining the data on regional and national attachment in the Eurobarometer survey series into an indicator equivalent to the Moreno question, it is possible to obtain a reliable and valid measure of the levels of regionalism across Western Europe. This allows for more generalizable conclusions regarding the distribution of regionalism across space, as well as more objective data on the levels of regionalism in particular regions. This chapter has presented some tentative data on the distribution of various types of regions on the regionalism index, and this might provide some insight into how levels of regionalism vary across Western Europe.

In the next chapter, the operational definition of regionalism is taken forward in an attempt to provide an explanation of why regionalism varies across space. The hypotheses developed in Chapter 2 will be tested by developing operational measures that can be used to explain variation in the levels of regionalism in a regression analysis. In this way, some of the most prominent theories of the causes of regionalism can be examined in order to achieve a greater understanding of how and to what extent they can influence regionalism.

4 Why some regions are more regionalist than others

The preceding chapter showed that there is a great deal of variation in the levels of regionalism across different regions in Western Europe. On the regionalism index, the scores range from 45.4 in the Basque Country (Spain) to 3.3 in Northern Savonia (Finland). There are large differences even within most countries when it comes to the levels of regionalism in individual regions. The rise of the regional level in Europe seems to be a phenomenon of highly varying strength. This variation might be considered a surprise, given that all regions are affected by the processes of globalization and European integration, which are expected to contribute to regionalism. Why are there such differences between European regions? Are these differences explained by culture and history alone, or are there significant differences in the economic and political processes taking place within the regions that can also explain variations in regionalism?

This chapter presents a model that can explain this variation within Western Europe, based on the theoretical framework discussed in Chapter 2. The model includes variables related to the theories on cultural distinctiveness, globalization, European integration, regional party systems and economic development, as well as control variables on geographical location and population size. The variables are fitted into a regression analysis, which will address the question of whether the model is capable of explaining why some regions are more regionalist than others, and it will also clarify which factors are most closely associated with regionalism. This will give an indication of how well the various theories on regionalism can explain variation across space, which will in turn provide a stepping-stone towards identifying some of the crucial causes of the development of regionalism in Europe.

Independent variables

The regression analysis contains indicators for each of the principal causal variables proposed in Chapter 2. The selected operational measures of cultural distinctiveness, globalization, European integration, party systems and economic development will be discussed. In some cases, more than one operational measure is included in order to capture different aspects of the independent variable. Cultural distinctiveness is measured by two separate indices, capturing linguistic differences and historical legacy. The operationalization of European integration includes a measure of public support for European integration and another of structural funds income. Finally, the regional party systems dimension is captured by an indicator of gross party system distinctiveness, and another on the existence of a regionalist party. The analysis also includes control variables for centre/periphery status and for absolute and relative population size.

Language

In the literature on cultural regionalism, linguistic differences are often quoted as the most crucial cultural difference that might lead to regionalism in a region (e.g. Anderson 1991). Linguistic differences create strong incentives to desire regional autonomy, as the regional institutions can be used to safeguard the status of the regional language and improve language education. Linguistic differences also make integration more difficult, as the cultural differences between the regional population and the national population are both obvious and a barrier to communication.

An index capturing the importance and indigenousness of the regional language has been developed in order to measure the impact of linguistic differences. The index is made up of the following items, with one point awarded for each item:

- There is an indigenous regional language that is different from the dominant language in the state.[1]
- The regional language is spoken by at least half the region's population.
- The language is not the dominant language of any state.[2]

Table 4.1 shows how the regions covered by this study rank on the regional language index. The seven regions that score the maximum three points all have an

Table 4.1 Distribution on the regional language index

3 points	2 points	1 point
Balearic Islands	Aquitaine	Alsace
Catalonia	Basque Country	Burgenland
Friesland	Brittany	Carinthia
Friuli-Venezia Giulia	Brussels	Central Macedonia
Galicia	Finnmark	Finland Proper
Sardinia	Flanders	Lorraine
Valencia	Languedoc-Roussillon	Navarre
	Norrbotten	Nord-Pas de Calais
	North Karelia	Piedmont and Aosta Valley
	Ostrobothnia	Saxony
	Scotland	Schleswig-Holstein
	Trentino Alto Adige	Sicily
	Wales	Kymenlaakso
	Wallonia	Thessaly
		Uusimaa

indigenous language that is spoken by a majority of the population: Catalan (or Valencian), Gallego, Frisian, Friulian and Sardinian. The second-highest category includes several other indigenous regional languages that are not spoken by a majority of the population, including most prominently Basque, but also Welsh, Breton, Gaelic and Sami. The remainder of this category is made up of regions where a majority of the population speak the language of a neighbouring state, such as Dutch and French in Belgium, Swedish in Finland and German in northern Italy. The final category contains regions where a substantial minority of indigenous people are native speakers of the language of a neighbouring state.

Historical sovereignty

Regions that have a history of independent statehood are likely to be less integrated into the state, and it also seems reasonable to expect them to desire a return of the political autonomy they once held. The problems of integrating with the state are likely to be present also in regions that were once part of different states from the one that currently has sovereignty over the territory. The problems should be particularly acute in regions that have been included fairly recently into the state of which they are currently part, given that the processes of cultural assimilation and nation-building will not have had as long to work.

The index of the region's historical sovereignty captures the extent to which the region has historically been governed by itself or by other powers than the state of which it is currently part. This can be taken as an indication of the extent to which its history might serve as a basis for mobilization. The index assigns the highest score to regions that have a fairly recent history as independent states, and the lowest score to regions that have formed part of the state since its establishment. Regions that historically have been part of several different states fall somewhere in between these two extremes. The index is based around three criteria, with one point awarded if the region possesses each of the following characteristics:

- The region has not been part of the current state since its formation.
- The region was not part of the current state for the entire twentieth century.
- The region has been an independent state.[3]

The distribution on this variable is shown in Table 4.2. Only one region covered in the study has been politically independent within the past 100 years: Crete, which was an independent republic from 1898 to 1913. The second-highest category is dominated by regions that changed hands at the end of one of the two world wars during the past century, including several Greek regions; Alsace and Lorraine in France; and Friuli-Venezia Giulia and Trentino Alto Adige in Italy. The category also includes some regions that have been independent *since* the formation of the state of which they currently form part, including Scotland,[4] Bavaria and Baden-Württemberg. The final two regions in this category are Catalonia and the Basque Country, because of the statutes of autonomy that

Table 4.2 Distribution on the historical sovereignty index

3 points	2 points	1 point	1 point (cont.)
Crete	Aegean Islands	Andalusia	Provence-Alpes
	Alsace	Brandenburg	Rhône-Alpes
	Baden-Württemberg	Epirus	Sardinia
	Basque Country	Franche-Comté	Saxony
	Bavaria	Halland	Saxony-Anhalt
	Catalonia	Hesse	Schleswig-Holstein
	Central Macedonia	Jämtland	Sicily
	East Macedonia	Langued.-Roussillon	Skåne
	Friuli-Ven. Giulia	Lombardy	Thessaly
	Lorraine	Mecklenburg W. P.	Thuringia
	Scotland	Navarre	Tuscany
	Thrace	Nord-Pas de Calais	Valencia
	Trentino Alto Adige	N. Rhine-Westphalia	Veneto
		Piedmont and Aosta	Västra Götaland

these regions enjoyed prior to the Franco dictatorship. The final category includes several regions that have older histories of independent statehood or of belonging to different states, including a large number of regions in Germany and Italy, where state-building was a late and gradual process.

Globalization

Globalization is expected to create incentives for regional mobilization as a result of the blurring of national borders and the increased competition between regions for investments and labour. While globalization also encompasses the increased movement of people, culture and ideas, it is almost exclusively conceived in the political science literature in terms of the increase in international trade of goods and services. The most common operationalizations therefore use total trade as a proxy for globalization, for instance by looking at the sum of exports and imports as a proportion of gross domestic product (GDP) (Garrett 2001: 7). Unfortunately, figures on international trade are unavailable on a regional level in most countries, and it is therefore not possible to use this measure here. The same is true for foreign direct investments, which are another common proxy for globalization.

Instead, one can look at a different aspect of the concept and use movement of people as a proxy for globalization. The theory predicts globalization to have an effect on the regional labour market, with successful regions becoming clusters of growing businesses. The number of people who immigrate into the region from abroad should give an indication of how strongly globalization affects the region. This variable therefore measures the annual number of foreign immigrants as a proportion of the region's population. Eurostat (2004) provides data for most regions[5] for at least parts of the period 1990–99, and by taking the average levels for the years in which data are available it is possible to obtain a decent measure of relative levels of globalization. Admittedly, this is not a perfect measure of globalization, but it does at least capture one aspect of the phenomenon.

European integration

Theories on the impact of European integration on regionalism hold that the EU is increasingly becoming an alternative to the nation-state, undermining the traditional dominance of the national level in territorial politics. As discussed in Chapter 2, there are three different aspects of European integration that can cause regionalism: economic integration across national borders, transfer of political authority from the national to the European level, and the construction of a European identity. The first two aspects of European integration can be expected to vary mainly across time rather than space, and there are indeed no indicators on how individual regions have been affected by these developments. However, the third aspect, identification with Europe, can be expected to vary across regions.

This can be measured by looking at the extent to which people in a region are willing to let the EU extend its political authority, based on the idea that citizens want to be governed by a unit that they identify with. The need to improve the legitimacy of the EU institutions was arguably a crucial part of the rationale behind the EU's attempts at building a European identity (Bruter 2005: 67ff.), so this operationalization should capture the concept reasonably well.[6] This rationale is also similar to the connection between regional identity and regional institutions, discussed in Chapter 3. Furthermore, the instrument partly captures the first two dimensions of European integration as well, as EU institutions are likely to be more successful in creating a new economic and political framework for the regions if the regional public supports the transfer of powers to the European level.

A useful operational measure of Europeanization can therefore be obtained by measuring preferences for state or EU responsibilities in different policy areas. Several Eurobarometer surveys present respondents with a list of policy areas, asking for each of them whether they think it should be the responsibility of the EU or of national governments. By looking at the average number of policy areas that people believe should be the responsibility of the EU rather than the state, it is possible to get a measure of the extent to which the EU is seen as a viable alternative institutional framework to the central state, which conforms closely to the theoretical mechanisms predicted by the literature.[7] The top ten and bottom ten regions on this measure are presented in Table 4.3.

The top ten list is dominated by regions from Italy and Spain, which between them contribute seven of the eight most pro-EU regions in Europe. Italy alone provides five of these, with three regions in the north-west of Italy in the top five. The two Spanish regions at the top of the list, Cantabria and Galicia, are also in the north-western part of the country. The list is completed by the French region Aquitaine, the Belgian province Limburg and the German state Hamburg.

Table 4.3 Most and least Europeanized regions

Top ten		Bottom ten	
Umbria	2.02	North Trøndelag	−2.46
Friuli-Venezia Giulia	1.79	Kainuu	−2.16
Cantabria	1.45	Buskerud	−1.96
Tuscany	1.32	Burgenland	−1.94
Liguria	1.24	North Savonia	−1.73
Galicia	1.24	Finnmark	−1.66
Aquitaine	1.18	Satakunta	−1.62
Calabria	1.17	North Ostrobothnia	−1.56
Limburg (B)	1.11	Telemark	−1.55
Hamburg	1.08	Nordland	−1.54

Source: Eurobarometer.

As the other end of the spectrum, the non-member Norway unsurprisingly provides a large number of the most Euro-sceptic regions. Five of the ten most Euro-sceptic regions in Western Europe are in Norway, and a further four are in Finland. In terms of geography, three of the four northernmost regions in each of these two countries are included within the list of the ten most Euro-sceptic regions. The only non-Scandinavian region in the bottom ten is Burgenland, a south-eastern Austrian border region.

Structural funds

While the Europeanization variable looks at the effects of the construction of a European identity, another approach is to examine whether the union's direct relationship with specific regions has fuelled regionalism. One can study the effects of the EU's direct efforts at strengthening the regions through looking at whether there is any connection between the union's structural funds expenditure and regionalism in the recipient regions. This variable is based on data from the 1999 annual report on the structural funds (European Commission 2000), and it measures the total payments to each region through all of the various objectives in the structural funds programmes for the period 1994–99. The indicator is adjusted on a per capita basis, with one unit being equal to €100 per capita of structural funds payments.

Party systems

Part of the purpose behind devolution of power is changing the policy outcomes. However, diverging policy outcomes depend to some extent on different parties being in power at the regional and national level. The likelihood of this occurring increases when the difference between the regional and national party systems increases. The distinctiveness of the regional party system is measured through comparing the distribution of votes on the regional level with the state-wide distribution. For each region, the regional party system is compared to the state party system through a formula known as the Lee index[8] (see Caramani 2002). Table 4.4 shows the ten regional party systems in the study that were most distinctive from their respective state-wide party systems, as well as the ten least distinctive party systems, in the parliamentary election falling closest to 1995.

Unsurprisingly, the completely regionalized Belgian parties take Wallonia and Flanders to the top of the list. Both regions have party systems that are unique to their specific region, without any state-wide parties contesting the elections. The parties thus achieve state-wide results that are on average slightly less (in Wallonia) or slightly more (in Flanders) than half their regional vote share. Between the two Belgian regions on the list are two regions where regionally organized parties win a higher share of the vote than state-wide parties. In Bavaria, the Christlich-Soziale Union (CSU) won an absolute majority, while it did not run elsewhere in Germany. In the Basque Country, the regional vote was split between three different regional parties: the Partido Nacionalista Vasco (PNV), Eusko Alkartasuna and Herri Batasuna. Combined, these three parties won more votes than the state-wide Partido Popular (PP) and Partido Socialista Obrero Español (PSOE), which dominated the national election. A further three regions in the top ten list are characterized by one large regionally organized party competing with the state-wide parties and winning a large share of the vote. These are the Convergéncia i Unió in Catalonia (30 per cent), Svenska Folkpartiet in Ostrobothnia (20 per cent) and the Union für Süd-Tirol in Trentino Alto Adige (8.5 per cent).

The final three regions in the top ten do not have any specifically regionally organized parties. Rather, the vote share for the national parties is highly distinctive in these regions, with some state-wide parties enjoying substantially more success than others. In the two northernmost Finnish regions, Lapland and Kainuu, the Keskusta (Centre Party) and the Vasemmistoliito (Left Alliance) performed much better than on the state level, whereas the Suomen Sosialidemokraattinen Puolue (SDP – Social Democratic Party) and the Kokoomus

Table 4.4 Most and least distinctive regional party systems

Top ten		Bottom ten	
Wallonia (average)	60.5	Salzburg	1.5
Bavaria	45.1	Östergötland	1.8
Basque Country	43.5	Epirus	2.3
Flanders (average)	36.3	Vorarlberg	2.8
Lapland	31.5	Västra Götaland	2.8
Catalonia	29.5	Thessalia	2.9
Ostrobothnia	27.2	Uppsala	3.0
Trentino Alto Adige	25.9	Champagne-Ardennes	3.1
Kainuu	25.9	Peloponnese	3.1
Saxony	25.6	Gelderland	3.4

Source: Caramani (1999) and Ministero dell'Interno (1996).

(National Coalition Party) fared much worse. In both regions, the Keskusta dominated, winning close to 40 per cent of the vote, while the Vasemmistoliito was larger than the SDP. In Finland as a whole, the SDP was by far the largest party, with 28 per cent of the vote compared to the Keskusta's 20 per cent and 11 per cent for the fourth-placed Vasemmistoliito. Finally, Saxony's place in the top ten is explained by the fact that it was the strongest region for the Christlich Demokratische Union (CDU) and the weakest region for the Sozialdemokratische Partei Deutschlands (SPD) in this election. The post-communist Partei des Demokratischen Sozialismus (PDS) also performed relatively well in Saxony.

The list of the least distinctive regional party systems features regions from five different countries: Austria, France, Greece, the Netherlands and Sweden. Thus, they cover a range of different party systems, from the Austrian three-party system to the more fragmented Dutch and Swedish systems. Notably, none of the bottom ten regions are capitals, although some are situated close to their respective state capitals (Uppsala, Peloponnese and Champagne-Ardennes). Capitals tend to be rather distinctive areas, particularly in terms of the composition of their electorate, and it is therefore not surprising that the election results are fairly different in capitals compared to the state-wide results.

Regionalist parties

In addition to the variation in support for national parties, the question of specifically regionalist parties is of particular interest in this connection. Regionalist parties have an interest in mobilizing regionalism, as this is likely to increase their electoral support. Although the success of regionalist parties is to a large extent a function of regionalism itself, their existence as such might be regarded as being less dependent on regionalism. The variable is therefore a dummy that takes the value 1 if the region has a non-trivial ethno-regionalist party and 0 if it does not. In this way, it can examine whether the existence of regionalist parties has an impact on the levels of regionalism, regardless of whether or not they achieve electoral success. The ethno-regionalist parties are drawn from the handbook of Lane *et al.* (1997: 138ff.). Parties listed as ethnic in these authors' classification are included, provided that they have a specifically regional basis.

Economic development

The theories provide contrasting predictions on the relationship between regionalism and economic development. Internal colonialism holds that poor regions will be likely to rebel against the state in order to improve their lot, while theories on prosperity and regionalism claim that prosperity provides fiscal incentives for mobilization and boosts regional self-esteem. In country-level studies, economic development is usually measured in terms of GDP per capita. The equivalent of this for regions is the GDP per region (GDPR) per capita data calculated by most national statistical agencies, as well as by Eurostat at the European level.[9]

Control variables

Fundamental centre–periphery theories hold that states are formed as centres conquer and colonize surrounding areas, which subsequently form peripheries in the national states. From this perspective, one would expect resistance to the centre in the form of regionalist sentiments in the peripheries. The peripheries might be expected to want to take back autonomy over their own affairs, while centres should be expected to remain faithful to the state that they created themselves. This effect is captured by a dummy variable that distinguishes between regions that border the capital, and are hence classified as being in the centre, and those that do not.

The population variable reflects the assumption that size matters, which is implicit in some of the literature on regionalism. For instance, some writers (such as Hooghe and Marks 2001) do not count regions in the Nordic countries as regions because they regard them as too small,[10] which certainly seems to reveal an expectation that a certain population size is necessary for the development of regionalism. One would also expect populous regions to be better equipped for autonomy, as they resemble nation-states to a larger extent. For instance, North Rhine-Westphalia, with its 18 million inhabitants, would have been a fairly large European country if it had been an independent state. Conversely, a small region might be expected to be more dependent on the central state, and it might be considered too small to be able to function efficiently as a unit of governance. The population variable tests these hypotheses by measuring the population size of the region (in millions) and examining to what extent it explains variation in the regionalism index scores. A separate variable measures the regional population as a proportion of the state population, in order to examine whether relative size matters.

Why regionalism varies across Western Europe

The operational measures of independent and control variables can be applied to the regionalism index in a regression analysis to examine their ability to explain variations in the levels of regionalism across Western Europe. This will make it

Table 4.5 Expected effects

Independent variables		*Control variables*	
Regional language	+	Periphery	+
Historical sovereignty	+	Population	+
Globalization	+	Relative size	+
Support for the EU	+		
Structural funds	+		
Vote distinctiveness	+		
Regionalist party	+		
Economic development	+		

possible to test the central hypotheses about the relationships between various potential factors and regionalism, as well as to look at the relative impacts of specific factors when controlling for other possible explanations. Table 4.5 summarizes the predicted relationships between each independent variable and regional identity. Each of the independent variables is predicted to have a positive impact on regional identity.

Regression analysis

In Table 4.6, the independent variables outlined have been regressed on the logged regionalism index scores.[11] The 'model 1' column contains the full model with all the independent variables, whereas the 'model 2' column contains the parsimonious model that resulted from backwards stepwise selection.

Overall, both the full model 1 and the parsimonious model 2 can explain around 56 per cent of the variance in regionalism. Among the independent variables, one indicator related to each theoretical hypothesis has a significant effect on regionalism. In terms of cultural distinctiveness, regional languages are positively associated with regionalism. On the other hand, there does not appear to be a significant relationship between regionalism and historical sovereignty. The historical sovereignty index is positively related to regionalism, but not significantly so.

Globalization emerges as the strongest of the independent variables in both model 1 and model 2. Economic development also has a strong and significant

Table 4.6 Examining the model of regionalism

	Model 1			Model 2		
	Coeff.	*SE*	*Beta*	*Coeff.*	*SE*	*Beta*
Regional language	0.148***	(0.054)	0.17	0.182***	(0.050)	0.21
Historical sovereignty	0.051	(0.059)	0.05			
Foreign immigration	0.035***	(0.007)	0.28	0.035***	(0.007)	0.28
Support for the EU	0.096*	(0.050)	0.11	0.102**	(0.046)	0.11
Structural funds	−0.014	(0.010)	−0.07			
Vote distinctiveness	0.009**	(0.004)	0.14	0.010***	(0.004)	0.16
Regionalist party	0.113	(0.122)	0.06			
GDPR per capita	0.311**	(0.124)	0.16	0.333***	(0.113)	0.17
Periphery	0.283***	(0.069)	0.23	0.310***	(0.065)	0.25
Population, millions	0.019	(0.013)	0.09	0.025**	(0.012)	0.12
Relative population	−1.008***	(0.321)	−0.20	−0.984***	(0.304)	−0.19
Constant	1.678***	(0.146)		1.601***	(0.125)	
Adjusted R^2	0.56***			0.56***		
n	212			212		

Notes
Dependent variable: log (Regionalism index).
* *p* (two-tailed) < 0.10; ** *p* < 0.05; *** *p* < 0.01.

positive impact in both models. The impact of Europeanization is somewhat weaker, and only one of the two variables is significantly related to regionalism. The main indicator, measuring support for the EU, has a significant positive impact in both models. On the other hand, the structural funds variable does not have a significant impact on regionalism when the model controls for other variables. Indeed, the direction of the relationship even goes in the opposite direction to what was expected, as regions receiving more structural funds tend to be less regionalist than other regions. This is reasonable given the relationship between economic development and regionalism, as structural funds are mainly provided for the poorest regions. However, the findings do question the idea that income from structural funds would lead to growing regionalism, particularly when structural funds expenditure does not appear to be associated with regionalism even when economic development is controlled for.

Differences in regional party systems also appear to be closely related to regionalism, as the relationship between the Lee index and regionalism is significant and positive in both models. On the other hand, the existence of specifically regionalist political parties does not appear to have an independent effect once the distinctiveness of the regional party system as a whole is controlled for. The relationship between the regionalist parties dummy and regionalism is positive, as expected, but it is not statistically significant.

Among the control variables, the centre/periphery variable has the strongest effect on regionalism, with levels of regionalism being significantly higher in peripheral regions. The two population variables relate to regionalism in somewhat contradictory ways. The analysis shows that large regions are indeed likely to be more regionalist, as expected, but the same is true for regions with a small share of the state's population, once other variables are controlled for. It thus seems that there is a tendency for relatively high levels of regionalism in small regions in large countries, whereas lower levels of regionalism would be expected in large regions in small countries. It is worth noting that the two variables are closely connected, so that if one of them is removed from the model, the other ceases to be significantly related to regionalism. The relationship between population size and regionalism thus appears to be fairly complex, and it is necessary to take relative as well as absolute population size into account.

As the regression model explains variation in the logarithmic transformations of the original regionalism index scores, the results are less straightforward to interpret than for an ordinary regression model. However, model 2 can be used to calculate predicted scores on the regionalism index for regions with specified values on each of the variables. This will make it easier to interpret the results in terms of the effect that each variable is expected to have on regionalism. Table 4.7 demonstrates how the predicted regionalism index scores change when each variable is specified as taking a low, average or high value.

Varying the regional language index score has the strongest impact on the predicted regionalism index scores. Regions with a score of 3 on the regional language index are expected to score 21.2 on the regionalism index, compared to 12.3 for regions with no regional language. Regions with low levels of globali-

Table 4.7 Predicted regionalism index scores

	Low	*Average*	*High*
Regional language	12.3	14.8	21.2
Foreign immigration	10.8	12.3	14.2
Support for the EU	11.0	12.3	13.6
Vote distinctiveness	11.3	12.3	13.7
Regional GDP per capita	11.1	12.3	13.6
Periphery	9.0		12.3
Population size	11.8	12.3	13.0
Relative population size	12.8	12.3	11.2

Note
The table shows the predicted scores on the regionalism index when all variables are kept constant at the series mean, except for the independent variable listed in the first column of each row, which is varied to the 10th and 90th percentile levels. For regional language, 'low' represents a score of 0, 'average' a score of 1, and 'high' a score of 3. For periphery, 'low' represents a region that borders the state capital, while 'high' represents a region that does not border the capital. The score of 12.3, listed in the average column of most rows, represents the expected regionalism index score for a region that does not border the state capital and does not have a regional language, while it is precisely average with respect to all other variables. The figures in the low and high columns represent how the predicted regionalism index score changes when the relevant independent variable is varied to a low and high level (i.e. to the 10th and 90th percentile, respectively).

zation are predicted to score 1.5 points lower on the regionalism index than an average region, while regions with high levels of globalization are predicted to score 1.9 points higher. The other variables have similar, but slightly weaker, effects on regionalism. A low level of Europeanization reduces the regionalism score by 1.3, while a high level increases it by 1.3 points. Economic development has almost precisely the same effect. Finally, regions with party systems that resemble the national party system are predicted to score 1 point lower than average on the regionalism index, while regions with distinctive party systems score 1.4 points higher. Among the control variables, the centre–periphery variable has the strongest effect on regionalism. At 9.0, regions bordering the national capitals have the lowest predicted regionalism score. Absolute and relative population sizes have more modest effects on regionalism.

Country-specific effects

The regions in this data set are governed by different states with various types of political institutions. There is a chance that the effect of some of the independent variables could depend on which country the region is in. Regions might cluster in groups according to their country, and the model could then be expected to fit in a reasonably similar way to all regions within any given country, while being a poorer fit when it comes to explaining variation across countries. This hypothesis can be tested by introducing a dummy variable for each country into the model. Through introducing country dummies, it is possible to check whether the model is capable of explaining variation within each country, in which case the independent variables will still have a significant impact on regionalism even when country dummies are controlled for. It is also possible to test whether the model can explain variation across different countries, in which case the country dummies themselves will not have a significant effect on regionalism.

In model 3 of Table 4.8, such country dummies have been included for each of the countries in the study. This produces a large increase in R^2. When the country dummies are introduced, the model can explain 76 per cent of the variation in the regionalism index. This suggests that the model has been underspecified, or that there is a substantial national element to the phenomenon of regionalism. The political structure and the political culture of the country might be part of this explanation.

The country dummies broadly cluster into three or four different groups. Germany forms a separate cluster where regionalism is underestimated by the model compared to all other countries. At the other end of the spectrum, Greece, Spain and Finland form a cluster of countries where regionalism is overestimated by the model. Most other countries form one large cluster, although the differences within this cluster are fairly large. Four of the independent variables of the model remain significantly related to regionalism. Europeanization is actually even more strongly associated with regionalism once the analysis controls for country, with the effect of an increase in Europeanization being more than twice as strong as in model 2. The impact of regional language is also markedly stronger than in model 2, as is the effect of regional party systems. The relationship between economic development and regionalism remains approximately the same whether or not countries are controlled for, with only minor differences in the coefficients.

Conversely, the relationship between the globalization variable and regionalism changes completely when country dummies are controlled for. The variable

Table 4.8 Exploring cross-national validity

	Model 2			Model 3		
	Coeff.	*SE*	*Beta*	*Coeff.*	*SE*	*Beta*
Regional language	0.182***	(0.050)	0.21	0.256***	(0.038)	0.29
Foreign immigration	0.035***	(0.007)	0.28	−0.013	(0.009)	−0.10
Support for the EU	0.102**	(0.046)	0.11	0.208***	(0.064)	0.23
Vote distinctiveness	0.010***	(0.004)	0.16	0.013***	(0.004)	0.21
GDPR per capita	0.333***	(0.113)	0.17	0.326**	(0.141)	0.17
Periphery	0.310***	(0.065)	0.25	0.170***	(0.050)	0.14
Population, millions	0.025**	(0.012)	0.12	−0.011	(0.013)	−0.05
Relative population	−0.984***	(0.304)	−0.19	−0.330	(0.345)	−0.06
Country dummies	Excluded			Included		
Constant	1.601***	(0.125)		1.848***	(0.127)	
Adjusted R^2	0.57***			0.76***		
n	212			212		

Notes
Dependent variable: log (Regionalism index).
* *p* (two-tailed) < 0.10; ** *p* < 0.05; *** *p* < 0.01.

now actually has a negative impact on regionalism, although the relationship is not statistically significant. This suggests that the observed relationship between globalization and regionalism in the previous models might have been an arte-fact of variations in average globalization index scores across different countries. Certainly, one plausible explanation would be that the globalization index actu-ally picked up some of the impact of the country dummies, rather than being sig-nificantly related to regionalism in itself. One of the control variables, centre/periphery location, still has a significant impact on regionalism, although its impact is drastically reduced. However, the two population variables are no longer significantly related to regionalism once countries are controlled for, and the impact of absolute population size actually changes direction and becomes negative in the country dummy model.

The analysis of the country dummies shows that the regions cluster around the countries in which they are located. It is possible to take this into account in the analysis by running a random intercept model where the regions are clustered by countries. As the variances of the regionalism index estimates differ across regions, the analysis still needs to be weighted. This has been achieved using the gllamm software for Stata and applying robust standard errors. The results need to be treated with caution, owing to the difficulties concerning weighting in mul-tilevel modelling, but they are still instructive in combination with the weighted least-squares regressions presented earlier in this chapter. Table 4.9 presents the results of a random intercept model that clusters the regions by country.

Table 4.9 Clustered regression

	Model 2		Random intercept model	
	Coeff.	S.E.	Coeff.	S.E. (robust)
Regional language	0.182***	(0.050)	0.275***	(0.048)
Foreign immigration	0.035***	(0.007)	0.009	(0.006)
Support for the EU	0.102**	(0.046)	0.104***	(0.033)
Vote distinctiveness	0.010***	(0.004)	0.016***	(0.003)
GDPR per capita	0.333***	(0.113)	0.189*	(0.115)
Periphery	0.310***	(0.065)	0.183	(0.118)
Population, millions	0.025**	(0.012)	0.001	(0.001)
Relative population	−0.984***	(0.304)	−0.517	(0.329)
Constant	1.601***	(0.125)	1.694***	(0.144)
n (level 1)	212		212	
n (level 2)			13	
R^2	0.57***			
Log likelihood			−106864***	
Level 1 variance			0.092***	(0.016)
Level 2 variance			0.200***	(0.059)

Notes
Dependent variable: log (Regionalism index). Clustered by country.
* p (two-tailed) < 0.10; ** p < 0.05; *** p < 0.01.

The clustered regression analysis produces similar results to those produced by the analysis that controls for country dummies. Except for globalization, all the independent variables retain their impacts on regionalism, with regional language, Europeanization, vote distinctiveness and economic development still having significant positive effects on regionalism. Relative and absolute population sizes are still not significantly related to regionalism. The same is true for globalization, although its impact now resumes being positive, with a p value of 0.105. Location in the periphery of the country also no longer has a significant effect on regionalism ($p=0.119$), although the direction is still positive. Around a third of the remaining variance in the data is between regions and two-thirds between countries.

Conclusion

The cross-sectional analysis shows that regionalism is likely to be more prevalent in regions with a regional language, a high level of economic development and highly regionalized party systems, and which are closely integrated into the European Union. All of these relationships are statistically significant even when country dummies are controlled for and in the clustered regression analysis. There are also some indications that regionalism is more prevalent in highly globalized regions. Globalization did have a significant positive effect in the original regression, but its impact ceased to be significant and even turned negative when country dummies were controlled for. This might suggest that the original impact was a result of variations in average levels of globalization across different countries, and it is still unclear how globalization impacts on regionalism.

As the introduction of country dummies creates uncertainty around some of the results from the cross-sectional analysis, the model needs to be tested further. It is also interesting to examine how some of the variables that are closely associated with the distribution of regionalism across space perform in explaining regionalism across time. The following chapter examines the model of regionalism in the form of longitudinal case studies. The cases have been selected to maximize variation across time in the levels of globalization, economic development and Europeanization. The developments along these variables will lead to a set of predictions about how regionalism has developed across time in the regions, and these predictions will be tested by a study that seeks to measure the levels of regionalism at different points in the recent history of the regions. Regional language and centre/periphery do not change across time, but the selection covers one region where there is an indigenous regional language and one region where the national language dominates, in order to examine how the model performs at different levels of this variable.

5   Territorial mobilization in Scotland and Rogaland

The cross-sectional analysis leaves some questions unanswered, both with regard to the regionalism model as a whole and when it comes to the relationship between globalization and regionalism. This merits further testing of the model, and the next step of the analysis examines how the model performs when it is tested using a completely different research design. This chapter tests the model's ability to predict developments across time in two Western European regions. This serves two purposes. First, it makes it possible to examine the similarities and differences between the variables that can explain variation in the levels of regionalism across space and those that can explain variation across time. Second, it allows the regionalism model to be tested on a new set of data, which will make the analysis more robust.

The regions are selected to maximize variation across time *within* each of the two regions. On the other hand, it is not necessary for there to be variation *between* the two cases on these variables, because the case studies aim to explain longitudinal rather than cross-sectional variation. For these purposes, the analysis focuses on the development of two petroleum regions since the 1960s: Scotland in the United Kingdom, and Rogaland in Norway. As oil was discovered underneath the sea between the two regions in the early 1970s, they have both experienced considerable changes in their economic fortunes and in their relations with the global economy. This combination of circumstances allows for the variation across time on the economic development and globalization variables that is necessary to test the model properly.

While both regions have experienced fairly similar developments on the two above-mentioned variables, the processes of Europeanization have been present in different degrees in the two regions. When the United Kingdom joined the European Community (EC) in 1973, a majority of the Norwegian public voted against joining in a closely contested referendum. The longitudinal study of Scotland will thus reveal how Scottish nationalism[1] was affected by its inclusion in the EC and the subsequent deepening of integration through for instance the Maastricht Treaty. Meanwhile, the longitudinal study of Rogaland will examine the development of regionalism across time in the absence of EC/EU membership.

The final independent variable, party systems, has not been used purposely in case selection, but it seems highly likely that there will have been some degree of variation on this variable across the forty years covered by the case studies. In every region, there is a degree of fluctuation in the support for the various political parties across time, and it is unlikely that this will follow the variations on the national level across the entire time period. Hence, it was not necessary to select the cases on the basis of their values on this independent variable.

Regional language and centre/periphery will be controlled for in the case studies, as there have not been any major changes in the status of either of these variables across the time period under study in either of these two regions. However, the two regions are also quite different with regard to the language variable, as Scotland does have an indigenous minority language, while Rogaland does not. Indeed, this is indicative of a broader difference in the history and culture of the two regions. Scotland would qualify as an *ethnie* in Smith's (1986) understanding. It is a historic nation within the United Kingdom with a history of independent statehood and a distinct religious tradition, and it continues to define itself as a nation in its own right. Scottish identity has always been strong, and there are long traditions for the use of symbols such as flags, clothes, music and sports teams to express this identity. Rogaland, on the other hand, is certainly no *ethnie*. It is a much smaller region that forms part of the fairly homogeneous and integrated Norwegian nation, and there are no claims to nationhood within the region. It does not have any major historical symbols on which to base a regional identity, and it has no recent experiences of autonomy, or indeed of regional political power to any significant extent.

The difference between the two cases in terms of their historical and cultural distinctiveness is interesting, as it allows for the examination of whether the influence of other causal factors is different in regions with high and low degrees of cultural distinctiveness. In other words, it makes it possible to look at whether there is an interaction effect between culture and other independent variables, and, if so, how this interaction works. The diversity in terms of culture and regionalist histories will also make the findings more generalizable, as they can tell us something about both stateless nations and ordinary regions.

This chapter tracks developments within the two cases across the time period from 1960 to 2005 on each of the independent variables in the regionalism model. This forms the basis of a set of predictions with regard to the development of regionalism in each of the cases across the period. The predictions are then tested in order to examine whether the model can predict changes in the levels of regionalism across time within individual regions. The analysis discusses various indicators of the variation across time in Scottish nationalism and in regionalism in Rogaland, with the aim of examining whether these developments conform to what the regionalism model would predict on the basis of the changes in the independent variables in each region during the period covered.

Model predictions

Ideally, the regionalism model should be capable of explaining variations in the levels of regionalism across time as well as space. If it is truly a causal model, the model that was developed on the basis of variation across space should also be able to explain variation in regionalism across time. This proposition can be examined through studying how each of the independent variables has changed across time in individual regions, and using this information to make predictions about how this will have affected regionalism. The predictions can then be compared to how regionalism actually developed across time to assess whether the model can successfully explain variation in the levels of regionalism across time.

This section examines how four of the independent variables from the regionalism model have changed through the period from the 1960s to the 2000s in Scotland and in Rogaland. The variation in the independent variables is used to make a set of predictions about how regionalism will have developed in each of the two regions over the same time period. In the next section, these predictions will be compared to actual measures of the levels of regionalism in the two regions through the same period.

Scotland: European integration, British divergence

The recent history of Scotland is characterized by a growth in each of the independent variables of the regionalism model. The region has become increasingly integrated into the EU, and also increasingly positive about European integration. Meanwhile, the Scottish economy has been affected by globalization, and it has gone through periods of strong growth both in the 1970s and in the 1990s. There has also been an increasing tendency towards divergence between the Scottish and British voting patterns, in particular because of the Scottish rejection of the Conservative Party under Margaret Thatcher's government. On the basis of the regionalism model, the levels of nationalism in Scotland should therefore have gone through major changes since the late 1960s.

The Scottish economy has traditionally depended on trade with the outside world. Scotland's small population size has meant that the domestic market is not large enough to provide a basis for modern industries, and the economy has therefore been export oriented (McCrone 1993: 5). It was also an early industrializer, and the British Empire provided connections with foreign markets. Scotland is still among the most export-oriented regions of the United Kingdom. According to Zürn and Lange (1999: 21), Scotland accounts for more than 10 per cent of UK exports, yet only around 8.5 per cent of the population. Driffield and Hughes (2003) furthermore show that foreign direct investment (FDI) also increased sharply in Scotland during the 1980s, both in absolute terms and as a share of UK FDI.

The proportion of immigrants in Scotland has increased gradually over the period from 1965 to 2005. However, the country has not had particularly high rates of immigration compared to other areas of the United Kingdom. In 1991, 2.5 per cent of Scotland's population was born outside the United Kingdom, whereas the foreign-born made up 5.8 per cent of the population in the United Kingdom as a whole. In 2001, the proportion in Scotland had risen to 3.3 per cent, while the corresponding proportion for the United Kingdom had risen to 7.5 per cent. In both of these years, Scotland had a lower proportion of immigrants than any of the English regions except the North East, although it did have a higher proportion of immigrants than Wales. The proportion of immigrants in Scotland grew at roughly the same rate as the proportion in the United Kingdom as a whole through the period from 1991 to 2001 (BBC 7 September 2005; Kyambi 2005).

As an early industrializer, the Scottish economy relied mainly on heavy industries at the beginning of the twentieth century. The decline of these industries subsequently led to an extended period of economic decline lasting well into the 1960s, and the regional GDP per capita stood at below 90 per cent of the UK average as recently as 1967. The economy grew strongly in the late 1960s and early 1970s with the discovery of North Sea oil and had almost caught up with the national average by 1976, when the Scottish GDPR per capita was 98.5 per cent of the UK average. Scotland maintained its relative economic position more or less until 1983, but suffered from economic decline through the latter half of the 1980s. In the 1990s, the economy picked up again with the development of a knowledge-intensive economy, with the Glasgow–Edinburgh area refashioned as Silicon Glen because of the new high-tech industries. By 1994, Scotland's GDPR per capita even exceeded the UK average – a rare feat in the centralized British economy.[2] Figure 5.1 shows the development of Scotland's GDPR per capita relative to the UK average from 1967 to 2005.

Owing to a lack of consistency in the wording of questions, it is hard to track the levels of support for European integration in Scotland across time using survey data. However, a comparison with data for the United Kingdom as a whole does provide a good indication of the development of attitudes towards the EU in Scotland. These suggest that Scots have become increasingly positive towards the European level. In the 1975 referendum, the support for continued

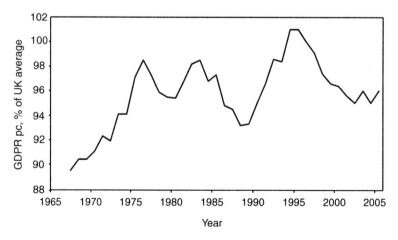

Figure 5.1 Development of Scotland's relative GDPR per capita (source: Office for National Statistics).

UK membership of the EC was markedly lower in Scotland, at 58.4 per cent, than in England (68.7 per cent) and Wales (64.8 per cent). Data from the British Social Attitudes Survey series suggest that Scottish views on European integration[3] gradually converged with those in the rest of the United Kingdom, catching up in the mid-1980s. Figure 5.2 shows the proportion of people in Scotland and the United Kingdom as a whole who thought that the United Kingdom should leave the EEC, and later the EU. Since the late 1980s, the Scottish public have consistently been more positive about European integration than the English and Welsh. In the United Kingdom as a whole, support for continued membership of the EEC/EU grew from 52.7 per cent to 77.1 per cent between 1983 and 1991. However, UK attitudes turned against the EU between 1993 and 1999, with a growth from 37.6 per cent to 56.1 per cent in the proportion favouring reduced EU influence.

The most obvious development in the Scottish party system since the 1960s is the emergence of the Scottish National Party (SNP) in the late 1960s. While the SNP created a new political dynamic in Scottish politics that differed from the British political competition, its emergence is also essentially a cause of Scottish nationalism, and it must therefore be disregarded in an attempt at predicting the development of said nationalism. The Lee index scores for Scotland therefore consider only the differences between Scotland and Great Britain in terms of the support for the national parties – that is, the Conservatives, Labour and the Liberals (later the Liberal Democrats). The development of this variable across the parliamentary elections from 1964 to 2005 is shown in Figure 5.3. The data reveal a steadily increasing difference between the Scottish and British electorates, with the Lee index growing steadily from 3.4 in 1966 to 16.5 in 1987, before dropping over the next decade to 9.7 in the 1997 elections.

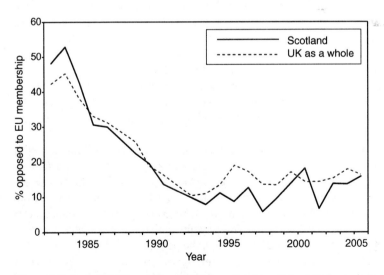

Figure 5.2 Opposition to continued UK membership of the EU (source: British Social Attitudes Surveys).

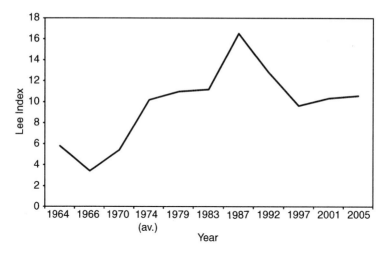

Figure 5.3 Scotland, divergence from national party system (source: Author's compilation).

Scotland has seen each of the four independent variables grow through the period from 1965 to 2005. Compared to 1965, Scotland was more prosperous, more dependent on the global economy, more deeply integrated into the EU, and more distinct from the rest of the United Kingdom in terms of the distribution of support for political parties in 2005. The regionalism model would thus unequivocally predict that levels of nationalism would have grown in Scotland during this period. Yet if one looks more closely at the developments along each of the four dimensions, it is clear that the growth in the variables has not been uniform. The Scottish economy grew mainly in the early 1970s, and again in the 1990s, but experienced a recession through most of the 1980s. The party system dissimilarity also grew during the 1970s, but it continued growing well into the recession of the 1980s, and declined during the early 1990s. Hence, these two variables predict different evolutionary paths for Scottish nationalism from the mid-1980s onwards, with the party systems variable predicting a growth and then a decline, whereas the economic development variable predicts precisely the opposite.

The European integration variable predicts a more steady development, with a gradual deepening of European integration, and a gradual growth of support for the EU, through the entire time period. Yet key events such as the UK accession in 1973, the introduction of the single European market in 1986 and the Maastricht Treaty in 1992 should be reflected in growing levels of regionalism in the wake of these developments. Similarly, the globalization variable also predicts a steady growth in regionalism through the period.

The evolution of Scottish nationalism through the period from 1965 to 2005 can potentially reveal a great deal about which of the independent variables from the model have had the strongest impact on the development of regionalism across time. The suggested paths of steady growth or growth interrupted by decline in the 1980s or in the 1990s form three separate predictions for how Scottish nationalism will have evolved through the period.

Rogaland: economic and social transformation

Rogaland's emergence in the 1970s as a centre for the international oil industry brought sudden changes to the region both in the form of economic growth and in opening up the region to the global economy. If the regionalism model is correct, this will have improved the conditions for regionalism in the region, and it seems likely that there will have been changes in the levels of regionalism in the wake of the economic transformation in the early 1970s. On the other hand, Rogaland has not been affected by European integration to any great extent, being part of a state that has not joined the EC/EU, and the regional party system has become more similar to the national system since the 1970s.

The regional economy has grown increasingly dependent on foreign investment over the past forty years. The principal reason for this is the discovery of oil resources on the Norwegian continental shelf in the North Sea in the late 1960s, a lot of which were located off the coast of Rogaland. The region's major city, Stavanger, soon became the country's oil capital,[4] home to the Petroleum Directorate, the state-owned oil company Statoil and some thirty international companies in the period 1971–73 (Nordvik 1987). The internationalization continued as the development of the petroleum industry progressed, primarily caused by the demands for skilled labour imposed by the industry. For the same reason, the country welcomed foreign oil companies to take part in the development of the industry, and major international businesses such as Phillips, Mobil, Elf, Shell and Exxon set up large operations in Stavanger. In addition, a host of international subcontractor businesses operate in relation to the oil industry. There has also been a growth in foreign exports, as the technologies of local companies have become increasingly sophisticated and hence interesting outside the domestic context.

As a result of the demands for skilled labour imposed by the industry, immigration to Rogaland has soared since the start of the oil age, particularly from the Netherlands, France, United Kingdom and the United States. In addition, the refugee and asylum population has grown steadily since the early 1970s, with Vietnamese, Bosnians and Turks making up the largest numbers (Pettersen 2003: 25). In 2001, around 22,500 foreign nationals lived in Rogaland, making up 6 per cent of the population. Just under half of these were of Western descent, and 70 per cent lived in the Stavanger area, which had the second largest proportion of immigrants in the country, behind Oslo (Lie 2002: 29). Figure 5.4 shows the increase from 1970 to 2008 in the proportion of the population who had no Norwegian-born parents. As the figure shows, the immigrant population in Rogaland has risen steadily throughout the period. Rogaland had a higher proportion of immigrants than the national average from approximately 1974 to 1994, but it has had a smaller proportion than the average since 1995. This is mainly due to the high concentration of immigrants in and around Oslo.

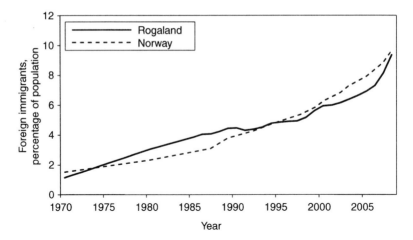

Figure 5.4 Foreign immigrant population in Rogaland and Norway (source: Dybendal (2006)).

Figure 5.5 shows the development of Rogaland's GDPR per capita as a proportion of the national average. In 1965, GDPR per capita was only 88 per cent of the national average. By 1973, the region was at par with the national average, and it remained so throughout the 1970s. Since 1983, Rogaland's GDPR per capita has been well above the national average, peaking at 112 per cent in 1993, and averaging 107 per cent in the period 1983–2000 (Statistisk Sentralbyrå 1970–2003). In most of the years for which data exist, Rogaland and Oslo/Akershus were the only two regions to produce more than the national average. In short, apart from the centre, Rogaland is in a league of its own among the counties when it comes to economic development. Rogaland has developed from being an economically disadvantaged, peripheral region to a position at the centre of Norwegian economy (Nordvik 1987: 162).

The increased production had a direct effect on the personal income of the average citizen in Rogaland. In 2000, the average worker had an annual income of 246,000 Norwegian kroner. Only in Oslo/Akershus did the average worker earn more (Statistisk Sentralbyrå 2003). Among the major cities, Stavanger went from having the lowest average income in some years before 1970 to the highest in 1990. Oil-related production dominates the labour market, especially in and around Stavanger, where estimates suggest that around 30 per cent of the population work in businesses that are directly related to the petroleum industry (Melberg 1997: 12ff.).

When it comes to European integration, one major objection is that Norway is not a member of the EU, which clearly limits any effects that this institution might have had on regionalism in Rogaland. The country is indeed not very strongly affected by several of the EU-related developments hypothesized to have an effect on regionalism. Rogaland has access to structural funds only

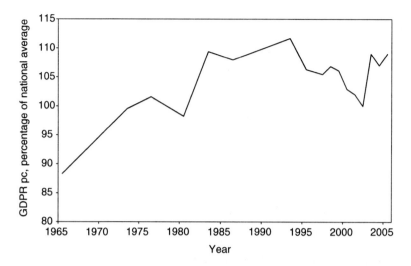

Figure 5.5 Development of Rogaland's relative GDPR per capita (source: Statistisk Sentralbyrå).

through its participation in Interreg programmes, and the direct pull from Brussels is thus not very strong in this case (Grindheim 2004: 71f.). Yet European integration has clearly affected Norway as well, most obviously through its membership of the single market through the EEA agreement. The country is also a signatory to the Schengen Agreement, which could be expected to aid the construction of a European identity in Norway (see Bruter 2005: 159).

However, data on European identities in Rogaland suggest that there has not been much variation on this variable that could explain the growth of regionalism in the region. The voting behaviour of the regional public in the referenda on Norwegian accession to the EU certainly fails to show any development in the construction of European identities in Rogaland. In both 1972 and 1994, a majority of around 55 per cent of the region's population voted against Norwegian membership of the EC and EU, respectively (Statistisk Sentralbyrå 1995: 56), making the region more Euro-sceptic than the country as a whole on both occasions. Seven Norwegian counties had higher levels of support for membership than Rogaland in 1972, whereas in 1994 six did.

The regional party system in Rogaland has become increasingly similar to the Norwegian party system during the period from 1961 to 2005. Figure 5.6 shows the development of the Lee index of dissimilarity between the vote distribution in Rogaland and Norway in elections to the national parliament. Across this period, the Lee index dropped from a high of 18.0 in the 1961 election to a low of 10.2 in the 1993 election. The largest changes in the regional relative to the national party system took place between 1973 and 1989, when the index score dropped from 17.5 to 11.1. In contrast, the index scores were relatively stable until 1973, and again from 1989 onwards.

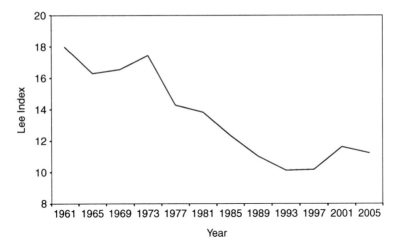

Figure 5.6 Rogaland, divergence from national party system (source: Statistisk Sentralbyrå).

The model provides contrasting predictions for the development of regionalism in Rogaland across time. The globalization and economic development variables both clearly suggest that regionalism will have grown during the period from 1960 to 2000. In particular, the oil boom of the 1970s should result in a growth in regionalism, but a steadily growing economy and increasing globalization throughout the period suggest that the levels of regionalism will have gone steadily up in the 1980s and 1990s as well. However, the party systems variable provides the opposite prediction, with the Rogaland party system becoming increasingly similar to the Norwegian system, particularly from 1973 to 1989. This suggests that regionalism will have declined gradually throughout the period. Finally, European integration has not changed a great deal through the period and should therefore not affect the levels of regionalism.

Summary

This section has presented indicators of the evolution of Scotland and Rogaland along each of the independent variables in the regionalism model developed in Chapter 4. The model has subsequently been used to predict developments across time with regard to regionalism in the two regions. These predictions will now be put to the test against some indicators of actual levels of regionalism in the two regions in the period from 1960 to 2005. The following two sections will examine whether the regionalism model is capable of explaining variation in the levels of regionalism across time within individual regions through assessing whether it can correctly predict developments in Scotland and Rogaland.

The analysis in Chapter 4 showed that regionalism tends to be more prevalent in regions that are strongly affected by European integration, have distinctive regional party systems and are economically developed. In both Scotland and Rogaland, there have been important changes along these dimensions in the period from 1960 to 2005. Scotland has joined the EU and the single market, and its population has become increasingly Euro-friendly. Its party system became increasingly distinctive until the late 1980s, before converging with the British party system through the 1990s. The Scottish economy grew strongly in the early 1970s as well as in the 1990s. Have these changes had any effect on the development of Scottish nationalism through the same period? Similarly, Rogaland has also undergone large changes, both in terms of strong economic growth since the early 1970s and in the form of convergence with the national party system. What effect have these changes had on regionalism in Rogaland? Finally, the effects of globalization were unclear in the cross-sectional analysis. The economies of both Scotland and Rogaland have become increasingly globalized throughout this period. What effect has this had on regionalism?

The analysis of longitudinal variation in the context of a particular case requires a different approach to measuring regionalism. The cross-sectional measure of regionalism relied on survey data, where respondents had stated their level of attachment to their regions and states. However, this approach is not available in the longitudinal study, as researchers have only recently started to survey regional identities and regionalist attitudes. The first surveys of popular attachment to the regional level in Rogaland were conducted as recently as the mid-1990s, and even then the number of respondents was too low to allow for any meaningful conclusions to be drawn. The data on Scotland are more reliable, but even there the Moreno question has been asked only since 1986. In order to compare levels of regionalism across time, it is necessary to measure past levels of regionalism in a reliable and valid way. The analysis discusses several methods that can be used for such purposes, with the aim of describing the development of regionalism in the two regions as accurately as possible by combining the data collected through the various measures.

Scotland: the path to parliament

In the case of Scotland, there is a wide range of indicators that can provide an insight into the development of nationalism across time. This section looks at four such types of indicators. Most obviously, the two referenda on devolution, in 1979 and 1997, provide the most solid measurements of opinions towards Scotland as a political community. These referenda are accompanied by a series of surveys measuring both attitudes towards constitutional change and political identification for a wider number of years. Furthermore, the development in support for the party political vehicle of Scottish nationalism, the SNP, also provides a valuable insight into changing levels of nationalism across time. Finally, a newspaper content analysis of two Scottish newspapers – the *Daily Record* and the *Press and Journal* – determines how the position of Scotland has changed across time in the minds of its inhabitants.

Devolution referenda

The obvious change from the 1979 referendum on devolution of power, which failed, to the 1997 referendum, which was successful, provides a puzzle that has generated a degree of interest in the development of Scottish nationalism across time (e.g. Dardanelli 2005a). The referenda are probably the most solid measures of the extent of nationalist sentiments in Scotland. They encompassed the entire voting population, and voters had both the information and the time to make a considered decision, as the referenda came at the end of political campaigns during which one can assume that political learning had taken place. The potential impact of the voting decision also contributes to a more considered decision, allowing the study to tap into revealed, rather than stated, preferences. At the referenda, voters did not merely state their preferences towards hypothetical institutions; they contributed to making actual decisions about whether or not to change the political system profoundly.

In addition to the outcomes of the referenda themselves, the very fact that they took place gives an indication of the demand for constitutional change. Devolution was not a major issue in Scottish politics before 1965, but by the mid-1970s the idea was backed by a clear majority of the Scottish public. Support was consistently stronger in surveys than in the actual referendum of 1979, but a majority of voters (51.6 per cent) still supported the idea in the referendum in a turnout of 63.6 per cent. However, the bill eventually collapsed because of a stipulation that 40 per cent of the entire electorate needed to vote in favour. The desire for devolution never really disappeared, and surveys throughout the 1980s and 1990s showed strong support among the Scottish public. By the time a new referendum was held, in 1997, the support for devolution had risen to a massive 74.3 per cent, and as many as 63.3 per cent voted in favour of giving the new parliament tax-raising powers, in a turnout of 60.2 per cent (Lynch 2001).

Scottish nationalism in surveys

While the referenda provide the most solid measure, they cover only two points in time and can give little information on the development of public opinion in between. Fortunately, the study of Scottish nationalism benefits from the availability of several surveys that track similar indicators across time. The issue of constitutional preference itself was measured in a wide range of surveys between 1974 and 2003, which have been compiled into a time series by Martínez-Herrera (2005). These data show that the proportion of Scots favouring independence remained fairly stable at around 21 per cent through the 1970s, before increasing to a peak of 36 per cent in 1986 and dropping off to 23 per cent again in 1992. In the 1990s, support for independence again increased steadily, to a level of around 30 per cent from 2000 to 2003. In the period 2003–08, support for independence has varied between 30 and 50 per cent across different polling agencies. The support for home rule (devolution) was very unstable through the

1970s, but stabilized in the early 1980s and started growing gradually from 1984 to 2000 (ibid.: 325).

Several other surveys have attempted to measure relative identification with Scotland and Britain, mostly using the Moreno question. This was introduced in a survey in *The Herald* in 1986, and has since been used by various researchers and in a wide range of contexts. Although the intervals have been irregular and the methodology and questionnaire frames have been different on each occasion, responses to the question still provide broadly comparable data across time.

Martínez-Herrera (2005: 321) has compiled data from fourteen surveys into a time series. The data show a fairly stable level of relative identification with Scotland and Britain over the period from 1986 to 2003. The proportion of *primarily* Scottish identifiers remained reasonably constant throughout the period. On the other hand, the proportion of *exclusively* Scottish identifiers dropped steeply from 1986 to 1992, before increasing steadily through the 1990s. It subsequently started to decrease again after 2001 (ibid.: 323).

Brown *et al.* (1998: 208ff.) look more closely at one of the surveys covered by Martínez-Herrera, the 1997 Scottish Election Survey, finding that Scottish identity is given prominence over British identity across all political parties, social classes, regions, religious affiliations and both genders. In terms of political parties, Scottish identity is, unsurprisingly, strongest among SNP supporters and weakest among Conservatives. However, twice as many Conservatives still give preference to their Scottish identity as do to their British identity. There are also slight differences when it comes to social class, with working-class people more likely to emphasize their Scottishness, and when it comes to religion, with Catholics appearing more likely than Protestants to identify as Scots. Scottish identity is also somewhat stronger in the central areas, particularly east-central Scotland, than in the peripheries.

In her study of political culture, Henderson (2007) confirms these findings using the 2001 British Election Survey. She also finds that Scottish identifiers had less respect for British political institutions such as the Westminster Parliament or politicians. The study also reveals differences between those who hold an exclusive Scottish or British identity and people who express a dual identity. Exclusive identities are associated with higher levels of cynicism towards the political system and lower levels of social capital.

Brown *et al.* (1998) also look at the connection between political identity and constitutional preference, finding a fairly strong connection. Respondents favouring independence were by far the most likely to identify themselves as Scottish, with 40 per cent claiming an exclusively Scottish identity, and 80 per cent a predominantly Scottish identity. However, there was also an overweight of Scottish identifiers favouring the status quo (prior to devolution), with 12 per cent in this group identifying themselves exclusively as Scottish, and 35 per cent as predominantly Scottish. Conversely, only 12 per cent in this group identified themselves as predominantly British. Finally, among the proponents of devolution, 18 per cent identified themselves as exclusively Scottish, and 61 per cent as predominantly Scottish (ibid.: 1998: 211).

Nationalist voting

Besides demands for self-government, Scottish nationalism has also been reflected in the emergence of a political vehicle, the Scottish National Party, which has been a significant party in the Scottish political landscape since 1970. Of course, the SNP's share of the vote does not equate to the share of nationalists in Scotland, as there will always be nationalists voting for other parties, as well as non-nationalists voting for the SNP. However, the SNP is essentially a centrist political party, with social democratic, liberal and conservative elements to its programme, and it is mainly the nationalist foundation that separates it from the other parties. This makes the SNP vote a reasonable proxy for Scottish nationalism, and one for which there are more complete historical data than any alternative measures. Recently, the party has had a political platform similar to that of Labour, with the crucial difference that it advocated independence for Scotland (Brown *et al.* 1998), and its rise to electoral prominence thus demonstrates that there was considerable resonance for politicizing the regional level in Scotland. The SNP has always been committed to the pursuit of an independent Scottish state, although a majority of party members have also tended to favour devolution as a move towards that goal.

The SNP was founded in the inter-war years, but it did not manage to elicit any widespread support before its major electoral breakthrough in 1970. In those elections, it won 11.4 per cent of the Scottish vote – a share that was to rise to 30.4 per cent by the time of the October 1974 elections (Leeke 2003: 13). Figure 5.7 shows the percentage of the Scottish population each year who voted or intended to vote for the SNP in Westminster elections. It should be noted that the growth in support for the SNP from 1979 to 1997 correlates with the growth

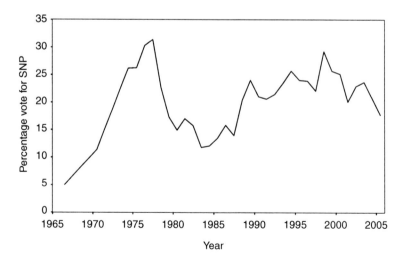

Figure 5.7 Support for the Scottish National Party (sources: Hassan and Lynch (2001) and author's compilation).

in support for devolution. This indicates that the development of the SNP vote provides a useful proxy for variation in the levels of Scottish nationalism over time.

As the figure shows, the SNP vote started growing in the late 1960s, reaching a peak in 1976. The support for the party subsequently fell as Labour fielded a proposal for devolution in the lead-up to the 1979 referendum, and it stabilized at around 15 per cent in the 1980s. However, the party reawakened in the 1990s, growing gradually to 29 per cent in 1997. The SNP then started to decline following the second devolution referendum. Its support dropped from 22.1 per cent in the 1997 Westminster elections to 20.1 per cent in 2001 and 17.7 per cent in the 2005 elections.

However, in the 2007 elections to the Scottish Parliament, the SNP won 31 per cent of the regional list votes and 32.9 per cent of the constituency votes, emerging as the biggest party in the Scottish Parliament. As a result, it formed a minority government, with Alex Salmond as First Minister. Opinion polls by YouGov show that support for the SNP continued to grow into 2008. It peaked in August 2008, when 36 per cent of respondents intended to vote for the party in the next Westminster election, and 44 per cent in constituency elections for the Scottish Parliament (YouGov 2008).

Newspaper content analysis

Completing the picture of the development of nationalism, a longitudinal content analysis of Scottish newspapers can reveal additional information about the saliency of Scottish nationalism, and of Scotland as a community, across time. If there has been a change in the amount of space devoted to Scotland as a whole across time, it would provide an indication that the region has become more (or less) important in the everyday lives of its inhabitants through the period of study. Thus, the data can complement the other indicators to provide a more complete picture of the development of Scottish nationalism. This is particularly important for the early part of the period, which is not covered by survey data and referenda. For this period, the data on the support for the SNP provide information on the politicization of nationalism, but the newspaper data will supplement this with information on the position of Scotland in the broader society.

Content analysis can be used to study the content in itself, but also the context in which it is produced. Through studying content, one can learn something about its writers, as well as its readers. Texts are means of communication between a sender and a receiver, and a text reveals both what a sender wants to communicate and how the sender thinks this message can be most effectively put across to the receiver. Through feedback, the receiver can also communicate to the sender what kinds of communication he or she wants to receive. In the media industry, the market provides a mechanism for readers to communicate to newspapers which kinds of material they find interesting. By watching its sales and circulation figures, the newspaper can adjust its contents to what the public want to read.

Bauer (2000) explains how a longitudinal content analysis design can be used to track changes in public opinion over time. He considers content analysis to be a form of public opinion research, as the texts express the values, attitudes and opinions of the community. Through newspaper archives, one can thus construct historical data to get an indication of public opinion in the past (ibid.: 135). The notion that press coverage is an expression of public opinion is something of an inversion of the common perception in discussions about the role of the media in modern society. It is often argued that the press influences public opinion, a view that has been prominent in media and communications research. However, Riffe *et al.* (1998: 9) distinguish between content analyses that seek to explain the effect of the message, and those that consider content an expression of antecedent social conditions. Although there are certainly indications that the media do to some extent influence public opinion, it should also be clear that a newspaper that was completely out of touch with pre-existing public opinion would have a short life span in a market economy. Such ties to public opinion can be the result of conscious editorial decisions to provide a product that is in public demand, as well as of more subconscious judgements on the part of the journalists, who are influenced by their social and cultural context in their decisions about which stories to cover (ibid.: 7).

Of course, the degree to which the newspaper content corresponds to public opinion might vary. An editorial change might for instance provoke a change in content without any corresponding change in public opinion, or a newspaper could differ from public opinion in certain areas while matching it more closely in others. Such considerations will have to be taken into account in the development of the research design, with particular attention being paid to the validation of the research findings. However, the connection between a newspaper and its readership can broadly be expected to hold in most cases, and it has formed the core of a rich body of content analysis research into a variety of topics across the social sciences.

Issues of measurement validity are sometimes problematic in content analysis research. Do the studies really measure what they are supposed to measure? One common method of validation is to look at the concurrent validity of the method – that is, the extent to which the results agree with those derived using different research methods. In this case, the content analysis can be validated by examining its correlation with the other measures of Scottish nationalism discussed in this chapter.

Another aspect to consider is the face validity of the method. This is a matter of whether the measure makes sense as a proxy for the phenomenon under study. In this case, it is reasonable to expect a connection between attention towards the region and regionalism. Regions are not naturally occurring phenomena; they have to be created in the public consciousness. Like nations, regions are imagined communities (Smouts 1998), and the more people talk about a region, the more the imagined community is reinforced. Imagined communities exist only as long as their members carry on imagining them. This requires them to remain visible in the public sphere: a region that no one talks about does not exist as a political community. Conversely, if people do feel a sense of community within their region, they will talk about the region and want to read about it. This general preoccupation with the region is a sign that people identify themselves as belonging to a regional community, as well as a contribution to the continued imagining of this community. A community in which everything that happens is viewed through the lens of the region is likely to be a regionalist community. The strength of the imagined regional community is therefore to some extent reflected in the frequency with which the region is talked about in the public sphere.

Several authors highlight the importance of reminding people of their identity and thus reinforcing the imagined community between them. Deutsch (1966) focuses on the role of social communication in constructing a national culture, emphasizing mass communication as the crucial technology that ties people together and makes nation-building possible. Billig (1995: 93) discusses 'flag-ging' of nationhood as a key mechanism, drawing particular attention to 'prosaic, routine words, which take nations for granted' and remind people of the imag-ined community. Wodak *et al.* (1999: 29) argue that discursive practice is important in both the construction and expression of identity. The writers' iden-tities are reflected in the media, which in turn reinforce the identities of the readers.

Law (2001) has previously studied the relationship between the press and Scottish national identity, applying a qualitative content analysis. He finds that the indigenous Scottish newspapers tended to use identical markers, referring to Scotland as 'the nation' or simply 'here', and to Scots as 'we'. However, refer-ences to the nation were often explicit, with the newspapers often talking about Scotland or Scots rather than using pronouns, and even deliberating on the content of Scottish national identity. Conversely, British newspapers, even Scot-tish versions thereof, often took a British deictic centre for granted, implicitly referring to Britain as 'the nation' and on some occasions regarding Britain as synonymous with England. Scottish nationalism thus appears to be less 'banal' than British nationalism in Billig's (1995) sense. See also MacInnes *et al.* (2007) for an analysis of banal nationalism applied to the Scottish newspaper market.

There is no single dominant newspaper that covers all sections of the Scottish market. Rather, there are several different newspapers that all have substantially different profiles and appeal to different segments of the population. The largest daily newspaper in terms of circulation is the *Daily Record*, with an average net circulation of 407,000 copies in 2005 (Audit Bureau of Circulation 2006). This is far more than any other Scottish newspaper, and it is matched only by the Scottish edition of the British newspaper the *Sun*[5] (395,000 copies). The *Daily Record* is based in Glasgow and it is regarded as a downmarket tabloid aimed at the working classes. It has a left-wing political outlook and remains affiliated with the Labour Party.

Owing to the size of its readership, the *Daily Record* should certainly be included in the newspaper analysis. However, the relatively segmented nature of its readership makes it difficult to make inferences about all of Scotland on the basis of this newspaper alone. Compared to the rest of the population, the *Daily Record* readership is more likely to live in urban areas and in the central areas of the country, have no university education, work in manual labour and vote left-wing. A 1998 survey put the readership at 40 per cent of the Scottish working class and 18 per cent of the Scottish middle class. The survey also showed that nearly 50 per cent of Glaswegians read the *Daily Record*, compared to 13 per cent in the north-east (McCrone 1999). These data are supported by the National Readership Survey, which indicates that the socio-economic composition of the *Daily Record* readership has not changed much since 1998. It would therefore be necessary to include an additional newspaper that would widen the representativeness of the selection.

The Scottish quality press lags far behind the tabloid newspapers in terms of readership, and the market is fairly evenly spread between four newspapers based in different areas of the country. The largest of these is the Aberdeen-based *Press and Journal*, with an average net circulation of 85,000 copies, followed by the Dundee-based *Courier & Advertiser* with 78,000 copies, the Glasgow-based *Herald* (73,000) and the Edinburgh-based *The Scotsman* (62,000) (Audit Bureau of Circulation 2006). Although the latter two are often classified as national Scottish newspapers, whereas the former are classified as regional ones, all four papers mainly have a regionally defined readership. *The Scotsman* is read by 34 per cent of people in Edinburgh and 9 per cent in Glasgow, while, conversely, the *Herald* is read by 19 per cent in Glasgow and only 4 per cent in Edinburgh (McCrone 1999). The distinction therefore seems to be a result of the geographical location of the printing presses of these two newspapers more than of their readership. All four rank far ahead of the largest-selling London-based broadsheet in Scotland, which is *The Times*, with a circulation of 30,000 copies.

As the *Press and Journal* is the largest of the Scottish broadsheets, it is the most obvious candidate for selection. However, it is also a suitable candidate because its peripheral north-eastern readership complements the central, Glasgow profile of the *Daily Record*. The *Press and Journal* covers the Grampians, Highlands and Islands – that is, northern and north-eastern Scotland. Another consideration is that it is popular among both middle-class and working-class readers across the political spectrum. According to the National Readership Survey (2006), its market share is 0.5 per cent of the British middle-class population, and 0.4 per cent in the working classes. It is read by 23 per cent of the population in north-eastern Scotland (McCrone 1999). Combined with the *Daily Record*, this selection makes it possible to cover as wide a range of the Scottish public as possible when making inferences about their readership.

The study covers the years 1965, 1985 and 2005, which provide an even distribution across the period of interest. This particular selection also avoids possible selection bias that might have occurred from including time-points close to the devolution referenda, which are in themselves likely to have led to more stories in the press about Scotland as a political unit. For the *Press and Journal*, the study analysed the main Aberdeen morning edition of the newspaper. For details on the sampling of issues within the selected years, see Fitjar (2007: 138).

The articles were coded according to the geographical level referred to. The regional category included articles that were mainly about the region as a whole. This could be articles on the Scottish economy, Scottish culture, how Scotland was affected by international developments or national policy decisions, or any other topic, so long as the geographical focus of the article was mainly on Scotland as a whole. Articles about specific places within the region, or about events happening at specific places within the region, were classified as local, or as national if they took place outside the region. Similarly, the European and international categories covered events occurring within or outside Europe. The study of the *Press and Journal* also looks at the proportion of articles dealing with the Aberdeenshire/north-eastern Scotland/Grampian region, in order to compare the level of identification with this region to the identification with Scotland. As the *Daily Record* does not have any particular regional profile,[6] the study of this newspaper looks only at the proportion of articles dealing with Scotland.

The coding scheme imposed a different standard on articles to be classified as regional compared to the other categories. Most regular news happens in specific places. The proportion of articles in the regional category could therefore not be directly compared to the other categories to measure the importance of the region. However, by applying a strict definition to the regional category, its contents corresponded more neatly to the phenomenon that it sought to measure, namely regionalism. The purpose of the study was to compare the proportion of articles on the region over time, thus indicating the level of public attention towards the region.

The analysis of the *Daily Record* showed a steady increase in the coverage of Scottish news stories across time, as shown in Table 5.1. The space devoted to stories about Scotland as a whole increased from 16.9 per cent of all articles in 1965 via 19.0 per cent in 1985 to 20.1 per cent of the articles in 2005. The increase came mainly at the expense of local news, and the *Daily Record* in 2005 appeared to be focusing more on stories concerning Scotland as a whole, and less on stories taking place in local areas within Scotland, than it did in 1965. The proportion of stories focusing on the rest of the United Kingdom (this includes stories about the United Kingdom as a whole, as well as local stories from outside Scotland) increased sharply from 23.3 per cent in 1965 to 36.8 per cent in 1985, but dropped to 24.9 per cent in 2005.

Considering only news stories – that is, excluding sports and culture news – as well as opinion pieces, the growth in focus on Scotland was even stronger. Whereas 16.1 per cent of all news stories in 1965 related to Scotland as a whole, the proportion was 17.8 per cent in 1985 and 20.6 per cent in 2005. Most of the growth in focus came in the shorter articles, with the focus on Scotland in single-column articles growing from 14.1 per cent in 1965 to 19.0 per cent in 2005, but the longer articles still focused more strongly on Scotland than the single-column articles and increased modestly from 20.7 per cent in 1965 to 21.6 per cent in 2005.

Table 5.1 The *Daily Record*, content analysis

Focus	1965	1985	2005
International	7.8	6.5	9.6
European	2.2	2.8	3.8
British	23.3	36.8	24.9
Scottish	16.9	19.0	20.1
Local	49.8	34.9	41.7
n	1,030	1,157	2,260

Source: Content analysis of the *Daily Record.*

Note
Share of articles referring to different geographical units in each year (%).

The *Press and Journal* focused less on Scotland than the *Daily Record* did, but it showed the same tendencies of a growing focus across time. While 7.3 per cent of articles focused on Scotland in 1965, this proportion increased to 9.3 per cent in 1985 and 12.5 per cent in 2005, as shown in Table 5.2. The focus on Scotland remained stronger than the focus on the north-eastern region throughout the period, despite the closer geographical proximity of the latter and the *Press and Journal*'s reputation as a regional newspaper for the north-east. The focus on north-eastern Scotland also did not appear to grow over time. The difference in focus was therefore growing. In 1965 and 1985, there were around 55 per cent more articles about Scotland than about the north-east, while the difference increased to 200 per cent in 2005. Again, the growth in focus on Scotland came mainly at the expense of local news, and it would appear that the newspaper focused more on Scotland as a whole, and less on local news stories within Scotland, in 2005 than in 1965. The space devoted to stories from other parts of the United Kingdom remained fairly stable across time, while there was a moderate growth in foreign news. Compared to the *Daily Record*, the *Press and Journal* focused less on Scottish news, but more on local/sub-regional and European news.

It makes little difference to the results if one looks only at news stories. The proportion of news stories focusing on Scotland grew slightly more quickly, from 7.0 per cent in 1965 via 9.3 per cent in 1985 to 12.5 per cent in 2005. The proportion of front-page news devoted to Scotland grew sharply over time, from 5.2 per cent in 1965 to 12.1 per cent in 1985 and 20.1 per cent in 2005, and there was a sharp drop in the proportion of British news on the front page, from 41.2 per cent in 1965 via 32.8 per cent in 1985 to 21.6 per cent in 2005. The same was true for back-page news, although the variation was not as large across time as on the front page.

The analyses of the *Daily Record* and the *Press and Journal* both show a steady increase in news stories relating to Scotland as a whole through the period of study. In both cases, this growth has to some extent come at the expense of local news stories, indicating that the coverage of developments in Scotland has taken on a more Scottish and less local perspective. As this development has taken place across two newspapers with very different profiles and readerships,

Table 5.2 The *Press and Journal*, content analysis

Focus	1965	1985	2005
International	5.4	6.7	7.0
European	3.4	4.0	4.3
British	28.8	26.2	28.4
Scottish	7.3	9.3	12.5
North East	4.7	6.1	4.1
Local	50.3	47.8	43.7
n	1,654	1,758	2,682

Source: Content analysis of the *Press and Journal*.

Note
Share of articles referring to different geographical units in each year (%).

the findings provide a strong suggestion that Scotland has strengthened its position in the minds of Scottish people.

The focus on Scotland is much stronger in the *Daily Record* than in the *Press and Journal*, which is perhaps not surprising given the former newspaper's geographical location in the centre of the country. This might also suggest that nationalism is stronger among the less educated, working-class readership of the *Daily Record* than in the population as a whole. Indeed, both of these findings are reflected in the survey data mentioned earlier. The highest levels of Scottish identity are found in east-central Scotland, and the lowest in north-east Scotland; and Scottish identity is also stronger among the working-class population than in the middle class (Brown *et al*. 1998: 211f.).

Summary

Most of the indicators broadly point towards a growth in Scottish nationalism across the period of study, although the extent and timeline of this development depend to some extent on which indicator one looks at. The devolution referenda show that nationalism grew from 1979 to 1997, while the content analyses suggest a uniform development of growing nationalism from 1965 to 2005. These findings are mutually consistent. They are also both consistent with the developments of the SNP, whose share of the vote was substantially higher in 1997 than in 1979, and also grew from 1965 to 1985, and from 1985 to 2005.

However, the SNP data provide more detailed information on the developments between these time points, suggesting that the strongest periods of growth in nationalism were the early 1970s and the 1990s. The 1980s, on the other hand, saw a slight decline, or at least a levelling out, in nationalism, and there was also a slight decline in nationalism in the aftermath of devolution. However, the performance of the SNP improved radically from 2005 to 2008. In the 2007 elections to the Scottish Parliament, the party won 32.9 per cent of the constituency vote and 31.0 per cent of the regional list vote, making it the largest party in Scotland for the first time in its history.

The survey data provide little information on Scottish identities in the period prior to the mid-1980s, but if one looks at the proportions of exclusively Scottish identifiers, they broadly support the story of a decline in nationalism in the second half of the 1980s and a steady increase throughout the 1990s. Similarly, the survey data on constitutional preferences also suggest a decline in the late 1980s and a steady increase through the 1990s. However, these data suggest that the first peak in nationalism did not occur until the mid-1980s, rather than in the mid-1970s as suggested by the SNP data.

In sum, all of the indicators appear to agree on the basic story, outlining a growth in nationalism in the early 1970s and the 1990s, and a slight decline at least in the latter part of the 1980s. For the period from 1975 to 1985 the data point in somewhat different directions, and therefore no firm conclusions can be drawn for this period. Still, it appears evident that there have been major changes in the levels of nationalism in Scotland across the time period under study.

Rogaland: a region constructed

While there are several indicators that tap into the development of Scottish nationalism across time, fewer data are available for regionalism in Rogaland. As a result, a different approach is needed in this case. This section begins with a qualitative interpretation of some political developments in the region that suggest an emerging regionalism. It then goes on to suggest possible quantitative indicators that may confirm or reject the general impression. Survey data have not been collected widely enough to give reliable results that would allow for longitudinal comparison on the regional level. A newspaper content analysis, mirroring the studies of the *Daily Record* and the *Press and Journal* outlined earlier, is therefore used to confirm that levels of regionalism in Rogaland have indeed grown across time.

The emergence of a new regionalism

Territory seems to have reappeared as a force for political mobilization during the 1990s. While Rogaland does not have any regionalist, or even regional, political parties, the regional branches of most national parties have on several occasions in recent years voiced regional interests at the expense of national party interests or ideology. The debate has been vocal enough to cause the newspaper *Dag og Tid* (4 July 2008) to proclaim a 'Rematch in Hafrsfjord', with the lead: 'Many *Rogalendinger* are now so dissatisfied with the Government in Oslo that they would like a new Battle of Hafrsfjord.'[7] The historical imagery recalls the battle of AD 872 in which King Harald I is popularly believed to have unified the Norwegian state through conquering Rogaland and three neighbouring petty kingdoms at Hafrsfjord in Rogaland. While the claims made by *Dag og Tid* are without doubt heavily exaggerated, they do express an increasing focus on the region and its interests among Rogaland elites in recent years. On a variety of political issues, the Rogaland party branches have mobilized along territorial, rather than functional, cleavages, leading them to unite in expressing regional interests that sometimes oppose the views of their national party organizations.

One example of this concerns the merger in 2007 between Statoil and Hydro Oil & Gas, the two major Norwegian petroleum companies. Statoil has had its headquarters in Stavanger since its establishment in 1972, while Hydro was based in Oslo. Regional elites in Rogaland feared that the new company, Statoil-Hydro, would be based in Oslo, thereby removing Statoil's headquarters from the region. Their worries grew when the merger agreement stated that StatoilHydro's main functions would be shared between Stavanger and Oslo, with the important International Exploration and Production business area based in Oslo. The issue was quickly politicized, as the Norwegian state was the largest shareholder in both Statoil and Hydro, and would own more than 60 per cent of StatoilHydro.

Reactions from Rogaland had a distinctly regionalist tone, with parties behaving in somewhat unexpected ways viewed from the perspective of national politics. Høyre (the Conservatives) and Fremskrittspartiet (FrP – the Progress Party) have been the most consistent supporters in Norwegian politics of a hands-off approach to public ownership in businesses. Both parties are ideologically committed to market-based solutions, arguing that businesses must be left to their own devices. However, in this case the Rogaland Høyre and the Rogaland FrP both demanded that the national government should intervene to force Statoil-Hydro to keep its headquarters and the International Exploration and Production division in Stavanger after the merger. Meanwhile, the Rogaland branches of the three national government parties, Arbeiderpartiet (Ap – the Labour Party), Sosialistisk Venstreparti (SV – the Socialist Left Party) and Senterpartiet (Sp – the Centre Party), were all up in arms, publicly accusing their own government of not doing enough to support Rogaland in the matter.

Similar stories have unfolded on a number of occasions in recent years, whether related to the location of military bases or to that of infrastructure investments. Disagreements over the provision of neurosurgical medical services at Stavanger University Hospital resulted in the dismissal in 2007 of Steinar Olsen, the Høyre chairman of Stavanger Health Trust, by Oddvard Nilsen, the Høyre chairman of Western Norway Regional Health Authority. Olsen was replaced by Odd Arild Kvaløy from the Sp, one of the coalition partners in Norway's left-wing government. However, the changeover from a right-wing to a left-wing chairman did not change the health trust's perspective on the matter, as all regional parties agreed on this issue across traditional cleavages.

Reactions to the 2003 closure of the local brewery in Rogaland, Tou, were also indicative of regionalist mobilization, this time extending to the mass public. Ringnes-Carlsberg decided in June 2003 to move production of the brand to Oslo as part of its long-term strategy of shifting towards large-scale production. This led large parts of the population to boycott all products related to the Ringnes-Carlsberg company, encouraged by the media and local political and business elites. The boycott included several of the most popular Norwegian brands of beer, soft drinks and mineral water, along with international brands such as Pepsi, 7-Up, Carlsberg and Guinness. The boycott soon gained widespread support, and sales of Ringnes-Carlsberg products in Rogaland almost halved within days of the decision, with regional newspapers bringing stories about people being harassed for including Ringnes-Carlsberg products in their shopping baskets. Ringnes-Carlsberg's main competitor, the Bergen-based Hansa-Borg Breweries, doubled its sales in the same period (*Stavanger Aftenblad* 29 July 2003).

Why were the reactions against the restructuring of Ringnes-Carlsberg's beer production so fierce? Obviously, all people have an interest in maintaining industry and employment where they live. But there was more to this issue than economics. The job question was suppressed, and the main issue at stake was the importance of maintaining ownership over local traditions and brands. The issue was framed mainly in terms of regional pride. In local understanding, 'Oslo', or the economic elite in the capital, had deprived the region of its beer-making history and traditions. One might regard this as a surprising spin on regional historical traditions, considering that only thirty years previously, Rogaland was noted mainly for its strong teetotal traditions as the heart and soul of Norway's powerful Lutheran temperance movement. Even the *Stavanger Aftenblad*, traditionally a major part of the temperance movement, moved to defend local beer culture. It printed a series of highly critical articles, and supported the boycott in editorials on 3 June 2003 and 5 July 2003. Within two months of the decision, two new local beers were on the market, both established in direct reaction to the closure of Tou Brewery and appealing heavily to regional identities in their marketing strategies.

All of the above are examples of a defensive regionalism, in which regional interests are mobilized in opposition to national political or business decisions that would hurt the regional status quo. However, there are also examples of more proactive expressions of regionalism, with regional elites cooperating across different sectors and political cleavages to generate positive changes from the bottom up. The 1997–2005 campaign to establish a new university in Stavanger is one example of such a development.

In the Norwegian system of higher education, there is a difference between universities, of which there used to be only four, and colleges. Universities have a reputation for conducting research at a higher level, while the colleges have offered more intensive teaching. There are various colleges in Rogaland, but until 2005 the region did not have a university, although the College of Stavanger had been trying to gain university status since the 1960s. Not much progress was made until 1997, when local and regional elites started to mobilize in favour of the idea. Instead of being the project of a limited group of academics, the campaign started to include local business interests, politicians from all political parties, and the local media (*Stavanger Aftenblad* 23 February 2001). The main reason for this broad support from regional elites was the near-universal consensus that a university would be pivotal in the development of the entire region, economically as well as culturally (*Stavanger Aftenblad* 1 April 2003).

The campaign was crowned with success when the University of Stavanger was formally opened on 17 January 2005. The university was a fundamental part of a long-term plan to transform Rogaland from an oil region into a knowledge region. Apart from the symbolic effect of having a university, which, it was believed, would attract students and skilled labour, the university would be used proactively in the development of communications between the various academic institutes in Stavanger. For instance, director Per Dahl explained that his institution would 'place considerable weight on having a good relationship with our environs that can be a foundation for increasing knowledge and production in the region' (*Stavanger Aftenblad* 21 August 2000).

The issue of devolution of power has also been on the agenda in Rogaland from time to time. National discussions over a reform of the regional level in Norway brought demands for devolution from various actors in Rogaland. In 2003, the county council pledged to 'work systematically towards achieving local/regional autonomy, more power, authority and resources to the directly elected regional level of government' (*Stavanger Aftenblad* 3 December 2003). The principle of decentralization of power to the regional level was supported by all parties except the FrP, which wanted to remove the regional level of government. In the debate, Ap's Frode Berge argued that there was a pressing need for decentralization in Norway, claiming that the state was among the most centralized in Europe. A few months later, he wrote an article together with his fellow partisan Eirin Sund, then deputy county mayor, entitled 'More power for Rogaland' (*Stavanger Aftenblad* 24 February 2004). Here, they argued that there was a need for an extensive reform of Norwegian democracy, demanding that local autonomy should be guaranteed by the Constitution and that local and regional governments should have more freedom to set their own tax rates.

Although most political parties in Rogaland agreed on the idea of decentralization of power, there were different perspectives on the future geographical structure of the regional level. One might say that all parties agreed that power should be moved away from Oslo, but they disagreed on where it should go instead. In 2005, Ap, Sp, Kristelig Folkeparti (KrF – Christian People's Party) and some members of Høyre (including county mayor Roald Bergsaker and six of the nine other Høyre councillors) were of the opinion that decentralization was realistic only if the regional level were restructured into a system of fewer and larger regions. SV voted to keep the current structure and work for devolution of power to Rogaland County. A section of Høyre (including key local mayors such as Stavanger's Leif Johan Sevland) wanted to expand the size of local governments and devolve power to what they called 'regional municipalities' (*Stavanger Aftenblad* 11 January 2005). However, by 2007, KrF and several Høyre councillors (including Bergsaker) had changed their minds and voted to keep the current county structure, resulting in a clear majority in favour of maintaining the present borders of Rogaland (*Stavanger Aftenblad* 13 June 2007).

Although all of these events suggest that some kind of regionalist movement is developing in Rogaland, it is still difficult to assess the extent of this change. A more systematic attempt at quantifying levels of regionalism would also be

necessary in order to test any hypotheses about the causes of the change. Therefore, a reliable and valid method for measuring regionalism is necessary. For this
purpose, the next section discusses potential quantitative indicators of the levels
of regionalism in Rogaland across time.

The inadequacy of survey data

During the preparation for the case study on Rogaland, it soon became apparent
that the inadequacy of existing survey data would be a major limitation. The
only available data set on regional identities in Rogaland was the National Identity Survey, carried out by the International Social Survey Programme in 1995,
so it was impossible to study trends in the strength of regional identities across
time on the basis of surveys.

Furthermore, there are obvious limitations to the use of this survey to study
regionalism even in a cross-sectional design. One major problem is that the
National Identity Survey inexplicably failed to ask respondents to rate their level
of attachment to Rogaland. They were only asked to indicate their attachment to
their city or municipality and the province of Western Norway, which does not
say anything about attitudes towards the region of Rogaland. Moreover, only
117 out of the 1,507 respondents in the survey were from Rogaland, which is too
few for any statistically significant results to be derived from the study.
However, the survey does include some data that are relevant in this context.
Respondents from Rogaland report stronger attachment to their cities and municipalities than respondents from other parts of the country. In particular, this is
true of respondents from urban areas. When it comes to attachment to province,
Norway and Europe, respondents from Rogaland do not differ much from
respondents from other parts of the country. However, none of the results from
this survey is statistically significant, because of the small sample size.

More luck is had by Baldersheim (2003), who reports a survey from 1993 by
Lawrence Rose that does ask about county attachment. In this survey, Finnmark
and Vestfold are the only counties with higher levels of attachment to the county
than Rogaland, but the differences between these counties and Rogaland are too
small to be statistically significant.[8] In his interpretation of the overall variation
in the data set, Baldersheim notes that the presence of large cities tends to
depress levels of regional identity. It is therefore notable that levels of regional
attachment are much higher in Rogaland, with 59 per cent of respondents claiming to be strongly attached to the county, than in Hordaland and Sør-Trøndelag,
where 47 per cent and 46 per cent, respectively, give the same response (Baldersheim 2003: 297). Among the regions dominated by large cities, Rogaland
clearly stands out as having the highest levels of regional identity.

Even though these surveys leave much to be desired, they do still indicate
that levels of regionalism are high in Rogaland compared to other Norwegian
regions. However, they cannot say anything about whether levels of regionalism
have increased or decreased over time, as there is only one point in time to go
by. There are no survey data that can say anything about levels of regionalism in

Rogaland in the 1960s and 1970s. However, a quantitative content analysis can provide an insight into the changes in regionalism over time. The next section presents the findings of such a study in the case of Rogaland.

Newspaper content analysis

The lack of data makes it far more difficult to study regionalism in Rogaland than in Scotland, particularly when it comes to the situation before the 1990s. Before 1993, no surveys were carried out on regional identities in Norway, and there has never been a regionalist party that could provide an indication of variation in the levels of regionalism across time. Hence, the only way in which a quantitative measure of regionalism in Rogaland in the past can be developed is through the analysis of written materials from the relevant period. For these purposes, the content analysis method provides a unique opportunity to construct a corpus of data on people's identities and interests in the past, which can be analysed to track the development of regionalism. Given the lack of alternative data in the case of Rogaland, this becomes even more important than in the previous case study.

The study[9] analysed a random sample of twelve issues of the main regional newspaper in Rogaland, the *Stavanger Aftenblad*, from each of three different years: 1960, 1980 and 2000. The *Stavanger Aftenblad* is widely read throughout the region: according to the Consumer and Media survey by TNS in 2005, it has 187,000 regular readers out of a population of 318,000 over the age of 12 – a coverage of 59 per cent (Futsæter 2005). No other regional newspaper comes close to these readership figures: the second-largest paper is the *Haugesunds Avis*, with around 85,000 readers, some of whom live in neighbouring Horda-land. On these grounds, the contents of the *Stavanger Aftenblad* can be considered a good indicator of regional public opinion. It is reasonable to assume that a newspaper that dominates to such an extent in the region has been success-ful in writing about what people are interested in.

One common method of validation in content analysis is to examine whether the results conform to the researcher's expectations. In this case, one can vali-date the findings by looking at whether the content analysis confirms the expec-tations of growing regionalism based on the qualitative study.

The content analysis of the two Scottish newspapers above provides a test of the concurrent validity of the method – that is, of whether the data derived from content analysis correspond to the data that other research methods produce. In the study of Scotland, the content analysis leads to conclusions similar to those reached from surveys and voting data on the development of nationalism across time, showing that there was a rise in nationalism between 1965 and 2005. They also concur with survey data on the geographical and socio-economic distribu-tion of nationalists, suggesting that levels of national identity are higher in Glasgow than in north-eastern Scotland, and higher among the working classes than among the middle classes.

The content analysis of the *Stavanger Aftenblad* shows a clear increase over time in the number of articles focusing on regional issues. Table 5.3 shows the

Table 5.3 The *Stavanger Aftenblad*, content analysis

Focus	1960	1980	2000
International	19.2	13.6	12.1
European	12.3	7.6	6.5
National	30.1	31.3	26.1
Western Norway	0.5	0.1	0.9
Rogaland	5.6	8.7	10.8
Local	32.3	38.6	43.7
n	1,068	1,496	1,750

Source: Content analysis of the *Stavanger Aftenblad.*

Note
Share of articles referring to different geographical units in each year (%).

distribution of articles relating to each geographical level for each year of study. Whereas only 5.6 per cent of articles referred to Rogaland in 1960, this figure almost doubled, to 10.8 per cent, in 2000. This amounts to an increase of 93 per cent. In the median position was 1980, with 8.7 per cent of articles focusing on the region, a 55 per cent increase from 1960. The increase in regional news is statistically significant for the period 1960–80 and non-significant for the period 1980–2000. A closer look at the data reveals that the associations retain approximately the same strengths when one controls for article type (for example by excluding culture and sports articles) and for article size. This clearly indicates that there has been a growth in regionalism from 1960 to 2000, in line with what was expected.

The study of regional papers shows that Western Norway hardly gets any attention at all. There is simply no discourse on issues relating to the province, and in no year do even 1 per cent of articles refer to Western Norway. The province clearly seems to be irrelevant to the people of Rogaland. This confirms the indications from the survey data about a low level of Western Norwegian identity. Meanwhile, local issues continue to make up the bulk of the news, and also exhibit a solid rise through the period studied, from 32.3 per cent in 1960 to 43.7 per cent in 2000. Taken together, news about regional and local issues went from comprising 37.9 per cent of the news in 1960 to 54.5 per cent in 2000, an increase of 43 per cent.

It is not national news that has suffered a loss of interest. Granted, the data do indicate a slight fall in the focus on national issues, from 30.1 per cent in 1960 to 26.1 per cent in 2000, but this change is not statistically significant. The main slump has come in the focus on international and, above all, European news. While the number of articles within each of these two categories has been fairly constant throughout the period, the size of the newspaper has increased, and therefore the proportion of European news in 2000 is little more than half of that in 1960: 6.5 per cent versus 12.3 per cent. International issues exhibit a similar trend, falling from nearly one-fifth of the articles in 1960 to less than one-eighth in 2000.

The content analysis supports the impression that levels of regionalism have risen in Rogaland since the 1960s. The region is talked about more frequently in the media, indicating a stronger sense of imagined community and hence greater interest in news stories pertaining to the region. This has had a political impact, as evidenced by the increasing tendency of political elites to mobilize to defend regional, rather than functional, interests.

Assessing the model

The preceding two sections have provided data on how regionalism has actually developed across time in the cases of Scotland and Rogaland. These development paths can now be compared to the predictions from the beginning of the chapter in order to examine the capacity of the regionalism model in explaining variation across time.

The development of nationalism in Scotland largely corresponds to the overall predictions of the model. All of the indicators suggested that there would have been a growth in nationalism across the period, and this does indeed appear to have been the case. The levels of support for autonomy, for independence and for the SNP have all grown between 1965 and 2005, and the coverage of Scottish issues in newspapers has also gone up. The changes in public opinion have been reflected in institutional changes, with the establishment of a devolved Scottish Parliament in 1999 serving as a major landmark.

A closer look at the trajectory of nationalism during the period reveals more support for some theoretical propositions than for others. The steady growth in globalization and European integration is reflected in the overall trend towards higher levels of nationalism throughout the period, but neither of these variables can explain the shorter-term variations within the period. In particular, the decline in nationalism in the second half of the 1980s does not correspond to the predictions on the basis of these variables. The Single European Act of 1986 should not have led to a decline in nationalism in the following years. On the other hand, the growing levels of nationalism in the wake of the Maastricht Treaty of 1992 match the predictions of the European integration variable.

The variables on economic development and party system dissimilarity provided more detailed predictions of peaks and troughs during the period. Overall, the development of nationalism matches the economic development curve quite well. Both of the strongest periods of growing nationalism – the early 1970s and the early 1990s – correspond to periods of growth in the Scottish economy, while the decline of the late 1980s coincides with an economic depression from 1983 to 1990. Similarly, the growth in party system dissimilarity in the early 1970s corresponds well to the growth in nationalism, and nationalism starts to decline at around the same time as party system dissimilarity in the late 1980s. Conversely, the growing nationalism in the 1990s is counter to the predictions of the party systems variable, as the Scottish and British party systems actually became more similar throughout the period from 1987 until the 1997 elections. However, the convergence of the party systems somewhat camouflages the fact that support for the ruling party at Westminster – the Conservatives – dropped sharply in Scotland during this period.

Overall, the model provides a fairly accurate prediction of the development of Scottish nationalism in the period from 1965 to 2005. The growing nationalism throughout the period reflects growth in each of the independent variables overall, suggesting that they are indeed associated with variations in the levels of regionalism across time as well. At the level of individual variables, economic development seems to have been most closely associated with the evolution of nationalism throughout the period, while other variables can only partially explain the developments that have taken place.

In the case of Rogaland, the development of regionalism in the period corresponds to the predictions on the basis of the globalization and economic development variables. There has been a steady growth of regionalism throughout the period, which corresponds to growing levels of globalization as witnessed by an increasing presence of foreign companies and foreign labour, as well as growing levels of immigration. The region also gradually became more prosperous during this period, evolving from a GDPR per capita well below the national average prior to the discovery of petroleum into the richest peripheral region in the country by the early 1980s.

However, the developments contradict the predictions of the party systems variable, as the party system in Rogaland became gradually more similar to the Norwegian party system, in particular between 1973 and 1989. Divergence between the regional and national party systems does therefore not appear to have explanatory potential in this case, even though the voting patterns in Rogaland remained fairly distinct by Norwegian standards throughout the period. Nor does European integration appear to have played a major role in the development of regionalism in Rogaland. Although ties between Norway and the EU became closer through the period, Norway is still not a member state, and it has therefore not been affected by many of the policy initiatives aimed at strengthening the regions. In Rogaland, there has also been a steady majority opposed to membership throughout the period, and it does not therefore seem likely that the regional public would prefer the EU institutional framework to that of the Norwegian state in any way.

The model is broadly confirmed by the two case studies, as most of the predictions on the basis of the development of the independent variables are reflected in the actual development of regionalism. In particular, economic development and globalization appear to be closely associated with levels of regionalism across time in both of the case studies. European integration also appears to be associated with levels of nationalism in Scotland, which is the only region that is actually a member, and this theoretical connection is therefore also supported by the case studies. On the other hand, the connection between party systems and regionalism in the cross-sectional study is reflected only to some extent in these longitudinal studies. Party system dissimilarity correlates with growing nationalism in Scotland in the 1970s, but the growth of nationalism in the 1990s as well as the rising regionalism in Rogaland throughout the period are accompanied by convergence with the national party systems.

Conclusion

This chapter has tracked levels of regionalism across time in Scotland and Roga-land, building an account of how regionalism has changed in different time periods in both regions. Through comparing these to the predictions of the regionalism model, it has been possible to assess whether the model is capable of explaining variation along the longitudinal dimension. The results are mainly positive, although some variables are more closely associated with longitudinal variation in regionalism than others in these two cases. The effects of economic development, globalization and European integration on regionalism are broadly confirmed by this analysis, while the effect of party system divergence is not as evident in these two cases.

The overall correspondence between the results of the cross-sectional and longitudinal analyses strengthens the model of regionalism. Three of the varia-bles are correlated with variation in the levels of regionalism across both time and space, and these relationships manifest themselves through different research designs and methods. This leads to the conclusion that there is a relationship between regionalism and economic development, globalization and European integration.

The next two chapters will probe these relationships further by examining the relationship between each independent variable and the development of region-alism in Scotland and Rogaland. Each theoretical relationship is critically assessed on the basis of existing literature and primary source material from newspapers and election manifestos. The main aim is to evaluate whether the effects of the independent variables follow the logic and mechanisms of the theoretical discussion in Chapter 2. The quantitative analysis up to this point has established the existence of these relationships, but the next two chapters will apply a qualitative analysis that can contribute to the understanding of how the independent variables affect regionalism in the context of these two case studies.

6 Scotland

From unionism to nationalism

The previous chapter demonstrated growing levels of nationalism in Scotland, which correspond fairly well with the predictions of the regionalism model. However, the longitudinal study was able to examine only the correlations between regionalism and the independent variables across time. This chapter analyses the relationships between the variables qualitatively, aiming to understand why and how they are related. It furthers the analysis through discussing causality, rather than correlation. The discussion focuses on whether the theoretical connections proposed in Chapter 2 can actually be discovered in the development of Scottish nationalism. The purpose is mainly to explore these connections, rather than to confirm them. The analysis draws on qualitative data from regional newspapers and SNP election manifestos, as well as on secondary literature on Scottish nationalism. The findings indicate that European integration provides an important reason for the growth in nationalism in the 1990s, whereas economic growth seems to be a crucial reason in both the 1970s and the 1990s.

Historical context

The United Kingdom of Great Britain and Northern Ireland was formed in 1800, when the Kingdom of Ireland was united with the Kingdom of Great Britain. Great Britain itself had been formed in 1707, when Scotland united with England and Wales. Scotland occupies the northern third of Great Britain and has 5 million inhabitants. Prior to 1999, the United Kingdom was a politically centralized unitary state, save for various attempts at devolution to Northern Ireland. Indeed, the UK regions were among the weakest in Europe in terms of their political autonomy. The state did not have an elected tier of regional government, and the regions were instead run by unelected regional assemblies with a fairly vague role in promoting economic development. Local government was and is run by elected councils, whose powers vary substantially across different types of councils (the main types are boroughs, districts, counties and unitary authorities).

However, Scotland did retain a certain degree of administrative separation under the terms of the Act of Union of 1707. The country retained its own legal system, Scots law, which to some extent is based on civil-law principles, as opposed to the common-law principles that underlie the legal systems of England and Wales, as well as Northern Ireland (Brown *et al.* 1998: 2). Furthermore, the Scottish education system has remained separate and substantially different from the English system in terms of the content of the syllabus as well as the length of study, with Scottish university degree programmes lasting for four years as opposed to three in England. The Scottish health system has also been organized independently. Finally, the Scottish Church (the Kirk) has remained independent from the state, and it follows a tradition of Presbyterianism that is decisively shaped by the Scottish Reformation. The Church of England, on the other hand, is a state church under the British monarch and follows the Anglican tradition. In sum, this all meant that the Scottish society did not fully integrate with the English and Welsh to create a unified British society. Rather, the United Kingdom remained a state that consisted of several different civil societies (ibid.: 40). This was possible in part because the United Kingdom of the eighteenth century was close to the prototype of the liberal nightwatchman state, with responsibilities mainly in the areas of foreign policy, defence and justice, and it did not seek to transform civil society.

The status of the Kirk is perhaps particularly important in this context, because prior to the establishment of the Scottish Office and the expanding role of the state, it played an important role in the social sphere, running several welfare institutions. However, in the second half of the nineteenth century the state was expanding its influence on society, particularly with the emergence of a welfare state, and the influence of the Kirk waned. This led to demands for Scottish influence on the way in which these institutions were run in Scotland. In 1885, this eventually resulted in the creation of the Scottish Office as a distinct bureaucracy that would govern Scotland, taking over from sector departments within the central administration. The Scottish Office ran the welfare state and acted as a state within the British state. It was accountable to the Secretary of State for Scotland, who was appointed by the UK prime minister and served in the central government. The Scottish Office has been regarded as a defender of the Scottish national interest (Brown *et al.* 1998: 13), and its policies were often the result of negotiations between the government and Scottish civil society institutions, rather than dictated from London.

Scotland also retained its independence in many areas of symbolic importance. The country has continued to be represented by its own national sports teams in a range of international competitions, including the football and rugby world cups and the Commonwealth Games. Scotland uses the British pound, governed by the Bank of England, but some Scottish banks are allowed to issue their own banknotes, with distinct Scottish imagery. The Scottish flag has also been widely used, along with several other national symbols.

The centralized nature of the United Kingdom was fundamentally changed by the devolution of power to the Scottish Parliament and the National Assembly for Wales in 1999. While sovereign power remains vested in the central UK Parliament, these two regions now have substantial powers to legislate in a wide range of policy areas. The United Kingdom can therefore now be classified as a regionalized unitary state. In Scotland, devolution established a Scottish Parliament with the power to legislate in all policy areas except those reserved by the central UK Parliament (mainly foreign, defence, economic and fiscal policies). Thus, the Scottish Parliament took over responsibility for all the policy areas that were previously governed by the Scottish Office, as well as gaining the right to vary income tax by up to 3 per cent and potentially legislating in new policy areas (Lynch 2001: 15). This makes it one of the most powerful regional assemblies in Europe in terms of the number of policy areas it controls. The Scottish Office itself was straightforwardly replaced by the Scottish Executive, which includes an administrative branch as well as a government appointed by the Scottish Parliament.

Nationalism in Scotland and the United Kingdom

On a European level, there have been fairly strong developments towards growing regionalism across the continent, along with a growth in regional identities as well as an institutional strengthening of the regional level in many countries. Many regionalist movements can be explained by this general trend, and their individual developments are thus not particularly puzzling at all. The first question to be faced in the search for an explanation of regionalism is therefore whether one should look for endogenous or exogenous causes. If the developments in Scotland are only the result of exogenous developments affecting all of Europe, these factors could be expected to have a similar effect on all regions in the United Kingdom. It is therefore useful to start by looking at whether developments on the central state level can explain what has happened in Scotland.

There was a general trend towards devolution in the United Kingdom under Tony Blair's Labour government, with the introduction of assemblies in Wales in 1999 and in Greater London in 2000, along with several efforts at establishing a workable Northern Ireland Executive. These trends notwithstanding, there is little doubt that Scotland has been in the forefront of developments. The plans for devolution were in many ways a response to the strength of demand for it in Scotland, not least because Labour needed to win back votes from the SNP. The demands for a parliament were certainly far stronger in Scotland than in Wales, with 74 per cent voting in favour of a Scottish Parliament in 1997, whereas only 50.3 per cent (in a turnout of only 50.1 per cent) voted in favour of a considerably less powerful Welsh Assembly. Compared to the English regions, the contrast is even stronger: in 2004, only 22.1 per cent in a turnout of 47.7 per cent voted in favour of the establishment of a regional assembly for North East England, widely considered the most regionalist of the English regions. As a result, the Labour government cancelled plans for similar referenda elsewhere in England.

Similarly, survey data confirm that feelings of national identity are much stronger in Scotland than in other parts of the United Kingdom. Brown *et al.* (1998: 213) present data from the 1997 British Election Survey showing that 61 per cent of respondents in Scotland identified themselves primarily as Scottish, whereas 42 per cent of those in Wales identified primarily as Welsh and only 24 per cent in England identified primarily as English. Hence, national developments cannot properly explain the growth of regionalism in the Scottish case.

Cultural nationalism

The distinctive institutional framework that Scotland retained under the Act of Union ensured the continued existence of Scots law, the Kirk and a distinctive education system. The establishment of the Scottish Office furthermore created a separate bureaucracy governing Scotland. Thus, there were several institutions that enabled Scots to maintain a separate national identity within the United Kingdom over the 300 years following the Union of 1707. In explaining the continued importance of Scottish national identity within the United Kingdom, the importance of these historical developments cannot be dismissed, and accordingly they feature prominently in most scholarly accounts of Scottish nationalism (e.g. Brown *et al.* 1998; McCrone 2001; Henderson 2007).

McCrone claims that people identify as Scots 'not because there is some ancient folk memory, but because national identity is carried by means of the plethora of associations and organisations we call by way of shorthand "civil society"' (2001: 46f.). Scottish schools, the legal system and the press have contributed to sustaining a separate Scottish society, teaching its inhabitants to be Scottish through their daily praxis. However, survey data show that it is not necessarily the case that people who are more embedded in typically Scottish cultural institutions are also more nationalist. In fact, Presbyterians are less likely to favour independence than either Catholics or non-religious Scots (Henderson 2007: 77). Henderson argues that the differences in political culture between Scotland and the rest of the United Kingdom have more to do with perceived differences in values and attitudes than with actual differences. In terms of culture, the main divide in the United Kingdom is between southern England and the rest of the country, whereas northern England and Scotland are remarkably similar (Curtice 1992).

While political institutions may have maintained a sense of cultural distinctiveness, linguistic differences were traditionally far greater within Scotland (between the Highlands and the Lowlands) than between Scotland and England (Gellner 1983: 47). Although Gaelic is nowadays spoken by a tiny fraction of the Scottish population, it used to be the main language in parts of the Highlands, yet it never led to the development of a separate national identity in the Highlands. However, Henderson (2007: 27) argues that the lack of linguistic difference is easily made up for by the presence of other cultural markers. She cites tartan, bagpipes and other Highlands traditions as examples of this. These aspects of Scottish culture have been used actively as symbols of the nation, both from within and by outsiders.

In a longitudinal study that aims to explain change across time in Scottish nationalism, one is looking mainly for independent variables that vary across time. A key question when it comes to cultural explanations of nationalism is whether Scotland has become any more culturally distinctive between 1965 and 2005. Examining the main objective markers of culture would lead to the opposite conclusion: the number of Gaelic-speakers has fallen across time, and religion has become less important in a secularizing society. Meanwhile, the education and legal systems of Scotland and England were as separate in 1965 as they were in 2005. Cultural distinctiveness therefore does not seem to explain particularly well the mobilization of Scottish nationalism in the second half of the twentieth century.

Changing circumstances might nonetheless have made Scottish cultural distinctiveness matter in ways that it previously did not. The growth of the welfare state and the declining influence of the Kirk have made the UK state more important in the daily lives of Scots. In such a context, a feeling of cultural distinctiveness vis-à-vis other parts of the United Kingdom could matter more than it used to when the state had less of an impact on the daily lives of Scots. However, the development of a UK welfare state did not primarily take place between 1965 and 2005. It was already well developed by 1965, and it was partly being dismantled under Margaret Thatcher's government in the 1980s.

Although Scotland has not become more culturally distinctive across time, the status of Scottish culture might have improved, making it more attractive for people to identify as Scots. The revitalization of popular culture in Scotland might have contributed to this. Scottish cultural products have undergone something of a renaissance over the past thirty years, with Scottish literature, drama, music and arts becoming increasingly popular. Christopher Harvie likens the developments to the Scottish golden age of the eighteenth century Enlightenment, noting that 'works about Scotland and society of a seriousness rivalling anything printed in the place came from all the arts, as did scholars, artists and epicures' (2001: 496). The impact of popular culture on the development of nationalism in Scotland is noted by several authors. According to Pittock (2001: 141), 'it is certainly the case that Scottish culture has been one of the aspects of a Scottish agenda which has created a marked divergence in the outlook and nature of debate in Scotland and England'. Harvie mentions the example of the Scottish Poetry Library, established in the early 1980s, as a cultural institution that 'helped propel the Scottish constitutional movement' (2001: 521).

The processes were sparked by the literary revival from around 1980, with authors such as Kelman, Gray, Welsh, Warner and several others rising to fame. The large number of authors achieving international success has led some to argue that '[i]n terms of the novel, no period in Scottish culture has, perhaps, been as rich as the period between the 1960s and the 1990s' (Craig 1999: 36). In his study, Craig finds strong elements of a Scottish literary tradition in the works of these authors, and he links this tradition explicitly to the development of nationalism, arguing that because of it,

> Scotland went on imagining itself as a nation and went on constituting itself
> as a national imagination in defiance of its attempted or apparent incorpora-

tion into a unitary British culture, a defiance which has had profound political consequences in the last decade of the twentieth century.

(ibid.: 36)

Several of the above-mentioned writers have used the Scots language or Scottish dialects rather than the Queen's English, either in representations of dialogue or also in the narrative.

Slightly earlier, there was a revival of folk music. While this seems to have started in the 1950s, the golden age of Scottish folk music was mainly from the 1970s onwards, and it carried on into the 1990s. One important consequence of this movement was that it 'helped the movement for re-acceptance of Scots language' (Munro 1996: 177), which could certainly have had an impact on nationalism. More recently, Gaelic folk song has also been popularized by the success of bands such as Runrig and Capercaillie since the early 1980s, both singing in Gaelic (MacLeod 1996). This has arguably contributed to making Gaelic fashionable, thus helping to turn around the rapid decline of the language. Hutchinson (2005) discusses the revival of the Gaelic language since the 1970s, when the language manifested itself in several sectors of the modern arts.

The success was followed up by movies such as *Braveheart* and *Trainspotting*, both released in 1995. *Braveheart* is directly related to nationalism, being based around the life of Scottish national hero William Wallace and portraying the battle against the English occupation of Scotland in the thirteenth century. It also employs traditional tartan imagery. Even though it was criticized for its historical inaccuracy and 'Hollywood' perspective on Scotland, *Braveheart* was still exploited by the SNP to mobilize nationalist sentiments. As McCrone argues, '*Braveheart* may have been bad history but it made good politics' (2001: 128). On the other hand, *Trainspotting* portrays a picture of modern urban Scotland, using mainly Scottish actors and crew. It does not have a nationalist agenda, but its international success and cult movie status made it a source of pride among many young Scots.

Scotland's cultural distinctiveness, maintained by its separate institutional framework within the United Kingdom, is a crucial factor to take into account when explaining why it has sustained a separate national identity. However, it does not straightforwardly explain the sudden mobilization of nationalism from the 1970s onwards, when a growing number of Scots wanted to renegotiate their relationship with the United Kingdom and establish either a devolved Scottish parliament or an independent Scottish state. The expanding role of the state or the improved status of Scottish popular culture may have contributed to politicizing the existing cultural distinctiveness, but neither explanation is completely satisfactory. When one looks for an explanation of changing levels of nationalism across time, more dynamic factors need to be taken into account. Among the key structural changes affecting Scotland and most other Western European regions in this time period are globalization and Europeanization. The next two sections will discuss whether these might have had more of an effect on Scotland than on other UK regions, and hence whether they may be helpful in explaining the divergence between growing levels of Scottish nationalism and lower levels of regionalism elsewhere in the state.

Globalization: building institutions to attract capital

While the processes of globalization have affected all of the United Kingdom, it still seems likely that they could have had a stronger effect on Scotland. Scotland is one of the most export-oriented regions in the country, and it has traditionally had an open economy. This might be one reason why Scotland has developed an institutional infrastructure aimed at promoting the region's position in the global economy, in accordance with the theories on globalization and regionalism.

From the 1970s, there have been concerted efforts at promoting Scotland as an attractive place to invest. The Scottish Development Agency (SDA) was set up in 1974 to carry out industrial planning. It gradually lost influence through the 1980s, but was restructured as Scottish Enterprise in 1991, adopting a more market-based approach that focused on supporting private Scottish businesses. Meanwhile, another government agency, Locate in Scotland, was set up in 1981 in order to focus on attracting foreign investments. In 2001, it was replaced by Scottish Development International, which also incorporated promotion of Scottish exports. These agencies have frequently sought to mobilize particular aspects of Scottish identity that are seen as conducive to economic development, such as the education system and the Highlands landscape (Bond, McCrone and Brown 2003).

The regional organization of these economic development agencies would seem to conform to the expectations of the globalization thesis, and it certainly reinforces the point that the region is now seen as the most appropriate unit for economic development. This argument is made in the SNP's 2001 election manifesto, which focuses on the need to 'encourage the relocation of high-skill, value-added international investors to our country' and claims that 'because we stand for Scotland, we will be best placed to sell Scotland as a marketplace, as a holiday destination and as a key export partner' (Scottish National Party 2001: 9). Thus, the party suggests that the region is the most appropriate unit for economic development, and focuses on the need for regions to be proactive in attracting investment and promoting growth. This corresponds well with the theories on globalization.

However, the establishment of economic development agencies seems to have been as much a reaction to growth in regionalism as a cause thereof. Rather than preceding the growth in Scottish nationalism, they have been established at times when Scottish nationalism has been at its peak, or in the middle of an upward or downward trend. It is also frequently suggested that nationalism was a crucial factor in the decisions to establish these agencies. The SDA was set up between the two general elections of 1974, and its creation has been interpreted as part of Labour's strategy to win back votes in Scotland from the SNP (Mitchell 1997: 409). Indeed, during the period between these two elections, 'Scotland suddenly became very important to Labour and Scots voters found themselves lavished with attention' (Lynch 2002: 129). The establishment of the SDA itself was proposed in the first-ever Labour manifesto for Scotland, created for the October 1974 election. Similarly, its restructuring into Scottish Enterprise has been seen as a way to address the Thatcher government's political problems in Scotland. The SDA was considered by the Scottish public to be successful, but the Conservative government did not get the credit for this. Consequently, it needed to be restructured in order to become more closely identified with the Conservatives by voters (Danson *et al.* 1989: 72).

The relationship between globalization and regionalism is complex, with levels of regionalism determining how regions respond to the opportunities provided by globalization. Scottish nationalism played a part in the development of the institutional infrastructure that characterizes a region competing for capital and labour in the global market. However, globalization provided an opportunity structure that allowed the Scottish economy to compete directly with other regional economies across state borders. This has reduced its dependence on the UK state and made it more reasonable to devolve authority to the regional level. Parallel to the processes of globalization, European integration has contributed further to reducing Scotland's dependence on the United Kingdom, allowing some nationalists to view membership of the European Union as potentially making continued membership of the United Kingdom redundant.

European integration: independent in Europe

European integration has been put forward as one of the main reasons for the growth of nationalism in Scotland, not least because of the Europhilia of the SNP after the formulation of its 'Independence in Europe' strategy in 1988 (Dardanelli 2005a; Jolly 2008). The party argues that the existence of the European Union will make the transition to political independence easier and provide economic continuity (Lynch 2002: 187). In this framework, European integration offers a solution to the fear that the Scottish market would be too small under independence, reducing Scotland to the economic and political periphery of Europe. Through the single market, Scotland would have access to the same markets regardless of whether it were part of the United Kingdom or not. According to the SNP, 'the single market between Scotland and England is guaranteed by the 1957 Treaty of Rome and the 1987 Single European Act – not the 1707 Treaty of Union' (SNP 1992). Politically, independence would mean a move away from the periphery as Scotland would be given its own seat at the negotiating tables in Brussels, rather than having to work through the British delegation.

However, this still leaves the question of why these developments would have a greater effect in Scotland than in other parts of the United Kingdom. Institutionally, all regions within the United Kingdom are in the same situation with regard to their relationship to the EU vis-à-vis the United Kingdom. Even if one expects the impact to be different in a culturally distinct area such as Scotland, there should still not be any reason to expect a different development in similarly culturally distinct Wales. The only reason why the effects might vary across space would be if the attitudes towards European integration were different, so that the EU was seen as a favourable alternative to the United Kingdom in some parts of the country but not in others.

As the data presented in Chapter 5 show, the Scottish public has indeed been more positive about the EU than the English and Welsh since around the late 1980s. On the other hand, opposition to the EU seems to have been stronger in Scotland than in the rest of the United Kingdom during the 1970s and early 1980s. It would thus seem that European integration provides a reasonable explanation for the growth of regionalism in the late 1980s and 1990s, and this has indeed been offered as a key reason for the discrepancy between the devolution referendum results in 1979 and 1997.

Dardanelli (2005b: 337) argues that independence was regarded as a much more favourable option in 1997 than in 1979 because at the second referendum it was expected to entail continued membership of the European Union. In 1979, 'independence in Europe' was not a meaningful option. While the support for devolution itself actually dropped from 54 per cent to 43 per cent from 1979 to 1997, the support for independence increased from 7 per cent to 35 per cent. This was almost entirely due to the existence in the surveys of the new independence in Europe option, favoured by 26 per cent of the respondents (ibid.: 329). Furthermore, the possibility of independence in Europe led many devolutionists to prefer independence to the status quo in 1997, whereas in 1979 they preferred the status quo to independence. This effectively neutralized the unionists' argument that devolution would inevitably lead to independence (the 'slippery slope' argument), which was so effective in making many a priori devolution supporters vote against devolution in the 1979 referendum for fear that it would eventually lead to secession.

However, European integration does not appear to offer an explanation for the growth of nationalism in the 1970s, when the EC was not seen as a good alternative to the United Kingdom. In the 1970s, the SNP was opposed to European integration, and the levels of Euro-scepticism were higher in Scotland than in the rest of the United Kingdom. In the 1979 referendum, the issue of European integration was not utilized by elite actors, who did not consider it to be connected to devolution. The European dimension therefore did not make much of an impact on nationalism in the lead-up to the referendum. On the mass level, support for self-government was also linked to hostility to the EU (Dardanelli 2005a: 75ff.). Institutionally, the EC could not really be regarded as an alternative to the United Kingdom in the 1970s in the way that the Europeanization hypothesis stipulates. It would not have guaranteed market access before the Single European Act of 1987 paved the way for the single market.

Structural funds also fail to provide a sufficient explanation for the growth of nationalism in the 1970s, as they started to become important only from 1989 onwards – a couple of years after Scottish nationalism resumed its growth, from the mid-1980s. On the other hand, some areas of Scotland did receive structural funds in the 1990s, and they might therefore be part of the explanation in this period. However, Dardanelli (2002: 284) finds no evidence that the structural funds had any direct effect on nationalism. According to him, the structural funds issue was never raised in the pro-devolution discourse, and they seem to have affected nationalism only in so far as they made public opinion more positively inclined towards the EU. Even here, the impact seems limited, as the turning point for Scottish public opinion on the EU appears to have been the mid-1980s, which was before the structural funds had much of an impact.

European integration is a key factor in explaining the changes in Scottish nationalism between the 1979 and 1997 referenda, in particular the growing nationalism in the 1990s, following the introduction of the single market and the SNP's 'Independence in Europe' strategy. However, it does not contribute much to explaining the growth of nationalism in the 1970s, when European integration had not proceeded as far and was less popular in Scottish public opinion. Further factors are therefore needed to explain the development of nationalism more completely. In particular, it is necessary to look at endogenous processes of change. The final two sections of this chapter consider the two remaining factors of the regionalism model, both of which are dynamic as well as endogenous to the region: party system distinctiveness and economic development.

Party system: rejecting the Tories

Scotland has long had a distinctive party system from the rest of the United Kingdom, and the differences grew through the 1970s and 1980s. The most obvious manifestation of this is the SNP, whose successes in the 1970s and 1990s have been documented in the previous chapter. However, the Scottish party system differs substantially from the English and Welsh even if the SNP is kept out of the equation.

Most notably, the Conservatives ('Tories') have been weak in Scotland since the late 1960s, with their performance gradually worsening to the point that they did not return a single MP from Scotland in the 1997, 2002 and 2006 elections. This is a trend that has developed over the past forty-five years. In the general elections from 1951 to 1959, the Conservatives were the largest party in Scotland on every occasion, winning 50.1 per cent of the vote at their peak in 1955. However, from the 1964 election onwards they started losing ground. By the time of the 1979 election, the Tories won only 31.4 per cent, which was 10 points less than Labour and resulted in the Conservatives returning only 22 MPs compared to Labour's 44 from Scottish constituencies. At the national level, this was of course the election that brought Margaret Thatcher to power with 43.9 per cent of the vote – 7 points more than Labour. The Conservatives' performance worsened even further during their time in office from 1979 to 1997, with only 25.6 per cent of Scots voting Conservative in 1992, compared to 41.9 per cent of voters in the United Kingdom as a whole. In the 1997 general elections that brought Labour back to power in London, as little as 17.5 per cent of Scots voted for the Conservatives. At the national level, the party still won 30.7 per cent of the vote (Hassan and Lynch 2001: 349ff.). The decline was uniform across social class, gender, age and religion (Brown *et al.* 1998: 154).

Conversely, Labour has been the dominant party in Scotland since the Conservatives started to lose support, and it has been the largest party in every Westminster election since 1964. The Labour vote did suffer from the growth of the SNP and the Liberals, and the party was down to 35.1 per cent in the 1983 elections. However, this was still 7.5 points more than its share in the United Kingdom as a whole, and indeed Labour's share of the vote in Scotland has been higher than its UK share in every general election since 1974. The difference was biggest in the 1987 elections, when Labour won 42.4 per cent in Scotland, compared to 30.8 per cent in the United Kingdom as a whole (Hassan and Lynch 2001: 349ff.).

The Liberals (later the Liberal Democrats) have had their stronghold in the northern and western peripheries of Scotland. The party has won seats in the country in all elections since 1950. However, in terms of its overall support in Scotland, the performance of the Liberals has not been markedly different from its performance in the country as a whole. Indeed, since its alliance with the Labour breakaway Social Democratic Party resulted in a national electoral breakthrough in 1983, the party has attracted a lower share of the vote in Scotland than in the United Kingdom as a whole.

The discrepancy between the opinions of Scottish voters and the government ruling them has been forwarded as one of the key reasons for the mobilization of Scottish nationalism under the Thatcher government (e.g. Brown *et al.* 1998; McCrone 2001). The perceived democratic deficit of being ruled by a government that was supported by an ever-smaller minority of the Scottish population laid the foundation for a mobilization on regional grounds. Of course, the perception that this represented a democratic deficit was deeply associated with the nationalist idea that Scotland as a nation should be considered a political unit – a *demos* deserving to govern itself, if you will (Henderson 2007: 103). Labour dominated in northern England as well, but Conservative rule in northern England was not perceived as a democratic deficit by most voters or political elites, because the region did not consider itself an independent political unit.

The democratic deficit was made all the more obvious by the fact that Scotland was in some ways treated as an independent political unit by the British state. The Conservative government appointed the Scottish Secretary, who was head of the Scottish Office. Hence, the political leadership of Scotland itself was being decided by a political party that had little support among the regional public. In this context, devolution was seen by many as a way to ensure that Scotland would always be ruled by Scots, and that the policies being implemented in Scotland would have the support of a majority, or at least a plurality, of the Scottish public.

However, a further question remains: why do Scots differ so markedly from other Britons in their voting behaviour? Followers of the democratic deficit school usually put this down to the left-wing political culture of Scotland. Surveys show that Scots tend to be more communitarian and have greater faith in the welfare state than British people in general. Brown *et al.* (1999: 77) provide data on political values, showing that Scots on average are more social-ist and more cosmopolitan than the English and Welsh. Indeed, the differences between Scots and the rest of the United Kingdom remain even if one controls for social class, education, religion, or other social characteristics. They suggest that this is because Scottish political elites have managed to create a fusion of Scottish nationalism and socialism, so that 'a feeling of "Scottishness" goes along with left-wing values' (ibid.: 83). Both Labour and the SNP have com-bined nationalism and socialism in their political agendas, and this has made it difficult for Scots to be nationalist without also being socialist.

However, the differences in political values are still fairly small in compari-son with the large gaps in support for political parties, and they tend to change more slowly across time. It therefore seems unlikely that this can account for the entire difference in performance. Taking a different approach, several authors have pointed to Margaret Thatcher as an important source of the Tories' misfor-tunes, and even of Scottish nationalism itself (Harvie 2004: 219; Nairn 2000: 180). Certainly, Thatcher was extremely unpopular in Scotland, and the hostility towards her has perhaps increased even further since her resignation in 1990. Although she was a controversial prime minister in England as well, she still had a strong core of supporters south of the border. Indeed, the popularity of the Conservative Party did not begin to wane until she was forced out of office in 1990. Thus, Thatcher actually appears to have been fairly popular in England, regardless of what some of her detractors may later have claimed.

There are different opinions regarding what exactly it was about Thatcher that led her to become such an unpopular character in Scotland. Certainly, some spe-cific policies were detested, such as the poll tax, which was introduced in Scot-land one year before the rest of the United Kingdom. She also gained a reputation as a proponent of centralization, overruling the Scottish Office on a number of occasions and reducing the freedom of local councils over housing and education policy. Yet claims that she single-handedly destroyed the Scottish economy appear unfounded, as Scotland's economic decline actually started in 1976, three years before Thatcher took office, and the revitalization of the Scot-tish economy in the 1990s also took place under a Conservative government (see Figure 5.1 in the previous chapter).

The Scottish dislike of Thatcher seems to stretch beyond her actual policies. To some extent, it appears to be connected with Scottish nationalism itself. Indeed, Thatcher herself attributes her unpopularity to 'the national question on which the Tories are seen as an English party and on which I myself was appar-ently seen as a quintessential English figure' (Thatcher 1993: 624). The best explanation of the Conservatives' problems in Scotland may be that they have been regarded as the party of the political centre in the United Kingdom. The Conservatives have always been the most explicitly unionist party in Scotland – indeed, they were called the Scottish Unionist Party until 1965. They have espoused centralizing policies and been opposed to devolution of power. This was certainly true of Thatcher, who was a fervent opponent of devolution and also reduced the powers of local councils during her time in government. Support for the Conservatives has therefore been hard to reconcile with nationalism, and for many people it has probably been synonymous with support for 'London'. In many quarters, the party was even perceived as being anti-Scottish (Hopkin and Bradbury 2006: 142).

As is frequently the case, there is no unidirectional line of causation in this relationship. The distinctive party system has been as much an effect of nationalism as a cause thereof.[1] The weakness of the Conservatives in Scotland was partly a consequence of nationalism, but it also led to the perception that there was a democratic deficit that could be addressed only through devolution, thereby contributing further to the growth of nationalism. Meanwhile, Scottish support for Labour has led the party to favour devolution as a way to maintain its influence in the region, regardless of who is in power at Westminster. The support for devolution has in turn boosted the party's popularity in Scotland.

Party system distinctiveness has contributed to the growth of nationalism in Scotland, in particular when the idea of a democratic deficit became widespread during the 1990s. Nationalism and party system distinctiveness mutually reinforce each other, resulting in an upwardly spiralling trend on both dimensions. However, the model still misses the final link, explaining why nationalism itself was mobilized in Scotland across the period 1965–2005. The last factor of the regionalism model is economic development, which will be considered in the next section.

Economic growth: is it Scotland's oil?

In the late nineteenth and early twentieth centuries, the Scottish economy was strongly based on heavy industries, and the decline of these caused economic recession and pressures of structural adjustment (Brown *et al.* 1998: 74). However, Scotland has since become transformed into an economy based on services, technology and petroleum. The main economic centre of the country is the Central Belt, which includes the capital, Edinburgh, and the largest city, Glasgow. The area houses most of the major industries, as well as 70 per cent of the population. The financial centre in Edinburgh and the computer technology industry in the Silicon Glen between Edinburgh and Glasgow are particularly important, while Glasgow remains an important seaport and manufacturing centre. The rest of the country is sparsely populated, but the third largest city, Aberdeen, is situated outside the Central Belt in the north-eastern part of the country. It is the main centre for the UK petroleum industry, as well as a major fishing port. To the west of Aberdeen, the rural Highlands are home to most of the larger whisky distilleries, whisky being another major export.

In the past, economic development has notably been used to explain Scottish nationalism by internal colonialist theorists such as Michael Hechter (1975) and Tom Nairn (1977), who argued that underdevelopment or dependent development led to a powerful convergence of economic interests and a shared culture. However, contrary to the expectations of these theories, Scottish nationalism has actually increased with economic growth.

The development of Scottish nationalism seems to have followed the conjunctures of the Scottish economy relatively closely. As was mentioned earlier, all indicators suggest that nationalism grew most strongly during the early 1970s and the 1990s, and these were both periods of sustained growth in the Scottish economy, both in absolute terms and relative to the United Kingdom as a whole. Most indicators also suggest a decline in nationalism in the late 1980s, when the Scottish economy was receding. For the period from 1975 to 1985, the indicators on the levels of nationalism point in somewhat different directions. This corresponds to a period of economic stability.

Figure 6.1 shows the development across this period of the Scottish GDPR per capita relative to the UK average, as well as the nationalism indicator for which the data set is most complete: the SNP's support in the Scottish electorate.[2] As the figure shows, the SNP vote started to pick up at around the same time as the economy started to grow, towards the end of the 1960s, and it peaked when the economy was at its strongest in the mid-1970s. The stagnation and subsequent decline in the 1980s were followed by an even stronger collapse of the SNP, before the party reawakened with the economic resurgence in the 1990s.

The concurrence of growth in nationalism and in relative economic fortunes makes it interesting to look more closely at relative economic growth as a factor in explaining nationalism in Scotland. This section will look at two different theoretical mechanisms through which relative economic growth may be conducive to regionalism, as discussed in Chapter 2. The crucial question is how each of these has been at play in Scotland. The analysis will examine the evidence that economic growth has provided a direct fiscal incentive for nationalism and generated disaffection with the region's political peripherality.

Traditionally, the fiscal balance has been regarded as an important argument against Scottish independence, and thus as a disincentive to nationalism. In the past, unionists argued that Scotland was financially dependent on the United

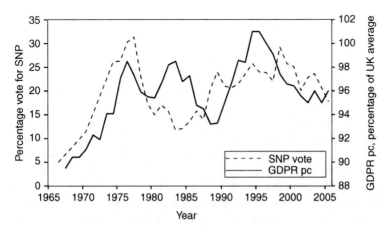

Figure 6.1 Regionalism and prosperity in Scotland (sources: Hassan and Lynch (2001) and Office for National Statistics).

Kingdom, and the Scottish economy would therefore suffer if independence were ever to become a reality. However, this started to change with the discovery of North Sea oil in the early 1970s. For the SNP, the oil argument had two strands. First, it offered evidence that Scotland was not dependent on the United Kingdom at all. According to McCrone (2001: 118), oil made the idea of an alternative Scottish future a real political possibility. The SNP argued that 'arguments in financial terms against self-government are going to lack credibility in future when Scotland's oil resources are recognized as of such immense magnitude as to put the advantages of independence beyond doubt' (*Scots Independent* 1972: 2, cited in Lynch 2002).

Second, it was argued that oil could make a substantial difference to the Scottish economy, whereas it would not make a big impact on the much larger British economy. In 1971, the SNP argued that 'the discoveries could make a vast difference to our basic standard of living. [...] If we remain in the UK the benefits of Scottish oil will be marginal' (SNP 1971). This gave rise to the slogan 'Rich Scots or Poor Britons'. Indeed, the party later considered the British state to be exploiting Scotland, arguing that most of the oil revenue was being used to fund tax cuts or infrastructure projects in England. The party's 2005 election manifesto still argued that

> [m]ore than 90 per cent of the UK's oil revenues come from Scottish waters. So it really is Scotland's oil. Since 1997, Scotland has pumped over £35bn worth of oil revenues into Treasury coffers. Yet we have had precious little to show for it.
>
> (SNP 2005)

The slogan 'it's Scotland's oil' became particularly effective and has been highlighted as perhaps the most crucial reason for the growth of the SNP in the early 1970s, indicating that these sentiments were shared by a substantial proportion of the Scottish population (Lynch 2002: 123). This interpretation is supported by a consideration of some of the constituencies where the SNP experienced the strongest growth. Robert McIntyre's success in the Stirling and Falkirk by-election in 1971 – up 20.1 per cent compared to 1970 – can be attributed to the oil campaign, as McIntyre campaigned mainly on this issue, and even became the SNP's oil spokesman. In the 1973 by-election in Dundee East, one of the areas that stood to gain the most from the oil boom, the SNP's support grew to 30.2 per cent, compared to 8.9 per cent in 1970. Later in the same year, the SNP won Glasgow Govan with 41.9 per cent of the vote, compared to 10.3 per cent in 1970. This by-election took place only a few weeks after the oil crisis of 1973 and the corresponding price rises (Lynch 2002: 127).

The balance of payments issue is still fraught with controversy, though, and far from everybody accepts the SNP's arguments. As we have seen, Scotland's GDPR per capita has actually been lower than the UK average for most years. Furthermore, Scotland also enjoys higher levels of public expenditure than the rest of the United Kingdom under the so-called Barnett formula. This is partly due to the fact that Scotland is more sparsely populated than England, making it more expensive to provide public services. However, the costs of running the Scottish Parliament have also contributed to increasing public expenditure. According to *The Scotsman* (24 June 2006), public expenditure per capita in Scotland in 2005/06 was £1,503 higher than the average for the United Kingdom as a whole. The discrepancy had risen from £875 per capita when Labour came into power in 1997.

The revelations about public expenditure led to a controversy over the subject – and not for the first time (Lynch 2001: 24). Polls showed that around 70 per cent of voters in England believed that the subsidy should be cut (*The Scotsman* 24 June 2006). London mayor Ken Livingstone jokingly commented that the government needed to support London's economy 'so that we can continue to pay for the Scottish to live the lifestyle to which they are accustomed' (BBC 7 June 2006). The SNP retorted that the figures excluded the revenue from petroleum, which, if included, would turn the balance upside down and show that it was actually the Scots who subsidized the rest of the country with around £3,000 for an average Scottish family. According to the party, 'Scotland could become one of the wealthiest nations in the world' if it were allowed to retain tax revenue from North Sea oil and gas (*The Scotsman* 24 June 2006). The party produced calculations showing that under devolution, Scotland's GDP per capita[3] ranked eighteenth in Europe, whereas under secession – and with control over the oil resources – it would rank eighth (SNP 2006).

Economic arguments are also used in other sectors, with financial services and high-tech industries being put forward as other sectors that would be better off without the Union, and which are allegedly harmed by the UK government's policies. According to observers interviewed by Zürn and Lange (1999: 15), the growing economic self-consciousness of Scots was among the main reasons for the success of the 1997 referendum.

However, fiscal incentives are only one part of the economic development argument. The other aspect is the growing disconnect between economic centrality and political peripherality. In the twenty years leading up to the devolution referendum in 1997, the discrepancy between Scotland's economic position and its political position grew dramatically. As Scotland was becoming more prosperous, in particular during the early 1990s, its political influence kept declining, creating the democratic deficit discussed in the preceding section. The Conservative governments under Thatcher and Major had little support in Scotland, and their popularity kept declining throughout the period. This resulted in fewer Scottish Conservative MPs with every election held, which naturally led to fewer Scots being represented in the Cabinet and central government positions. This increased the sense of peripheralization, as Scots had less influence on government policymaking.

As was mentioned, the democratic deficit argument has been put forward by several authors as one of the key factors in building support for devolution (e.g. McCrone 2001; Brown *et al.* 1998), and it is essentially an argument about political peripheralization. While grievances over political peripherality have not been linked to economic centrality by any of these authors, it is nonetheless interesting to note that the theories presented in Chapter 2 predict that peripherality becomes an issue in economically prosperous regions, which is indeed what happened in Scotland in this period. However, this came on the agenda mainly because Scotland was actually being peripheralized politically in this period, rather than because it was growing economically.

Since 1997, it has been increasingly difficult to sustain the political peripherality argument. All the three major parties in Westminster have been led by Scots at some time during this period: the Conservatives by Iain Duncan Smith (2001–3, though representing an English constituency), the Liberal Democrats by Charles Kennedy (1999–2006) and Sir Menzies Campbell (2006–07), and finally Labour by Gordon Brown, prime minister since 2007. Scots have also held several key positions in the Labour Cabinet in Tony Blair's and Gordon Brown's governments.

In terms of parliamentary politics, the Scottish electorate was overrepresented in the UK parliament prior to the reduction of Scottish MPs in 2005. Scotland used to have around one MP for every 70,000 inhabitants, compared to one for every 90,000 in the United Kingdom as a whole. Indeed, the influence of Scots over United Kingdom, and since devolution even exclusively English, legislation has increasingly been questioned in discussions over what is commonly known as the West Lothian question. With a growing number of policy areas being devolved to the Scottish Parliament, the legislation in these areas at Westminster does not affect Scots at all, yet Scottish MPs retain the right to vote on them. Thus, Scottish MPs for instance helped introduce university top-up fees in England, although the Scottish Parliament had ruled them out in Scotland (BBC 27 January 2004). This state of affairs has increasingly come under fire, with the Conservatives arguing that Scottish MPs should not be allowed to vote on legislation that affects only England (*The Economist* 8 July 2006). The Scottish electorate has also gained direct control over several policy areas through devolution, as was outlined earlier. In this situation, Scots cannot credibly claim to be politically peripheral any more.

Economic development and nationalism have followed each other closely throughout the forty years studied in this book, with a remarkable concurrence of the periods of growth and decline of each variable. The expectation that this will create fiscal incentives for nationalism is borne out by the SNP's argument that 'it's Scotland's oil', and the party's determination to demonstrate that Scotland would be better off as an independent state. However, higher public expenditure in Scotland has reduced the impact of the argument, and there is much disagreement over whether Scotland is a net contributor or recipient of fiscal transfers. Secessionists and unionists are usually on different sides of these arguments, underlining the importance of fiscal incentives to the debate. The political peripherality argument was also important, at least until 1997, with the weak Scottish influence in Westminster seen as a driver of nationalism. However, this has not tended to be linked to Scotland's economic position.

Causes of nationalism in Scotland

Several of the independent variables in the regionalism model are closely related to the development of nationalism in Scotland since 1970. Because of the maintenance of uniquely Scottish institutions under the Act of Union, a separate Scottish civil society developed, preserving its cultural distinctiveness compared to England and Wales. However, it is less clear why these differences resulted in the development of a political nationalism in the 1970s. Globalization and European integration might be part of the story, providing an opportunity structure for the development of nationalism. However, the establishment of regional economic institutions in Scotland was more a consequence of nationalism than a cause thereof. European integration had an effect on the development of Scottish nationalism in the 1990s, but was not a major factor in the growth of nationalism in the 1970s. Scotland's party system diverged from that of the rest of the United Kingdom in the 1970s and 1980s, contributing to a sense of democratic deficit under the Conservative government from 1979 to 1997. This is an important factor in explaining the growth in nationalism during this period, although nationalism in itself also contributed to the unpopularity of the Conservatives, as well as to the perception that this represented a democratic deficit.

Economic growth and prosperity were closely related to the rise of nationalism across the time period under study. The resurgence of nationalism coincided with the upturn of economic fortunes from the late 1960s, related to the discovery of petroleum in the North Sea. However, the movement stagnated with the economic decline of the 1980s, only to pick up again with the renewed economic growth of the 1990s. Economic prosperity has led to increasing disgruntlement about the perceived unfairness of current fiscal arrangements. This rhetoric is reinforced by the fact that the prosperity is based on natural resources, with claims that the central state is squandering the region's resources. Economic growth has represented a significant resource that regional elites could draw on in their attempts at mobilizing the general public, providing a direct economic rationale for desiring more political power for the region.

7 Rogaland
Petrolization and region-building

Chapter 5 discussed different indicators pointing towards growing levels of regionalism in Rogaland between 1960 and 2000. This was demonstrated both through a quantitative content analysis and through references to political developments reflecting a politicization of the region. The rise of regionalism covaried with regional economic growth and increasing globalization, while the regional party system became less distinctive in this period. This chapter examines each of the variables in the model of regionalism – cultural distinctiveness, globalization, European integration, party systems and economic development – analysing to what extent they are useful in explaining the observed growth of regionalism in Rogaland. It argues that the massive economic growth that took place in Rogaland after the region emerged as Norway's oil capital in the early 1970s created the conditions for a mobilization of regional identities in the region. As the region became richer, the incentives to mobilize on a regional basis grew, and the discourse on local grievances over shortfalls in public investments assumed greater resonance in regional public opinion.

Peripherality in a centralized state

Norway has been a sovereign state for little more than a hundred years. It gained independence from Sweden as recently as 1905, but by then the process of nation-building was already well under way. Since Sweden took Norway from Denmark after the end of the Napoleonic Wars in 1814, Norway had been a separate entity under the Swedish Crown. The country had its own parliament, its own language (adapted from Danish) and its own constitution. Rather than being integrated into the Swedish state, Norway was ruled as a colony, with most decisions being made in Oslo. The colonial bureaucracy had asserted its power and *de facto* ruled Norway independently of the Swedish metropolis, and after 1884 the Norwegian Parliament took over the same position (Seip 1974: 13). Oslo was therefore clearly established as the national centre by the time of independence in 1905, when it became the capital of an independent monarchy.

Norway was a late industrializer in the Western European context, and the process of industrialization did not fully start until the beginning of the twentieth century. Even then, the country continued to rely on the export of fish as its main source of income, and it remained less urbanized than most other industrial countries. Forestry and agriculture also employed a large number of people throughout the twentieth century. The main industries were aluminium and hydroelectricity (Hodne 1975). The discovery of oil and gas resources on the Norwegian continental shelf in 1969 was the impetus behind an unprecedented period of growth, restructuring and modernization in the Norwegian economy. By 1980, production of oil made up 15.7 per cent of GDP, and Norway is now the world's third largest exporter of oil. In 2001, revenues from oil accounted for almost a quarter of GDP and half of all exports, and the oil industry deserves most of the credit for making Norway's GDP per capita the second largest in Europe (OECD 2002: 21f; Economist Intelligence Unit 2002).

After declaring independence in 1905, Norway pursued a policy of neutrality that it managed to maintain through the First World War. However, in the Second World War Norway was occupied by Germany from 1940 to 1945. The Høyre and Venstre (Liberal) parties dominated domestic politics and alternated in government until 1936, but after the Second World War Ap won hegemony for the next twenty years, establishing itself as the default party of government. Since 1965, Ap has met competition from various coalitions of centre-right parties. Norway applied for EU membership in 1972 and 1994, but the population in popular referenda narrowly rejected joining on both occasions. Voting patterns revealed an important cleavage between the mainly Europhile urban centres and the overwhelmingly Euro-sceptic rural peripheries (Valen and Aardal 1995; Pettersen *et al.* 1996). However, Norway has been part of the EU's internal market since its inclusion in 1995 into the European Economic Area.

In terms of territorial organization, Norway is divided into 19 counties and 434 municipalities. For analytical purposes, the country is also often divided into five provinces, or *landsdeler* – Eastern, Southern, Western, Central and Northern Norway – although there are no formal political institutions that correspond to these provinces. Western Norway consists of the counties Rogaland, Hordaland, Sogn og Fjordane and Møre og Romsdal. These provinces are sometimes referred to as regions, which is confusing in this context. In this book, 'regions' will refer to the counties, and 'provinces' will refer to the five *landsdeler*.

Counties and municipalities both have directly elected councils, but the county councils have limited powers and operate under strong fiscal constraints. The municipalities are also restricted in terms of taxation, but they do have a substantial degree of autonomy over local policymaking in areas such as education, care for the elderly, area planning and culture. In 2001, municipalities and counties were responsible for 37 per cent of total public sector expenditure, but most of this went towards welfare state obligations that were delegated to them from the central state. Health, education and social protection accounted for 78 per cent of local government expenditure (Statistisk Sentralbyrå 2002: 451).

The county structure has been in place with few changes since the early nineteenth century. The last major reform was in 1976, when directly elected county councils were introduced, replacing a system in which municipalities appointed a number of representatives to the county councils. At present, counties are responsible for secondary education, regional planning, regional development, cultural institutions and public transport, having lost control over hospitals to the state in 2002. However, actual policymaking takes place at the central level even for most of these policy areas, leaving councils mainly responsible for implementation of policy and provision of services (Leknes *et al.* 2008).

There is also a top-down component of regional government in the form of county governors, who are the regional representatives of the central state with responsibilities for implementation of national policy and supervision of counties and municipalities. Besides the county governors, there are more than forty regionalized branches of the state bureaucracy, each operating their own definition of regions, resulting in more than thirty-five different ways of subdividing the country into regions.

Rogaland is in the south-western part of the country, and has 381,000 inhabitants. As a result of economic growth, the population has grown rapidly over the past forty years. During this period, Rogaland has had by far the most rapid population growth of any Norwegian region. From 1970 to 2000, the population grew by 37.6 per cent, from 260,000 in 1970 to 369,000 in 2000. No other regions had growth rates above 26 per cent during the same period, and in the country as a whole the population grew by 14.7 per cent. The twin cities of Stavanger and Sandnes constitute the largest urban area, with 162,000 inhabitants. This is also where most industrial and service production takes place. The southern part of the region, Jæren, is a predominantly agricultural area, although the short distances mean that an increasing number of commuters to Stavanger also live there. A total of 246,000 people live in Stavanger, Sandnes and Jæren. Haugesund is the main city in the northern part of the region, with 40,000 inhabitants, nearly half of North Rogaland's total population of 86,000. The main industries in this part of Rogaland are shipping and fisheries. Ryfylke, to the east of the county, is more scarcely populated, and mountainous. Only 23,000 people live there, and the population is ageing: 26.3 per cent of the population is over the age of 55, against 21.9 per cent for the region as a whole (Statistisk Sentralbyrå 2002: 73).

Rogaland in the Norwegian context

The emergence of regionalism in Rogaland is somewhat surprising, as Norway is not generally known for its regionalist movements. Rather than a growth of regionalism in other parts of the country, recent trends have been increasing centralization and the weakening of the regional level, along with attitudes and identities related to it. The institutional developments in Norway have gone in the opposite direction compared to the rest of Europe: towards a dismantling of the regional level of government (Baldersheim and Fimreite 2005). The Norwegian counties have lost competencies, most notably in the health sector, which was taken over by the central state in 2002. Both Høyre and FrP want to remove the regional level altogether and move towards a system of central and local governments only. An attempt between 2004 and 2008 to restructure the regional level into a system of fewer and larger regions with more competencies collapsed when few counties wanted to merge with their neighbours and the government refused to impose a new structure from the top down. The promises of decentralization of power were also watered down substantially, with very few new competencies being devolved to the regional level in the end.

These developments have met with little protest on the regional level, and there has indeed been little interest in them in the national media and among the public. To the extent that people care, there does seem to be support both for transferring responsibilities from the regional to the central level and for dismantling the regions altogether (Baldersheim 2003). Both the lack of protest and the lack of interest point towards low levels of regionalism in the country in general. In Rogaland, on the other hand, there has been a great deal of interest in the media and among political and business elites in how the regional level should be restructured, with demands that the new regional level should be substantially strengthened in relation to the central level. The survey data discussed in Chapter 5 also suggested that levels of regional identity in Rogaland are higher than in comparable regions elsewhere in the country. This indicates that the developments in Rogaland should not be seen as part of a general Norwegian trend, but rather that one needs to look at developments that are specific to the region of Rogaland for an explanation of the growth of regionalism.

Counter-cultures and petrolization

Although the region is no different from the rest of Norway on objective cultural markers such as language, religion or ethnicity, Rogaland is not unaccustomed to being a centre of cultural opposition to the centre of the Norwegian state. Situated in the heart of the Bible belt along Norway's south-western coast, the region was one of the most obvious examples of what Rokkan (1967) called the 'counter-cultural' opposition against the expanding influence of the central state in the southern and western peripheries in the early twentieth century.

The peripheral reaction mainly took the form of a cultural opposition to the allegedly continental or international values of the central elites, and the response was a focus on religion and tradition. Specifically, the protests were concentrated around the counter-cultures in the peripheral south-west. These represented a cultural opposition to the values of the more central areas, and included elements of teetotalism, pietism, and support for the *nynorsk* version of written Norwegian.[1] These movements came together in the party Venstre, which later produced two major splinter parties; KrF and Sp (the Agrarian (later Centre) Party). These three parties all had strongholds in the western and southern parts of Norway, and they came to occupy a strategically important position between Høyre and Ap in domestic politics.

As the southernmost of the four counties that make up Western Norway, the influence from the counter-cultural movements was strong in Rogaland. In Berge Furre's words, the region was 'the buckle of the Bible belt' (1987: 6). Rokkan's (1967) data show that the temperance movement and the pietistic movement were especially strong in Rogaland. The language dispute did not come to dominate politics in Rogaland to the same extent as it did in other parts of Western Norway, but in 1957, 85.8 per cent of school districts in the region still used *nynorsk*. This was less than the average 94 per cent in Western Norway, but still much higher than the national rate, which was 49 per cent. However, the proportion of *nynorsk* users in the population was substantially smaller than these figures indicate. The *nynorsk* districts are generally far smaller than the *bokmål* districts, as they are overwhelmingly located in rural areas. In the capital, Oslo, not a single school district used *nynorsk*.

The temperance movement was considerably stronger (Rokkan 1967: 416). In a national referendum in 1926, 73.1 per cent of the Rogaland population opposed a motion to abolish the prohibition of liquor consumption. Only in Møre og Romsdal did the prohibition vote fare better (at 77.2 per cent). This contrasted sharply with the central parts of the country: in Oslo, 13.0 per cent supported prohibition, and in the country as a whole 44.3 per cent voted in favour of prohibition (Statistisk Sentralbyrå 1978b: 647).

However, the strongest of the counter-cultures in Rogaland was the pietistic movement, which had its core in the region. This movement embodied Lutheran orthodox movements, free churches and missionary societies, and it was primarily a reaction against the central authority of the State Church. As home of the missionary college, missionary organizations such as *Det Norske Misjonsselskap*, and the layman's movement, Stavanger has been called the religious capital of Norway (Furre 1992: 364). Other parts of Rogaland were certainly no less religious. Since the popular movement around the Stavanger priest Lars Oftedal in the second half of the nineteenth century, religious political parties and charismatic religious movements have enjoyed widespread support across the region. The two Christian Democrat parties in Norwegian politics – Moderate Venstre in the 1880s and 1890s and KrF since 1945 – have both had their strongest support bases in Rogaland (Rokkan 1967: 400f.). The same is true of several major religious associations that organized large parts of the population in religious work, such as Indremisjonen, Bethania and Ynglingen (Fossåskaret 1987: 357).

All of the counter-cultural movements have lost ground in Stavanger[2] since the 1960s. Melberg (1997) finds that participation in religious organizations dropped significantly from 1974 to 1994. Whereas in 1974, 16 per cent of the respondents to a Stavanger survey stated that they participated actively in their local congregation and the same number were members of religious organizations outside the State Church, the corresponding figures in 1994 were 6 per cent and 8 per cent respectively. Private religious activity decreased as well: whereas 41 per cent of the population in 1974 stated that they prayed regularly, this figure had dropped to 23 per cent in 1994. Melberg (1997: 54) also finds indicators suggesting that support for teetotalism has fallen sharply in the same period. Today, values and attitudes towards the traditional counter-cultures in the Stavanger area do not differ very much from those held by the general Norwegian population. Stavanger is no different from the country as a whole when it comes to levels of Christian faith, membership in religious organizations and attitudes towards abortion. Nor do levels of participation in religious services, or the proportion of teetotallers and of *nynorsk* users, differ significantly from those found in other major cities (Grendstad and Rommetvedt 1997: 193ff.).

The new form of peripheral protest in Rogaland differs substantially from the previous counter-cultural opposition in both its focus and its basis. The counter-cultural protests were based around the notion that the region was 'more Norwegian' than the internationalized centre and aimed at the cultural values of the centre. The new regionalism, on the other hand, focuses more strongly on economic and political issues. The main worries for regionalists today are the region's share of public expenditure and its influence in national politics. The changing values and attitudes of the regional public may provide an explanation for this shift.

Grendstad and Rommetvedt label the processes of cultural change in Rogaland 'petrolization', linking them to economic changes in the region. They find a strong relationship between occupation and cultural values and opinions, with counter-cultures having an even weaker position among people who work in oil-related industries, especially offshore (1997: 199). On these dimensions, petrolization has led to a convergence between the region and the rest of Norway. However, the petrolization processes have also contributed to cultural differences between Stavanger and the rest of the country on other dimensions, and its population today appears more modern in outlook, more open to change and libertarian than the rest of the country. People in Stavanger are also more right-wing and more inclined to prefer reward for effort to economic equality (ibid.: 228). This could reinforce the effect of economic growth in the region, as the prosperity-based regionalism agenda is distinctly non-egalitarian and emphasizes rewarding of the economically productive regions. The changes that petrolization has brought could thus increase the salience of the prosperity-based regionalism argument.

It seems likely that these cultural changes have taken place across the region, rather than being a limited Stavanger phenomenon. Smith-Solbakken (1997) explains how the offshore workers were mainly recruited from fishing and farming communities in the rural areas of Rogaland in the early stages of exploration and production. The platforms were under American management and dominated by southern US industrial culture. Local workers adapted well to this culture, mainly because of the cultural similarities between the two groups. The farming and fishing communities in Rogaland have traditionally placed a strong emphasis on hard work, frugality and individualism – all traits that applied equally to the drillers who were imported from the southern United States. Smith-Solbakken (1997) describes this as a meeting between 'cowboys from Texas and cowboys from Jæren'. The cowboys from Jæren were also drawn to US pop culture. This was an area where American music, movies, cars and clothing were particularly popular even before the petroleum boom. In this context, it seems reasonable to expect these workers to be affected by the American offshore culture, and also that they would contribute to the dissipation of this culture among non-offshore workers when they returned to their home communities between rotations.

Besides the changes in regional attitudes and perspectives, the prestige of regional culture also seems to have grown in Rogaland across time. This is primarily related to the growing use of the regional dialect in public space. Unlike its Scandinavian neighbours, Norway has always been a country where dialects have had a certain status, and many people have preferred to speak in their regional dialects rather than adapt a more standardized form of spoken Norwegian for public usage (Venås 1998). However, the use of dialects was long restricted in written materials and public broadcast media. This has changed substantially since the mid-1990s. Now it is common for people to write informal texts in local dialect, particularly when using modern technology such as e-mails and text messaging. These media have opened up a new sphere for informal writing. More often than not, young people from Rogaland today write text messages and informal e-mails using dialect (*Stavanger Aftenblad* 9 February 2001).

In the mass media, the use of dialects is growing as well, mainly as a result of the demise of the state monopoly on TV and radio broadcasting in the 1980s and early 1990s. Whereas presenters were not allowed to speak in dialect during the NRK state broadcasting monopoly, the opening for commercial radio and television has brought dialects into daily broadcasts. The main commercial television channel, TV2, encourages its presenters to use their own dialects, as do local radio stations (Roksvold 1998). These developments have subsequently forced NRK to reconsider its own policies on the use of dialects. The author Tore Renberg illustrated the radical change for television presenters well in a net meeting in 2004, when he commented on Stavanger's cultural awakening:

> We live in a region [...] that in an extremely short period of time has experienced a shock to its self esteem. I can remember when I worked for NRK in '98 and '99. Once, I was walking down the hall, on my way to the studio. Then I heard a voice behind me: 'Renberg?' I turned around. The voice had spoken Stavangerian. But behind me, I could only see Einar Lunde [a news presenter]. So I kept walking. But the voice was there again: 'Renberg?' I turned around again. Nobody from Stavanger there. Just Einar Lunde. Then Einar Lunde stops me and starts speaking in Stavangerian. He told me that when he first started in NRK, everybody spoke the Oslo dialect, and if they didn't, they had to learn. He just wanted to tell me that I was lucky to be a presenter in NRK who was allowed to speak my dialect, and that it was neat, he thought. When I was a kid, Mia Gundersen [a Stavanger actress] did not appear very often on TV. Once, I think, when she sang 'Onna ei større vinga' by Asfalt. Sometimes, Stavanger-ensemblet were on TV, and I was glued to the screen. Otherwise, Stavanger was only represented on the weather map. Then came the oil.
>
> (*Stavanger Aftenblad* 2 September 2004)

The latter part of Renberg's account hints at another important development on the cultural scene in Rogaland: the Rogaland dialect also conquered the arena of popular music in the 1980s and 1990s. The 'Stavanger wave' became a well-known term in Norwegian pop music in the 1980s, referring to the sudden invasion of music charts by bands from Stavanger, starting with Stavanger-ensemblet in 1980. What is important for these purposes is not that music from Stavanger became popular as such, but that it embodied a new form of expression: The lyrics were in local dialect. Local musicians stopped using standardized oral Norwegian in their music, opting instead to use dialect – and they were successful (Wold 2002). Bands such as Mods and Asfalt followed up on the trend that Stavanger-ensemblet started, and although some major bands sing in English today, there is also a considerable amount of music in the Rogaland dialects. Nobody uses standardized Norwegian any more. The cultural reassertion has also spread to other fields: in 2000, the term 'Stavanger wave' resurfaced, this time to describe the growth of movies from the region (*Dagbladet* 10 March 2000). In the period since 1980, cultural products in local dialect – music, movies, even literature – have achieved widespread success outside the local community for the first time.

Rogaland is not culturally distinctive in the traditional sense; no linguistic or religious cleavages separate it from the rest of the country. When culture was nonetheless an important aspect of regional mobilization in the early twentieth century, this was framed as being in opposition not to the Norwegian nation, but rather to the foreign ways of the central elites. The values that these counter-cultural movements were based on – teetotalism and pietism – have since lost influence, making the region even less culturally distinctive across time. On the other hand, changing values have led the regional culture to differ in other ways, not least on the left–right and authoritarian–libertarian dimensions. As in Scotland, the status of the regional culture of Rogaland – in particular its dialect – has also improved. On the whole, these changes do not appear to be sufficient for cultural distinctiveness to be a major factor in the mobilization of regionalism, but they form part of the context in which other factors have influenced regionalism. The following sections consider the impact of these other factors, starting with the processes of globalization.

Globalization: a petrol-protected nation-state

Arguably, the growth in regionalism has gone hand in hand with globalization in Rogaland. The discovery of petroleum brought a large increase in the presence of foreign businesses and foreign labour in the region from the 1970s, and there has been a steady growth in the number of immigrants throughout the period. As a result, Rogaland is now clearly part of the global competition for capital and labour, and it is actively promoting itself as an attractive region in which to work and invest. The growing foreign influence has also had a cultural impact, as discussed in the previous section.

Although petroleum has clearly led to an internationalization of the regional economy, developments in Norway only partially fit with the globalization thesis. Rather than weakening the Norwegian state, the petroleum industry has provided the resources to protect the state from the consequences of global competition. The state has maintained control over the petroleum industry through its ownership of the natural resources and control over licences for exploration and production. Businesses are therefore forced to relate to the state – indeed, to win its favour, as licences are awarded by politicians (on the basis of competence), rather than going to the highest bidder – and the scarcity of petroleum makes exit an undesirable option on the extraction side of the chain.

However, the petroleum industry is still essentially global in nature, with most major companies operating around the world, and certain aspects of its economy are still highly mobile. This is above all true of the labour force, as reflected in the immigration data. This has arguably had an effect on the regional culture, making it possible to construct a regional identity around the supposedly 'international' nature of the region as opposed to the provincial nature of the Norwegian nation.

There has also been a tendency towards centralization of planning, research and administration. In the processing stage, oil refineries are mobile, as witnessed by the closure of Shell's refinery in Tananger in 2000. The industry has also brought a service sector that is highly mobile, and there have been several successful exports from Stavanger in this sector over the past forty years. In this perspective, it is clearly important for the region to remain competitive in the international market, particularly in relation to other oil hubs such as Aberdeen and Houston. Regional elites have placed great emphasis on this in recent years, aiming to establish Stavanger as 'the European Houston' (*Stavanger Aftenblad* 10 November 2003; Reve 2003). In the domestic market, there is also competition from Oslo and several other cities for the location of businesses and investments.

The establishment of several agencies that seek to promote the regional economy are responses to increased competition between regions. Most notably, fourteen municipalities in the Stavanger area, along with the county council, are involved in Greater Stavanger Economic Development, an organization that seeks to promote regional economic development, bringing together government and businesses. It was established in 1999 as the Arena for Regional Business Development and Entrepreneurship (ARNE) and has grown rapidly to include most of the Rogaland population (only North Rogaland and Dalane are excluded). In 2002, the county administration itself initiated the business network Innovasjon Rogaland, which connects the major businesses in the region. Both of these are the results of a regionalist discourse that has convinced regional elites that they need to actively promote development in the region themselves instead of relying on the central state. Farsund *et al.* (2008: 149) argue that the willingness to act according to common regional interests across municipal borders is based on a common identity and sense of belonging, and they suggest that these institutions have been developed further in the Stavanger region than in other Norwegian city regions.

Another focal point has been the desire to move away from the dependence on petroleum. One the one hand, regional elites have pursued a strategy of transforming Rogaland from a petroleum region into an energy region in a broader sense, aiming to develop a business cluster in renewable energy. On the other, they have sought to diversify the regional economy by expansion into other sectors. The most concerted effort has been the attempt to build the brand *Matfylket Rogaland* ('Rogaland – a region of good food'), focusing on the development of the farming and fishing industries, as well as research centres related to the sector. The aim is that Stavanger will be an international centre for quality food. Similarly, Stavanger's spell as European Capital of Culture for 2008 represented a desire to focus on the development of culture in the region. Finally, the new University of Stavanger, mentioned in Chapter 5, is also seen as part of a wider strategy to transform Rogaland into a knowledge region. These campaigns all reflect a new regionalist understanding in which Rogaland is seen as competing with other regions in a globalized world, and the focus on fashionable ideas such as knowledge and culture arguably also reveals a new regionalist perspective. The strategy also follows new regionalism in its focus on making the region desirable for skilled workers in order to attract human capital for local businesses.

Overall, it seems that the pressures of globalization have had some impact on regionalism in Rogaland. As is predicted by the theories, it is becoming increasingly important for regional policymakers and businesses to cooperate in pursuit of economic development, and the region is seen as competing with other regions for investments and human capital. This perspective runs through the efforts to consolidate the leading position as a petroleum region, and the attempts to gain importance in other sectors. On the other hand, these political developments can also be seen as reflections of the growth in regionalism itself. The increasing identification with the region might well be the reason for the desire to join forces in working for regional development and increasing Rogaland's success in different sectors of the economy.

European integration has led to the markets being opened further to foreign competition, with Norway being a part of the single market through the EEA agreement. On the other hand, the impact of European integration on the political and cultural dimensions is limited by the fact that Norway is not a member of the EU. The next section discusses whether European integration has affected regionalism in Rogaland as a non-member region.

European integration: the EU as a non-member

Although public opinion has been fairly stable in opposing Norwegian membership of the European Union, regional elites frequently claim that Rogaland is closer to Europe than are other Norwegian regions. For instance, Stavanger's application to become European Capital of Culture for 2008 characterized the region as 'where Norway meets Europe' (Stavanger2008 2003: 42). In 1993, it became the first Norwegian region to set up a regional information office in

Brussels (a joint effort by the county and local councils, business organizations and research institutes). This has been used actively by regional elites as a symbol of the alleged European orientation of the region and the related need to loosen the ties to Oslo. In this perspective, the Brussels office represents an attempt to break the chain of command and establish a direct connection with the supra-national level – in this case, a supra-national level that the state itself is not even part of.

However, there is little to suggest that this connection between European integration and regionalism on the elite level has had any effect on the regional public. As is discussed in Chapter 5, a majority of voters opposed EC/EU membership in both the 1972 and the 1994 referenda, and there were no suggestions in the membership discourse that Brussels would ever become an alternative to Oslo, other than as a warning by the 'no' campaign. The content analysis also shows that the number of articles on European affairs remained fairly constant in absolute terms from 1960 to 2000. This translates into a decline in relative terms as the newspapers overall grew in size.

There are no indications that European integration has had any effect on the rise of regionalism in Rogaland. While many regional elites would undoubtedly have preferred a closer relationship with Europe, this sentiment is not shared by a majority of the regional public. Public scepticism towards the EU limits any political or cultural impact that the EU might have had on regionalism in Rogaland. Apart from the impact of globalization, the model has so far had limited explanatory potential in the case of Rogaland. However, the two internal dynamic factors party system distinctiveness and economic growth might still contribute to an understanding of the causes of regionalism in the region. These are discussed in the next two sections.

Party system: from the centre to the right wing

Although the same parties have been present in Rogaland as in the country in general, their respective strengths have traditionally differed quite markedly. In particular, Ap, which has been the largest party at the national level continuously since 1927, has always had a lower level of support in Rogaland than at the national level. On average, Ap's share of the vote in Rogaland between 1961 and 2001 has been 24 per cent lower than the party's share in the country as a whole. This proportion has been fairly stable over time, ranging from 20.6 per cent (in 1993) to 27 per cent (in 1981). Three times in this period (1981, 1985 and 2001), Ap was surpassed by Høyre as the largest party in Rogaland, and it was also smaller than FrP in the elections of 2001 and 2005. Other left-wing parties have performed even worse in Rogaland, and neither SV nor the various communist parties have ever won a higher proportion of votes in Rogaland than on the national level. In total, the left-wing parties were supported by 25.8 per cent fewer voters on average in Rogaland than at the national level in this period.

The main beneficiaries of this lack of support for the left have traditionally been the counter-cultural Venstre and its splinter parties – in particular KrF. The latter won almost twice as many votes in Rogaland as on the national level in the period 1961–2001, winning 17.4 per cent of the votes in Rogaland on average, compared to 9.7 per cent in the country as a whole. This difference has decreased over time, and the party won only 53 per cent more votes in Rogaland in 2001, compared to a peak of 145 per cent more votes in 1969 (19.1 per cent in Rogaland and 7.8 per cent in Norway). Venstre won 7.6 per cent of the vote in Rogaland on average across the same time period, whereas the party took more than one-third less than that in the country as a whole: 4.8 per cent. This difference has also fallen over time, and in the period 1993–2001 the party took only 25 per cent more of the vote in Rogaland than in Norway as a whole. In total, the four centrist parties (including Sp and Det Liberale Folkeparti – the Liberal People's Party) won 40 per cent more of the vote in Rogaland than in the country as a whole through this period. This difference was comparatively higher in the 1960s and 1980s, while it was lower in the 1970s and 1990s.

Since its establishment in 1973, the populist FrP has also performed well in Rogaland. The party's share of the vote was a third higher than the national average in the period 1973–2001, at 10.7 per cent in Rogaland compared to 8 per cent in the country as a whole. This difference has declined as the party has grown in size over time, but in the period 1989–2001 FrP still won 23 per cent more of the vote in Rogaland than in the country as a whole. At the 2005 elections, the FrP was the largest party in Rogaland for the first time. The rise of FrP has been accompanied by a similar tendency in the fortunes of Høyre, which has fared slightly better in Rogaland than on the national level in most elections since 1977, while the party's share of the vote in Rogaland was more than 10 per cent lower than the national average in the period 1961–1973. Overall, the right[3] has therefore gone from winning fewer votes in Rogaland than the national average until 1969 to winning more votes from 1973 onwards. In the period 1961–69, the right won 9.9 per cent less of the vote in Rogaland than the national average, while the right gained 9.4 per cent more than the national average in the period 1973–2001.

This disparity from the central level can be interpreted both as an expression of regionalist grievances and as a cause thereof. Ap has dominated Norwegian post-Second World War politics to such an extent that the party has tended to be closely associated with the state itself. Supporting Ap has tended to be associated with supporting the state, and therefore regionalists opposing the centralizing tendencies of the Norwegian state have tended to vote for other parties. On the other hand, the weakness of Ap in Rogaland has been mirrored by a weakness of Rogaland in Ap. The region has rarely supplied the party with promising politicians, and it has therefore been underrepresented in the Ap leadership and in Labour governments.

This has certainly contributed to the sentiment that Rogaland is being run from the centre, without sufficient control over its own affairs. For instance, when the 2000 Ap government was announced, the *Stavanger Aftenblad* (18 March 2000) ran an article about the region's historical representation in Ap governments, under the headline 'Closed for *rogalendinger*'. It concluded that

Rogaland had been severely underrepresented in Ap governments and slightly overrepresented in centre-right ones, compared to its share of the population. When the next Ap (coalition) government took office in 2005, it was the seventh time that the party announced a government with no ministers from Rogaland.[4] The Conservative MP Bent Høie commented that this was 'the way it usually is in Ap governments, and that's why little has been done for Rogaland when Ap has governed' (*Stavanger Aftenblad* 18 October 2005). Hence, the lack of support for Ap has contributed to regionalist grievances in Rogaland. However, the fact that the difference in support for Ap in Rogaland and on the national level has declined over time suggests that this is not a sufficient explanation of regionalism in this case.

The support for KrF and Venstre is also a reflection of regionalism in Rogaland. As was mentioned earlier, Venstre arose from the counter-cultural movement that opposed the international culture of the central elites. In Rogaland, the religious and teetotal electorate provided most of the support base for the party. KrF was the result of a split in Venstre, and as the name (Christian People's Party) would suggest, it focused mainly on its religious constituents. In its own words, it was a reaction to the secularization and materialism that were associated with the culture of the central elite. Above all, KrF became the party of the independent Christian movements, outside the state church.[5]

If Rogaland has traditionally been underrepresented in Ap, it has been overrepresented in Venstre and KrF. For instance, there has been at least one KrF minister from Rogaland each of the last three times KrF has been part of a coalition government. In recent years, KrF's position in Rogaland has been undermined by a succession of negative events for the party. First, in 2003 the county deputy mayor, Jan Birger Medhaug, was accused of rape by a former girlfriend. The party leadership sided with the ex-girlfriend and suspended Medhaug from his place as the party's first candidate for upcoming regional elections. However, Medhaug retained his popularity among the party faithful, and the strategy backfired on the party when he was later cleared of the allegations following a police investigation. Second, the regional party decided to place the party leader, Dagfinn Høybråten, from Oslo, at the top of the party list in Rogaland for the 2005 parliamentary elections to increase his chances of securing a place. This was regarded by many as an insult to regional pride, and the media questioned his knowledge of the region (*Stavanger Aftenblad* 8 September 2004, 26 November 2004). According to a survey by TNS Gallup at the time of the nomination, 37.8 per cent of voters in the region said that they were less likely to vote for KrF if Høybråten was the first candidate on the list, with only 2.4 per cent saying that they were more likely to do so (TV2 15 September 2004). (In the event, Høybråten focused strongly on appeasing regional concerns during his first term as a Rogaland MP, frequently staying in touch with his constituents and voicing their concerns in parliamentary debates. As a result, there was much less criticism when he was renominated at the top of the Rogaland KrF list for the 2009 elections.)

The support for FrP fits less well with regionalist sentiments. As mentioned earlier, the party wants to abolish the regional level of government, mainly for economic reasons. The regions' current responsibilities would partly be taken over by the state and municipalities, and partly privatized. In this sense, FrP appears to be a distinctly non-regionalist party. However, the party is also the main anti-establishment party in Norwegian politics, taking much of the protest vote (Aardal 2003). For voters in Rogaland, support for FrP can therefore be seen as a statement of protest against the central elites. In this way, FrP may have taken over some of the counter-cultural aspects of regionalism in Rogaland. The party is also explicitly pro-market and ideologically committed to cutting taxes. This would result in less redistribution, and hence more of the resources would stay in the region. In this way, the support for FrP to some extent also fits with the theories of economic regionalism, which will be the focus of the next section.

Although the distinctiveness of the regional party system has declined over time, it is still the case that the centre-right has dominated regional and local politics through much of this period, while Ap has been the main government party at the national level. As a result, regional politicians from the centre-right have been able to blame the national government for problems affecting the region, and they have frequently seized the opportunity to do so. Rogaland has also been underrepresented in Ap governments, mainly because of the party's weakness in the region, and this has further contributed to regional grievances. In both these ways, party system distinctiveness continues to be a factor in the mobilization of regionalism. However, the main factor contributing to regionalism in Rogaland is the economic growth of the region, which will be discussed in the next section.

Economic growth: petrolization and regional self-esteem

The economic history of Rogaland is a story of ups and downs. Since 1800, the region has experienced three major waves of growth and prosperity based around successes in different sectors. Between 1820 and 1870, herring fisheries and the related shipping trade made the region one of the wealthiest in the country. However, owing to the domination of fisheries and agriculture, industrialization got off to a late start in Rogaland. The period from 1870 to 1890 was therefore one of stagnation, as the region lost its dominant position in the fishing industry. When the region did industrialize, it did so explosively. Between 1900 and 1920, Rogaland almost trebled its share of national industrial labour, even though this was a period of rapid industrialization in the entire country. The first major spell of industrialization in Rogaland was again related to fisheries and shipping. The main industry was the canning industry, specializing in exporting canned brisling and mackerel. Shipping remained an important trade, and the region also became home to a burgeoning shipyard industry. However, all of these industries collapsed after 1920, when the reduced stocks of brisling in the North Sea severely hampered supplies, and prices fell on the world market (Nordvik 1987). The period of stagnation lasted until 1970, when the discovery of petroleum in the North Sea made Rogaland the most prosperous Norwegian region apart from

Oslo. In no area have the effects of Norway's economic transformation into a petroleum-exporting country been stronger than in Rogaland.

The covariation between relative economic growth and regionalism is reasonably clear in Rogaland. Figure 7.1 shows the development of regionalism and relative GDPR per capita between 1960 and 2000, with the growth of regionalism accompanying the growth of the regional economy fairly well. The region was not very strongly politicized when the economy was doing poorly in the 1960s, but by 1980, regionalism was already picking up. The development continued with concurrent growth in regionalism and the economy until well into the 1990s.

The correlation between economic growth and regionalism across time makes it interesting to look more closely at relative economic growth as a factor in explaining regionalism in Rogaland as well. In order to establish the connection between these two developments, one must consider the ways in which economic growth and prosperity have been used to promote regionalism in Rogaland. The following analysis will establish the empirical connection between prosperity and regionalism by demonstrating how regional elites have used the region's prosperity to construct a regionalist discourse that centres around two major arguments: first, that the region is not getting its fair share of public investments considering what it pays in; and second, that the region's political position does not match its economic importance.

References to the region's strong economy are often explicitly used in discussions about politics in Rogaland. Two statements made by regional representatives to the Storting in 2000 typify the way in which issues in regional politics are commonly framed. In a discussion about the lack of public investments and fund transfers, Høyre MP Jan Johnsen argued that 'we knew already when our country was created that we would have to give some of our bread to others. But

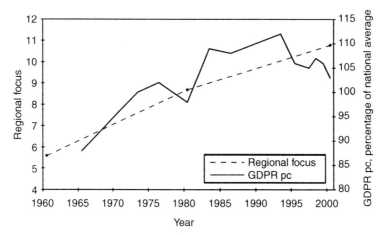

Figure 7.1 Regionalism and prosperity in Rogaland (sources: Statistisk Sentralbyrå and content analysis of the *Stavanger Aftenblad*).

nobody thought that it would go this far' (*Stavanger Aftenblad* 1 March 2000). Similarly, FrP's Jan Simonsen commented, 'We give the most and get the least in return. It is unreasonable that the state, through its transfers, should convert the richest region initially into the poorest' (*Stavanger Aftenblad* 13 October 2000).

In particular, the economic card is often played in discussions over infrastructure investments, a topic that has been a focal point for regionalists in Rogaland. The region receives a substantially smaller share of national infrastructure investments than its population share would suggest, and this is a source of frustration at the perceived centralization of the Norwegian state. For instance, Roald Bergsaker, the Høyre mayor of Rogaland, commented in 2003 that public funding for infrastructure in Rogaland fell well short of requirements. He suggested that the reason for this was either that the region was too rich or that it was too far from Oslo (*Stavanger Aftenblad* 3 February 2003).

More pertinently for this debate, the elites of Rogaland are not satisfied with bringing the levels of infrastructure investment up to a par with the region's share of the population. Rather, it is often suggested that Rogaland should receive a larger share of investments because of the region's importance to the national economy. For instance, in an editorial under the headline 'Rogaland gives much, gets little', the *Stavanger Aftenblad* (9 October 2000) wrote: 'Rogaland is one of the losers in the battle for public investments [in infrastructure], even though our region is at the top of the table when it comes to production'. In this way, a conflict with the centre is linked to the region's economic strength to create a powerful regionalist discourse. The opposition to the centre is also highlighted in the tendency for regional elites to focus explicitly on comparing infrastructure grants to Rogaland with those to the capital, noting that much more is being invested in and around Oslo.

The infrastructure discourse is particularly significant considering the importance of infrastructure policy in Norway. Fjords, valleys and mountain ranges make road construction difficult, and the standard of the road network is therefore relatively low by Western European standards. On the western coast, there are several ferry crossings because of the many long fjords. This makes communications difficult, and goods are likely to be transported via Oslo because of the prohibitive toll and ferry costs along the west coast (around US$600 for a lorry between Stavanger and Ålesund, for instance). Rogaland itself is divided into three parts by the Boknafjord, with a half-hour ferry crossing. This has always been a source of internal division. Two major proposed road projects seek to overcome these divisions through building long underwater tunnels: Ryfast, between Ryfylke and the Stavanger area, and Rogfast, between the Stavanger area and Haugesund.

Comments on the subject have unmistakably taken on a regionalist hue. The projects are portrayed as necessary to build a strong region, to strengthen the links between Rogaland and the other regions in Western Norway, and to oppose the centralizing power of the capital (see, for instance, *Stavanger Aftenblad* 31 January 2001, 4 January 2003). The county administration describes the rationale behind Rogfast as establishing Stavanger as the new hub for trade and transport between Western Norway and Europe, thus eliminating the need to send products via Oslo. Furthermore, it notes that 'Rogfast will also tie North Rogaland and South Rogaland closer together and contribute to making "the deep Boknafjord" less of a cultural cleavage' (*Rogaland i utvikling* 2004).

The conflict is particularly acute at the mass level because these major infrastructure developments, along with several others in Western Norway, will be funded by road tolls. As the regional elites can deflect responsibility onto the central elites who do not give the region what it supposedly deserves, the issue feeds directly into regionalist sentiments at the mass level. As an example of this, the regional council presented figures in 2003 showing that 70 per cent of infrastructure developments in Rogaland would be financed by tolls in the future – more than for any other region (*Stavanger Aftenblad* 3 February 2003). Statements from regional political elites reveal a similar agenda. On one occasion when such figures were presented by the *Stavanger Aftenblad* (3 October 2000), the head of the transport committee in Rogaland County, Ola Steensnæs (of KrF), commented that they confirmed that Rogaland had been 'ripped off'. In a similar debate a year and a half later, the head of the municipal administration in Stavanger, Ole Hetland, commented to the *Stavanger Aftenblad* (7 May 2002) that the lack of public responsibility for financing was disconcerting. The lesson was that the region would be much better off if it could retain control over the resources that it produced, instead of having to rely on the central state.

Chapter 2 also noted the psychological effects of relative economic growth. Prosperous peripheries should be expected to demand a more central position in political and cultural affairs to match their economic power. This mechanism is reflected in discussions about a variety of political issues in Rogaland, from central government representation to public broadcasting, by politicians across the ideological spectrum. When the 2000 Ap government was announced, for instance, Rogaland Ap's Jone Handeland complained, 'It is worrying that a county that – in terms of population and production – is so important, is not represented in the government' (*Stavanger Aftenblad* 17 March 2000). Similarly, the *Stavanger Aftenblad* described the more general scarcity of local representatives in central decision-making bodies, protesting that '[t]he oil and gas region, Rogaland, creates national values in the billions. But it is Oslo and Akershus that is represented on central boards, committees and agencies' (*Stavanger Aftenblad* 5 July 2001). Finally, the main argument of Stavanger's Høyre mayor, Leif Johan Sevland, when he tried to convince the government that the new national radio station, P5, should be based in Stavanger, was that the region did not get as much media coverage as other metropolitan regions, and that this 'did not match the region's role in the national economy' (*Stavanger Aftenblad* 7 April 2003).

Economic growth has been an important factor contributing to the growth of regionalism in Rogaland. It has provided fiscal incentives for regionalization and related claims for increased public expenditure in the region, and it has boosted regional self-esteem, creating demands for Rogaland to take a more central position in national politics. As was discussed earlier in the chapter, economic growth has also contributed to changes in the regional culture and the party system, thereby further strengthening regionalism.

Regional elites have used several strategies in their attempts to renegotiate Rogaland's position in national affairs. In the early 2000s, cooperation with the other counties of Western Norway in the creation of a new super-region was seen by many as the best way to increase public expenditure in the region and gain influence in national politics. The final section of this chapter will discuss this debate and how it can be interpreted in light of the data presented in this book.

A note on Western Norway

From 2004 to 2008, there was a debate between abolitionists and revivalists over the structure of the meso level of government in Norway. One of the key proposals from the 2004 Commission on Regional Reform was to scrap the counties and reorganize the regional level around five to seven provinces, which would gain competencies from the central state in several policy areas.

Initially, the political elites in Rogaland took a proactive approach to this, with most regional parties placing themselves in the revivalist camp, often opposing the views of the national parties.[6] The region aligned itself with its three northern neighbours with the aim of promoting the interests of Western Norway. The Council of Western Norway was established in 2003 as part of the preparations for the expected national debates about the restructuring of the meso level. It sought to promote cooperation in the campaign for better infrastructure funding, and to support business and culture in the region.

The Council also embarked on an ambitious strategy of region-building, commissioning a major work on the history of Western Norway (Helle 2006) in order to demonstrate the common identity of the region. When starting work on the book, its editor, Knut Helle, readily admitted that the book would serve a political purpose: 'That is not unusual for such a project. [...] In fact, it is the historian's duty and responsibility to shed light on the past based on the needs of today' (*Stavanger Aftenblad* 11 February 2004). The project was initiated by the president of the employers' association (NHO) in Rogaland and funded by a major regional bank, underlining the collaboration of political and economic elites in the promotion of regional identity.

Economic development played an important part in the establishment of the Council of Western Norway as well. For instance, Roald Bergsaker, leader of the Council and mayor of Rogaland for Høyre, commented to the local magazine *Rosenkilden* that

> [i]f we ask where values are created in this country, the answer is, no doubt, primarily in Western Norway. In my opinion, it is therefore both appropriate and reasonable that we try to ensure that more of the values created here in Western Norway remain in the region.
>
> (*Rosenkilden* 2003: 7)

Similarly, Ellen Solheim, who headed the KrF party list in regional elections in 2003, argued that 'we have to develop together with those who are strong. The money we make here in the West go into the big state coffers. Then the state spends most of it in Eastern and Northern Norway, while we westerners have to beg for funds' (*Stavanger Aftenblad* 23 August 2003). Her former party colleague Jan Birger Medhaug thought that 'the day we have a united Western Norway, the central powers in Oslo will not be able to carry on with a policy that favours the East over the West' (*Stavanger Aftenblad* 27 September 2003). This point of view was supported by the media. In an editorial, the *Stavanger Aftenblad* supported the development of closer interregional links because strong regions would be a necessary counterweight to the centralist state. Again, the connection to a strong economy was made explicit: 'With oil, fish, waterfalls and fjords, Western Norway is a great net contributor to the state. We do not have any reason to go cap in hand' (*Stavanger Aftenblad* 12 November 2003).

However, collaborative relations between the counties broke down within a few years, and Rogaland county council officially rejected the idea of merging into a Western Norway region in 2007. It was joined by Møre og Romsdal, reluctant from the outset, and Sogn og Fjordane, leaving Hordaland as the only county still in favour of creating the region of Western Norway. By that time, regional politicians in Rogaland had become disillusioned concerning Western Norway, in part owing to a disagreement with the Western Norway Health Board over the provision of neurosurgical services at Stavanger University Hospital, which reawakened a long-standing rivalry between Stavanger and Bergen, the main city of Hordaland (see Chapter 5).

The lack of a Western Norway identity at the mass level, as indicated by the newspaper content analysis in Chapter 5, was probably another key factor working against the development of a Western Norway region. If the *Stavanger Aftenblad* mainly focuses on local and regional news within Rogaland, the same goes for the other main media outlets in the province (Amdam 2008). There are simply no media that try to integrate the province, and there would most likely be no market for such news. Furthermore, all of the counter-cultural opposition movements that used to unite Western Norway have lost ground in Rogaland, including teetotalism, pietism and the *nynorsk* movement, as mentioned earlier in the book.

Western Norway region-building is perhaps most accurately described as a strategy followed by regionalists in Rogaland with the aim of improving their political influence and addressing the fiscal imbalances. Regional politicians believed that they could achieve more by cooperating than by working individually, creating a counterweight to the dominance of the centre (i.e. Oslo and the central state) in Norwegian politics. However, the cooperation was based on common interests rather than a common identity, and it was therefore vulnerable when regional interests came in conflict. While the Council of Western Norway did embark on a region-building project, this was instrumental to creating stable collaborative relations rather than an aim in itself. When Western Norway no longer seemed to serve the interests of Rogaland, the region broke out and embarked on a new strategy for promoting regional interests.

The political scientist Frank Aarebrot reawakened the idea of a Western Norway regionalism in 2008, when he warned against the possible creation of a Western Norway Party in response to the lack of public investments in the region (*Dag og Tid* 6 March 2008). According to him, Western Norway produced 70 per cent of national wealth, yet received only 28 per cent of the public expenditure. The message was well received, prompting responses from regional politicians across the province agreeing that the region was being mistreated. Comments by Ap's party secretary, Martin Kolberg, who characterized the claims that public expenditure was unevenly distributed between the East and the West as a myth created by the opposition, further inflamed the debate. Bent Høie, MP for Rogaland Høyre, commented that

> It's one thing that the attitude of Ap and [Prime Minister] Jens Stoltenberg's Oslo mafia is that Oslo contributes the most and gets the least in every area. But this government is also engaged in a continuous attack on the opportunities of Western Norway to deliver growth and production.
>
> (*Stavanger Aftenblad* 14 March 2008)

Tore Nordtun, MP for Rogaland Ap, criticized his own government, arguing that Rogaland and Hordaland were important for the national production and that the government had underestimated the cultural differences between Eastern and Western Norway. He urged the government to correct the imbalances in public expenditure across different parts of the country (*Stavanger Aftenblad* 19 July 2008).

The economic prosperity discourse related to Western Norway region-building mirrors that of Rogaland, with regional elites tending to use the same arguments whether they are seeking devolution to Rogaland or to Western Norway. This further underlines the significance of economic growth in explaining the development of regionalism. However, the strategies of Rogaland elites concerning Western Norway have changed frequently across time, depending on how realistic the prospects of achieving regional reform were at a particular time and on how cooperative relations with the neighbouring counties were. At times, regional elites have seen the construction of a Western Norway province as the only way in which the aims of increased regional autonomy could be achieved. At other times, they have backed away from interregional cooperation, fearing that Rogaland would become a periphery in a province dominated by Bergen. In both cases, their main concern has been to secure the interests of Rogaland, rather than those of Western Norway as a whole. This reflects higher levels of identification with the county level than with the province.

Causes of regionalism in Rogaland

Although globalization and party system distinctiveness have also had an effect on the rise of regionalism in Rogaland, the case study points towards economic growth as the main cause of the strong increase in regionalism since 1960. The region has not been very strongly affected by European integration, at least not in the ways hypothesized to affect regionalism, and there are no issues of language, culture or historical identity that can explain its regionalism. The only major development that seems to be able to adequately explain the growth of regionalism is the advent of the petroleum industry, and the economic growth that followed in its wake.

The oil boom and the related economic and social changes have caused the economy and society of the region to differ from that of other Norwegian regions, thus making it easier for the local population to separate 'us' from 'the other'. As a region becomes increasingly unlike the nation, the population can be expected to gradually develop a stronger regional identity. Rogaland has an economic structure that is clearly distinct from that of other Norwegian regions because it relies to such an extent on the petroleum industry. The immigrant labour relating to the oil industry may also have given it a distinct social structure.

The effect of economic growth is both direct and indirect. It is indirect in the sense that economic growth seems to boost self-esteem, allowing the inhabitants to take greater pride in their region and become more assertive on its behalf. However, economic growth can also have a direct effect on the level of regionalism in that it makes it more rational to demand greater political autonomy and, particularly, economic independence. People seem more likely to politicize their regional identity if their region, and they themselves, will gain economically from this. In Rogaland, the politicians are open about this to the extent that they make their economic centrality an explicit argument in discussions about a range of political issues. In doing so, they create a powerful discourse that resonates strongly with the general public.

8   Petro-regions and other prosperous peripheries

Despite the fact that Scotland and Rogaland are very different in terms of size, ambitions and cultural differences on which to base regionalism, the factors contributing to the development of regionalism across time are similar in the two regions. Economic development appears to have played a key role in both cases, and for largely the same reasons. In neither region is the effect of economic growth restricted to the fiscal incentives provided by these developments, although these do play a part in both regions. Just as important is the impact of economic success on regional self-esteem. It seems that political peripherality is seen as unacceptable by people in economically central regions.

The cultural reawakening that has taken place in the wake of the economic boom has arguably also contributed to regionalism. These developments in popular culture in both regions may be associated with their economic growth. In a growing economy, people are wealthier and have more money to spend on funding the popular culture sector. For instance, successful businesses may fund regional arts projects, allowing the cultural scene to develop. This may be important in order to attract human capital to the region, thereby improving the labour pool for the businesses operating in the region. Political elites may devote public resources towards culture for the same reason, but they may also use culture consciously in a bid to promote regionalism. In turn, successful regional cultural exports can reinforce the regional identity through making the identity itself as well as regional languages or dialects seem more attractive. This may contribute to reframing the regional identity as forward-looking and successful.

The case selection consciously included two regions with different relationships to the European Union in order to examine whether European integration would interact with the other variables in any way. This does not appear to have been the case, but European integration has had an effect in its own right in the more recent surge of nationalism in Scotland. Thus, EU membership does seem to matter to the development of regionalism, and the institutional incentives that it provides can be crucial in building support for specific proposals such as devolution of power.

The relationship between regional party systems and regionalism is complex. In some ways, the low levels of support for parties that have dominated national politics can be seen as a result of regionalism itself. The Norwegian Ap and the

British Conservatives are seen by many as opponents of regionalism – by some even as opponents of Rogaland and Scotland themselves – and have lost support partly because of voter concerns for what is best for the region. On the other hand, the low levels of regional representation in the national governments of these two parties have led to disaffection with the regions' influence in national politics and a desire to regionalize politics in order to win back power over regional affairs. In Scotland, this was framed as a desire to address a democratic deficit in the political system. The people of Rogaland did not see themselves as a *demos*, but they were nevertheless dissatisfied with the lack of regional representation in the national government.

Finally, globalization is correlated with regionalism in both regions. In Scotland, the establishment of political institutions aiming to support the region in the global economy corresponds to the globalization theories, but it seems likely that the establishment of these organizations is largely a consequence of nationalism, rather than a cause thereof. In Rogaland, the weakening of the central state never occurred in the manner expected by the globalization school, as the public ownership of the petroleum resources forced businesses to relate to a powerful state that was far from being at the mercy of the whims of international capital. There has thus not been as much need for the establishment of regional organizations, although some have still been created in recent years (such as Greater Stavanger Economic Development in 1999 and Innovasjon Rogaland in 2002).

A particular feature of both Scotland and Rogaland is that they are the main hubs for North Sea petroleum production in their respective countries. This raises the question of whether the reliance on petroleum in itself has an impact on regionalism, or whether the findings, in particular on the impact of economic growth and prosperity, are generalizable to other prosperous peripheries. This final chapter raises some theoretical perspectives as to why petroleum regions might differ from other regions, before discussing the impact of economic development in other European regions. This will shed light on whether the relationship between economic development and regionalism works in a similar fashion in regions whose prosperity is not based on petroleum resources.

Admittedly, the reliance on petroleum is far stronger in Rogaland than in Scotland. Rogaland is a much smaller region than Scotland in terms of population, and its economy is accordingly also smaller. Petroleum is therefore the dominant industry in the region, profoundly affecting the regional economy. Scotland has a more diversified economy, with petroleum production concentrated around the city of Aberdeen. The largest cities, Glasgow and Edinburgh, are based around other industries and are not particularly strongly affected by petroleum. This difference notwithstanding, the analysis in Chapter 6 showed that the presence of petroleum resources off the Scottish coast has been important in framing a fiscal incentives discourse in Scotland, and it is therefore highly relevant to ask what the impact of economic development on regionalism would have been in the absence of these natural resources.

Petroleum-based regionalism

When a region's prosperity is the result of natural resource endowments, local elites have an added incentive to mobilize the population on a regionalist agenda in order to gain control over the natural resources in the region. This is especially true where states claim ownership over the natural resources within their territories, and allow property rights and production rights over such resources to individuals and companies only at their own discretion. If the region is rich in resources, assuming regional control over those resources would be a potential source of revenue, as the spoils would not have to be shared with the rest of the country.

Among the natural resources, petroleum holds a special position in the contemporary world economy. Oil and gas are the most important sources of energy in the modern industrial world, and this has made them valuable natural resources. On top of this, the export controls of the main producers have contributed to keeping prices far above market clearing levels, allowing for even larger potential earnings. The value of these resources is likely to lead to regionalism in regions producing them, as the regions try to gain control over local resources and keep more of the wealth in the region.

In both Scotland and Rogaland, regional elites are claiming some sense of ownership over the petroleum resources, albeit in different ways in the two regions. The claims are more pronounced in Scotland, with the SNP slogan 'it's Scotland's oil' as the best example. Accusations that British governments have been squandering Scotland's natural resources are an important part of a discourse that aims to establish as a fact that an independent Scotland would be economically viable. Through claiming ownership of the petroleum resources, the SNP can add petroleum income to the regional balance sheet, turning a balance of payments deficit into a surplus.

The situation is different in Rogaland for two reasons. First, there are no political actors advocating separatism in the region, and everybody therefore accepts the Norwegian state's ownership of the resources. Second, unlike in Scotland, the petroleum is not mainly to be found off the coast of Rogaland. The oil fields on the Norwegian continental shelf span the entire coast of the country. Most of the active fields at present are to be found along the coast of Western Norway and Trøndelag, but future resources are largely in Northern Norway. Therefore, claims of ownership by regional elites are mainly associated with Western Norway regionalism, such as the *Stavanger Aftenblad* editorial claiming that Western Norway has 'oil, fish, waterfalls and fjords', or Hjellum's (2000) lament that petroleum revenues are not credited to regional GDPs, but to an artificial 'extra-region'.

At least three other factors make petroleum regions especially likely to develop regionalist discourses. First, when petroleum is discovered in an area, it is usually developed extremely quickly. The discovery of petroleum produces an economic shock that is strongly concentrated in the region. Keating (1998: 27) touches on the capacity of economic shocks to cause political changes and new identities. He cites de la Granja's (1995) account of Basque history as an example of this. Economic shocks are important because they are instantly noticed by the local population, and thus help to create an awareness of wealth in the area. This boosts regional self-esteem and pride. They also create a distinctive economy in the region, as shocks are often concentrated in one particular area and do not affect neighbouring regions to the same extent. This makes it easier to define the region and to distinguish it from other regions in the state.

While the boom leads to a rapid increase in the economic importance of the region in the national economy, the political importance of the region is likely to lag behind. This discrepancy between economic and political weight can be a source of frustration and lead to demands for status and political influence to match the importance of the region in economic terms.

While petroleum may not have created an economic boom in Scotland in the early 1970s, its discovery was certainly noticed by the Scottish public, and the SNP aimed to create an awareness of the nation's newfound wealth. Meanwhile, Scottish politics changed rapidly during this period, with the explosion in support for the SNP as one of the main developments. Across the North Sea, Rogaland certainly did receive an economic shock in the early 1970s, and the cultural changes referred to as petrolization (Grendstad and Rommetvedt 1997) are good examples of the effect that this had on society. A popular myth in the region describes the effect of petroleum on the regional psyche is as one of moving from apologizing for coming from Rogaland to bragging about it.[1]

Second, exploiting petroleum resources requires a great deal of technological expertise and a lot of capital that the newly established oil producer is unlikely to possess (Karl 1997). In the early stages, the state therefore depends on foreign companies and skilled labour to extract the petroleum. This leads to extensive immigration of foreigners into the region, causing its demographic composition to diverge from that of the rest of the country. This makes it easier to establish the cultural distinctiveness that regionalism thrives on. In addition to having immigrants of a different type compared with other regions, the influx of foreign skilled labour is also likely to affect the culture of the local population through social contact.

Again, the effects of this were stronger in Rogaland, both because the proportion of foreign workers to the native population was much higher and because the cultural differences between the immigrants and the natives were larger. The American oil workers immigrating to Rogaland arrived in a region that was almost completely unaccustomed to foreign immigration. They spoke a different language and were immediately noticed in the pubs and nightclubs of Stavanger. Smith-Solbakken (1997) describes the effect that this had on the culture of the resident population.

Finally, the market for petroleum is global, and hardly any other sector is as embedded in the global economy as the petroleum industry. This is also connected to the capital-intensive and technologically demanding nature of the industry. The effects of globalization are therefore likely to arrive in full strength in petroleum regions. Their economy is different from the national one, and this makes the region the most meaningful unit of economic activities and planning. In addition, they have to compete with other petroleum regions to attract investments and businesses.

Both Scotland and Rogaland have established regional development agencies and are actively competing with other regions for capital and skilled labour. In Rogaland, this is a fairly recent development, but the regional economy has been strongly globalized for some time. However, petroleum is also the most important national industry in Norway, and the central state has therefore been heavily involved in controlling the activities in this sector. In Scotland, the Scottish Executive has some control over the regional economy, and the SDA, and later Scottish Enterprise, played an important role in this area even before devolution. However, the British state is also strongly involved in governing the petroleum industry.

Lessons from elsewhere

With the particularities of a petroleum-based economic boom having had an independent impact on the development of regionalism in both Scotland and Rogaland, there remain some questions about the relationship between economic development and regionalism in other peripheral European regions. Can the findings from the petroleum regions around the North Sea be generalized to other prosperous Western European regions, or are the developments described in the preceding two chapters unique to petro-regions? In addressing this question, this section briefly discusses the role of economic prosperity in regionalisms in five other Western European states, as well as in Slovenia's secession from Yugoslavia in 1990–91.

Spain

The Spanish state was formed as early as 1469, with the union of the kingdoms of Castile and Aragon. However, the state spent most of its resources on overseas imperialism and did not focus much on internal cultural homogenization. As a result, minority cultures and languages remained, notably in the Basque Country, Catalonia and Galicia. When the ideology of nationalism was popularized in Europe in the nineteenth century, these cultural differences were politicized, partly in reaction to more forceful attempts at nation-building by the Spanish state.

Moreno notes that economic development played an important part in this early development of minority nationalism in Spain. In his words, both Catalan and Basque nationalism 'could be seen as political manifestations of a vigorous and prosperous periphery, which contrasted with the inept and parasitical centralism of the Spanish state to which it was subordinated' (2001: 52), and this incongruity is key to understanding the territorial conflicts in the country. Although possessing a distinct language and history was the foundation of Catalan nationalism, these cultural differences were politicized because of 'the paradox that a politically subordinate territory of Spain had become the most vital centre of economic progress' (ibid.: 84). This non-'congruence between political and economic powers [...] has traditionally nourished the centrifugal tendencies present in modern Spanish history' (Moreno 2002: 399). Moreno's account echoes the argument that economic development fuels a regional self-esteem that results in the refusal of a peripheral position in national politics. Conversely, Swenden (2006: 31) notes that Galician cultural distinctiveness was not politicized to the same extent because Galicia's economy was less developed. Galicia depended on fiscal transfers from the central state and on employment in state institutions such as the army or the bureaucracy. This dependence restricted the development of Galician nationalism.

Several interpretations of the resurgence of Catalan nationalism in the late nineteenth century also focus on the role of economic growth in reviving Catalan popular culture. Catalonia was the first Spanish region to industrialize, and it was far more developed economically than the central areas of the country. Both McRoberts (2001: 17) and Hargreaves (2000) argue that the economic resurgence around 1800 lay at the foundation of the revival (the so-called *Renaixença*) of Catalan culture from the 1830s. The growth of Catalan literature, art and music subsequently sparked the creation of Catalan as a written language. This led directly to the political nationalism of the 1880s (Hargreaves 2000: 24), with the indigenous language at the heart of Catalan identity (McRoberts 2001: 139).

Since democratization in the early 1970s, Spain's regions have demanded and received a gradually increasing level of autonomy from the central state. This process of devolution has been highly asymmetrical, with some regions gaining wide-ranging competencies and independent taxation rights, while others have only a limited degree of self-rule. Catalonia and the Basque Country have been at the forefront of the developments, pushing for more autonomy. Both regions also have sizeable separatist parties. The survival of regional languages and a history of political autonomy have been important drivers of these developments, combined with Franco-era repression of their respective national cultures and the opportunities provided by democratization. However, the economic development of the Basque Country and of Catalonia have clearly also been a factor. In 2005, they had the second and fourth highest GDPR per capita of the Spanish regions, respectively (Eurostat 2008).

There are several other parallels between Catalan and Basque nationalism on the one hand, and Scottish nationalism on the other. As with the SNP, mainstream Catalan and Basque nationalist parties are strongly in favour of European integration. The party systems in the two regions also differ from the national Spanish party system, with nationalist parties in each region claiming a substantial proportion of the vote, and the conservative PP faring poorly.

Italy

The Italian state has also been devolving powers to the regional level, in particular in the late 1990s and early 2000s. Whereas five Italian regions (four of them containing linguistic minorities and two being islands) have long had statutes of autonomy, similar arrangements have recently been extended (or at least offered) to the other regions as well. Regionalist parties have been successful in several of the 'special' regions, most notably the Südtiroler Volkspartei in Trentino-Alto Adige and the Union Valdôtaine in the Aosta Valley. As the party names suggest, regional languages (German and French, respectively) are an issue in both regions. They are also among the most prosperous Italian regions. However, in national politics the demands for devolution of power have been made most effectively by the Lega Nord, a regionalist party emerging in northern Italy in the 1990s and participating as a coalition partner in several centre-right governments.

Northern Italian regionalism differed markedly from that in the Spanish regions discussed in the previous sub-section when it comes to the matter of a common regional historical legacy or distinctive regional culture. The various northern regions united only in 1860, ten years before the formation of the Italian state in 1870. In the unification process, the north-western region Piedmont played the role as centre, conquering the other territories. The capital region, Lazio, was the last to fall. In that sense, the traditional centre–periphery relationship is reversed in the case of northern Italy and Rome. The North built the Italian state, conquering Rome and making it the capital.

Furthermore, while there are clearly cultural differences between the northern and southern parts of Italy, these do not take the form of a separate language or ethnicity, nor is there a uniform regional culture across the different regions of the North. Instead, the economic development issue was one of the main drivers behind the success of the Lega Nord. In Italy, there are large discrepancies in economic development between the rich northern parts of the country and the poorer South. All the regions north of Rome, with the exception of Umbria, have a GDPR per capita above the Italian average, while all regions south of Rome are below the average. In 2005, Campania, Apulia, Calabria and Sicily had a GDPR per capita of around 15,000 PPS (purchasing power standard), while Lombardy's exceeded 30,000 PPS (Eurostat 2008). Although many political and economic factors combined to pave the way for the party, the region's economic prosperity was definitely among the most crucial (Gold 2003).

The fiscal incentives argument is one part of the story. The Lega Nord sought to convey to the electorate that the southern parts of the country were freeloaders, living off subsidies from the richer North. The party accused the Italian government of financing pork-barrel projects that benefited only the South, famously coining the term '*Roma Ladrona*' (Thieving Rome) as an insult to the central government. Consequently, the people in the North would be better off if they were to gain more autonomy, or even secede from the Italian state (Bull and Gilbert 2001: 14). The party suggested the creation of an entirely new state, which it called Padania, encompassing all of northern Italy. While the population of northern Italy may not have supported such drastic measures as secession, the electoral success of the Lega Nord showed that the fiscal incentives discourse resonated with large sections of the regional population.

In addition to the fiscal incentives for decentralization, the Lega Nord also seemed to embody a sense of regional self-esteem based on its economic success. According to Torpey, the hard-core supporters of the party were of the opinion that 'northerners are good because they are wealthier and more valuable to society, while southerners are bad because they are economic losers' (1994: 314). Given this perspective on regional differences, it is not entirely surprising that the party should demand a more central position for northern Italy in national politics.

Belgium

The linguistic cleavage between French- and Dutch-speakers has been a source of conflict since the establishment of the Belgian state in 1830. Although the majority of the population spoke Dutch, French became the official language. The elites mostly spoke French, were inspired by the French Revolution and sought to distance Belgium from the past Dutch rulers. The Dutch-speakers were concentrated in Flanders, the mostly rural and traditional northern region of the country, while the French-speakers mainly lived in the industrialized southern region, Wallonia. A 'Flemish movement' soon emerged, seeking and gradually winning linguistic rights for the Dutch-speaking majority. Belgium remained a unitary state, but relied on consociational mechanisms to maintain stability (Lijphart 1977).

In the 1960s, an economically growing Flanders surpassed a declining Wallonia in terms of GDPR per capita. This allowed Flanders to 'use its economic strength as a vehicle for strengthening language rights' (Swenden 2006: 40), and fuelled demands for stronger autonomy. A Flemish separatist movement emerged, at least partly motivated by the desire to stop tax transfers to Wallonia (Bolton and Roland 1997: 1066). Hooghe (2004) argues that the reversal of fortunes fuelled linguistic conflict between Flanders and Wallonia, consolidating the territorialization of the linguistic conflict. However, the demands for autonomy were most pronounced in Flanders, while the Walloons remained more loyal to the Belgian state. Separatist parties also enjoyed more success in Flanders. Swenden (2006: 150) claims that 'the relatively weak socio-economic status of the Walloon region is an important factor' in explaining the stronger loyalty to the Belgian state in Wallonia. In 2006, the GDPR per capita of Flanders was €29,992, compared to €21,559 in Wallonia (Belgostat 2008).

The regionalist demands led to a gradual devolution of authority from the central state to regions and linguistic communities between 1970 and 1993, turning the formerly unitary state into a constitutionally enshrined federation through a process of four major constitutional reforms. Since 1993, Belgium has been a federal state with most political competencies held by the sub-national entities. The three regions Flanders, Wallonia and Brussels have responsibilities for a wide range of territorially organized policy areas, while the Dutch-, French- and German-speaking communities are responsible for policies directed at individuals. The federal level is mainly responsible for defence, justice, security and social security (Hooghe 2004).

In addition to cultural distinctiveness and economic development, European integration was an important factor in the development of regionalism in Belgium. It reduced the costs of secession and allowed the regions to assume a greater role in the international arena. For instance, they frequently represent Belgium in the Council, using a system of rotation among the regional govern-ments and codetermination on their political positions (Kerremans and Beyers 1997). However, the presence of the EU headquarters in Brussels has arguably also disciplined the regional actors into moderate and cooperative action (Hooghe 2004).

A final part of the story is the diverging political preferences between a relatively right-wing and conservative Flanders and the more social democratic Wallonia. Bolton and Roland (1997) put forward the example of Walloon nationalists threat-ening separatism in order to pursue more redistributionary policies than the Flemish electorate would allow them. The Belgian party system is a peculiar case in that it has no national parties. All the major parties split into separate Flemish and Walloon parties between 1967 and 1978, and they compete in elections within their respective communities. The regionalized nature of the Belgian party system has provided a political logic that has further increased regionalism in the country. Regionalist parties are also present in both regions, with the separatist Flemish Volksunie (now the Nieuw-Vlaamse Alliantie – New-Flemish Alliance) and the extreme right separatist Vlaams Blok (now Vlaams Belang) being the most success-ful in electoral terms in recent years. In the French community, the Front Démocra-tique des Francophones (Democratic Front of Francophones) has promoted the interests of French-speakers in Brussels with some success, while the separatist Rassemblement Wallon (Walloon Rally) has become increasingly marginal.

France

France is frequently forwarded as the prime example of successful state-led nation-building in Western Europe. French state traditions were based on a unitary structure with strong state control of the entire territory. The Jacobin tra-dition builds on the equality of all citizens within a single and indivisible repub-lic and refuses collective group rights that may challenge this ideal. The central elites pursued cultural homogeneity across the territory, promoting the French language and seeking to eliminate regional cultures. Despite these attempts, several minority languages remain important, sparking protests against cultural standardization. France has taken a top-down approach to territorial politics, with reforms initiated from the centre and a strong role for the state in regional government. Until 1982, the ninety-six *départements* were the main regional institutions, and they were supervised by powerful, centrally appointed prefects. However, a reform introduced twenty-two *régions* with directly elected councils. In terms of political power, the *départements* remain more powerful than the *régions* (Swenden 2006).

The French economy is highly centralized, with the capital region – Île-de-France – being by far the most economically developed in the country. It therefore does not have many prosperous peripheries. Rhône-Alpes, an artificially created region with no historical roots,[2] has the highest GDPR per capita apart from the capital region. The regional council of Rhône-Alpes has perhaps also been the most successful of the French regions in building powerful regional political institutions, claiming authority and resources for itself at the expense of the *départements* and the prefects. This has been attributed to 'its image of dynamism and growth' (Keating 1998: 135). It has also engaged in a process of constructing a regional identity top-down (Lecomte 1994), again tied to economic development and modernization. Its membership of the 'Four Motors for Europe' network is another part of this strategy. Rhône-Alpes thus appears to be the best example of a French prosperous periphery where region-building has occurred on the basis of economic success.

However, regionalism in France has not been associated mainly with economic prosperity. Corsica is among the poorest French regions, but it has still developed a fragmented regionalist movement consisting of a variety of secessionist as well as autonomist parties. Since 1975, various groups have engaged in a violent campaign for the independence of the island. However, there has been limited support for independence in the mass population. There has been more support for autonomy within the French state, but a proposal by the national government in 2003 to devolve powers to a regional assembly was rejected by Corsican voters by a majority of 51 per cent. Linguistic distinctiveness, immigration and an isolated geography seem to have been the main factors encouraging the development of regionalism, along with French decolonization in Africa (Olivesi 1998). The protection of the Corsican language has been a key motive for political groups advocating greater autonomy, with the declining number of Corsican-speakers seen as a major concern.

Brittany is another culturally distinctive region in France, with a regional language (mainly Breton, spoken by less than a tenth of the population, but politically significant), a Celtic cultural heritage and an ancient history as an independent duchy. Although regionalist parties have not been particularly notable in the region, the regional branches of national parties frequently cooperate across national cleavages in promoting regional interests. Survey data also show a high level of regional identity and public support for regional political institutions. In 2001, 12 per cent of respondents were in favour of an autonomous Brittany, while another 34 per cent of respondents favoured replacing the regional council with an elected parliament that would have tax-raising and legislative powers (Cole and Loughlin 2003). Brittany is close to the French median when it comes to economic development. Centre-right parties have traditionally done well, but the regional vote has swung towards the left in recent years, making the regional party system less distinctive. None of these factors explains the persistence of regionalism in Brittany. However, the regional public have been supportive of European integration, and this, along with the cultural distinctiveness of the region, may be the main factors involved in this case.

Germany

After the Second World War, the Allied occupiers imposed a federal structure on West Germany, with regions gaining substantial autonomy and an important position in national politics. The main motive was to prevent concentration of political power, and there were few demands from the regions themselves for devolution of power. Erk (2008: 57) argues that German federalism 'ran against the grain of its unitary ethno-linguistic structure', and, as a result, the regions tended to voluntarily harmonize their policies to achieve uniform national policies in various areas. The regional borders were also redrawn, and the resulting *Länder* did not necessarily correspond to any historical or cultural regions. The same could be said about the East German *Länder* joining the federation in 1990 from the highly centralized communist German Democratic Republic. The present regional borders within Germany therefore cross-cut the borders of the polities existing before the 1871 unification of Germany to a significant extent. The potential for regional cultural distinctiveness was further diluted by internal migration and immigration from abroad (Erk 2008). However, a religious cleavage dividing the more Protestant northern half from the more Catholic southern half of the country remains.

Except for the city states, Bavaria corresponds most closely to a historical entity. Apart from Saarland, it is also the most Catholic region of Germany, and it is among the most economically developed regions of the country. In 2006, only Hesse and the city-states of Hamburg and Bremen had higher GDPRs per capita than Bavaria's €33,240. The German GDP per capita was €28,194 (Statistische Ämter 2008). On the basis of the regionalism model, it is therefore not surprising that it has a strong tradition of regionalism. Bavaria has been the main proponent for more regional autonomy in the German federation, arguing for both fiscal autonomy and legislative powers. Swenden (2006: 147) attributes this to the region's socio-economic position, likening it to Flanders. Bavarian politics have been dominated by a regional party, the Christlich-Soziale Union in Bayern (CSU), which drew heavily on historical traditions to build a Bavarian identity (Keating 1998: 46). In the immediate post-war period, a separatist party, the Bayernpartei, also enjoyed some electoral success. To a lesser extent, a similar story applies to neighbouring Baden-Württemberg, which is also to some extent based on a historical region, predominantly Catholic, and economically developed. It had the fifth highest GDPR per capita of the German *Länder* in 2006, €31,441 (Statistische Ämter 2008). It has notably tried to promote its interests as a rich region through the 'Four Motors for Europe' initiative.

Since reunification, another potential territorial conflict has emerged between the former West and East German regions, where different recent historical experiences of the two parts of the country have created cultural, economic and political differences. Culturally, the East Germans were socialized into a secular and collectivist society, and they remain more committed to values such as equality and solidarity. Economically, the East German regions took a while to adjust to a different economic system, and they have remained substantially poorer than the Western regions. In terms of political consequences, the East Germans had no experience of liberal democratic institutions. The former Communist regime also had a lasting effect in terms of the Partei des Demokratischen Sozialismus (Party of Democratic Socialism – PDS; now renamed Die Linke – The Left), which has been fairly successful in the East, while winning little support in the West. It has entered regional governments in Berlin and Mecklenburg-West Pomerania in coalitions with the SPD. Although the PDS does not have a regionalist political platform, its support has been interpreted as an expression of a sense of East German regionalism (Oswald 2004).

German regions have been assertive in their response to European integration, in part as a result of the EU gaining competencies in areas that the *Bundesrat* or the regions themselves previously controlled. The regions have pursued a role in EU policymaking, both through the domestic political system and directly in Brussels. They have achieved Council representation through the *Bundesrat* when certain policy areas are discussed, and they have played an important role in constructing the Committee of the Regions. As such, they have been key players in the campaign to strengthen the regions at the expense of the nation-states within the EU.

Slovenia

Slovenia's secession from Yugoslavia in 1990–91, sparking the disintegration of the Yugoslav state, is another example of an economically developed region rebelling against the central state. The secession of Slovenia from Yugoslavia took place in the context of the socialist state breaking down. As was the case in other multinational socialist states, such as the Soviet Union and Czechoslovakia, this provided opportunities for institutional change. The central state leadership could no longer exert its authority over the Yugoslav public, allowing regional elites in Slovenia to take their place.

Unlike the other Yugoslav republics, Slovenia had an ethnically homogeneous population consisting of ethnic Slovenians, who spoke Slovene and were culturally distinct from the neighbouring Croatians and Serbians. Before the formation in 1918 of the Kingdom of Serbs, Croats and Slovenes (which would later become Yugoslavia), Slovenia had been part of the Habsburg Empire. Other parts of Yugoslavia had been ruled by the Ottoman Empire or been independent states. The historical legacy of Slovenia was therefore fairly distinct from that of other Yugoslav republics, further increasing its cultural distinctiveness within the broader state. There were also few institutions that could integrate the state, as the media and educational systems were organized separately within each republic.

While a culturally and historically distinctive republic would always be likely to secede given the opportunities provided by the fall of the socialist state, the Zveza Komunistov Slovenije (ZKS – League of Communists of Slovenia) remained loyal to the state in the initial phases of democratization. The alliance between Serbia and Slovenia had been one of the cornerstones of the Yugoslav state, and until early 1990, Slovenian political elites were in favour of maintaining the state (Cohen 1993). However, growing Serbian nationalism under the leadership of Slobodan Milošević sparked worries that Serbia, the biggest republic, might become too dominant, and the ZKS wanted to ensure its own autonomy by further loosening central control. This led the political leaders of Slovenia in the late 1980s to promote a system of asymmetrical federalism, with each republic negotiating its own association with the federation. Although other republics, in particular Serbia, refused to accept this proposal, the Slovenian leadership pressed ahead unilaterally, adopting a declaration of sovereignty in July 1990 and staging a plebiscite on secession in December. This won support from 88.5 per cent of voters, and, following another round of failed negotiations over its position within the Yugoslav federation, Slovenia declared independence in June 1991 (ibid.).

When disagreements with the Serbian elites arose, fiscal incentives were an important driver of conflict. Cohen (1993: 59) argues that 'many Slovenes felt that their economically productive republic [...] was contributing an unnecessarily high price for the operation of the federation'. Even though only 8 per cent of the population lived in Slovenia, the republic contributed more than 25 per cent of the federal budget of Yugoslavia. This was a source of frustration, which was exacerbated when economic difficulties hit the Balkans in the 1980s. A considerable majority of the population wanted to loosen the economic ties with the rest of the country, and in particular they did not want to subsidize the poorer regions in the south of Yugoslavia. In a 1988 survey, 59.5 per cent of respondents agreed that Slovenia had 'too great an economic association with the federation and the underdeveloped areas' (ibid.: 60).

In addition to these fiscal incentives for secession, economic development also contributed to a sense of regional self-esteem and an idea that Slovenia was entitled to an elevated political position. Displaying these sentiments, the Slovenian defence minister, Janez Janša, commented in 1991 that '[t]here is no known case in history where the less developed part of a state would have commanded the more developed part' (Cohen 1993: 119). Many Slovenians viewed the less developed southern parts of the federation as backward, and feared that they would prevent modernization and a closer association with Western Europe and the EU.

Revisiting the regionalism model

Economic prosperity has contributed to the development of regionalism in several Western European regions across various countries. As in the cases of Scotland and Rogaland, prosperity has created fiscal incentives for regionalism and occasioned regions to demand more political influence. This has occurred in culturally distinctive regions such as Catalonia, the Basque Country, Flanders and Bavaria, creating influential separatist movements in the former three regions. In Slovenia, relative economic development contributed to the actual separation of a prosperous periphery from the state of Yugoslavia. However, economic prosperity has also contributed to regionalism in regions without such cultural distinctiveness, including northern Italy, Rhône-Alpes and Baden-Württemberg. The impact of economic development therefore does not seem to depend on a distinctive regional culture. Both factors have an independent effect on the development of regionalism.

Petro-regions do not appear to behave in different ways from other prosperous peripheries when it comes to the effects of economic growth or any of the other variables of the regionalism model, although the peculiarities of petroleum-based development may in itself have an added impact on regionalism.

Implications for future research

This book has attempted to address some of the deficiencies identified in the existing literature on regionalism through employing a different research design than most previous work in this field. Analysing regionalism from a new perspective has the inherent benefit that it allows for new conclusions to be drawn and new lessons to be learned. However, there are also drawbacks to this strategy, not least in terms of data availability, which has affected the confidence with which conclusions can be drawn in this research. The outcome has therefore been of an exploratory rather than a conclusive nature, and the book's main contribution is perhaps the development of an approach that future studies in the field can build on to produce new and more secure insights into how regionalism works.

The analysis has combined quantitative and qualitative research methods, building its conclusions to a large extent on survey data and quantitative content analysis. These data sources have been somewhat neglected in the study of regionalism, and some authors have even rejected the validity of survey data in this field. This book has presented a method for using survey data reliably and validly, and it has hence been able to draw on a rich source of cross-sectional data from across Western Europe. I hope that the analysis can inform other researchers of how these sources might be used, so that future studies in the field can have at least the option of using similar data. Since the early 1990s, researchers have had the benefit of regular surveys being conducted on issues related to regionalism, and this might help to solve the problems of data availability in the foreseeable future. These developments should make surveys an even more attractive source of data for researchers, whether they are conducting cross-sectional or longitudinal studies.

In the absence of historical survey data, the book presented quantitative content analysis as an option for constructing a corpus of data that could be used to analyse past levels of regionalism. While it would be costly and time-consuming to use this method to create a complete time series over a number of years, it was nevertheless useful to be able to draw on quantitative data for a few selected years in the analysis of the case studies in this research. The approach could be used in a similar way to construct a corpus of data on other regions where data availability is an issue, in order to avoid undue bias in the assessment of levels of regionalism in the past. Although data of this type neither present a complete picture of the past nor allow for sophisticated quantitative analysis, they could still be both instructive and helpful when used in combination with other sources of data to build an overview of how regionalism has changed over time.

The combination of cross-sectional and longitudinal elements in the analysis represents another departure from most of the existing literature in the field. Through combining the two approaches, this book has been able to examine which variables have an effect on regionalism across both time and space. This has allowed for the construction and testing of the regionalism model through different research designs, thus providing two different perspectives on regionalism within one book. While this dual approach has sometimes risked complicating the conclusions, it has also allowed for the study of independent variables that vary across time as well as those that vary across space, keeping in mind that these are not necessarily the same.

The cross-sectional study showed that there is a significant amount of variation in levels of regionalism across the continent. This suggests that it is necessary for researchers to consider the processes taking place within the regions themselves when attempting to explain regionalism. So far, much research on regions has focused on the national, European or global levels, which has made it poorly equipped to explain differences between regions within the same country. This study has focused on how external processes have affected individual regions, allowing for variation across regions in the impact of processes such as globalization and European integration. It has also highlighted the inherently regional process of economic development as a highly significant predictor of regionalism across both time and space. It is necessary to look at the processes on the regional level itself in order to explain the developments there, which is a lesson that should be remembered for future research and theory-building in this area.

Appendix

Regionalism index scores

Table A.1 Average regionalism index scores

Basque Country	45.4	Tyrol	21.7	Upper Austria	15.7
West Flanders	35.8	Derbysh./Notts.	21.6	Molise/Abruzzo	15.6
Highlands & Islands	34.2	Galicia	21.5	North Holland	15.5
Catalonia	34.1	Vorarlberg	21.3	Centre, FR	15.5
Mecklenburg W. P.	34.1	Dorset/Somerset	21.0	Navarre	15.4
East Flanders	34.1	N Rhine-Westph.	20.9	Hainaut	15.3
Canary Islands	33.6	Groningen	20.5	Cheshire	15.2
Berlin	31.4	Aquitaine	20.5	Drente	15.1
Azores	31.2	Poitou-Charentes	20.4	Salzburg	14.9
Saarland	30.9	Northumberland	20.3	La Rioja	14.8
Saxony	30.8	Cumbria	20.0	Liguria	14.7
Bavaria	30.3	Alsace	20.0	Emilia-Romagna	14.6
Saxony-Anhalt	29.6	Rhineland Palat.	19.9	Marche	14.3
Thuringia	28.6	Walloon Brabant	19.7	Centr. Ostrobothnia	14.3
Schleswig-Holstein	28.6	Hesse	19.2	Valencia	14.3
Balearic Islands	27.8	NE Scotland	18.9	Midi-Pyrénées	14.3
Bremen	27.7	Overijssel	18.9	Flevoland	14.3
Brandenburg	27.6	Sardinia	18.7	Hampshire	14.0
Hamburg	27.4	Friesland	18.7	Nord-Pas de Calais	13.9
Limburg, NL	26.6	Tuscany	18.6	Andalusia	13.8
Antwerp	26.5	Cleveland/Durham	18.5	Loire Country	13.6
SW Scotland	26.5	West Yorkshire	18.3	Friuli-Ven. Giulia	13.5
Trentino A. Adige	26.3	Burgundy	18.2	Kainuu	13.4
East Scotland	26.2	Sicily	17.8	London	13.2
Zeeland	26.2	Brussels	17.5	Rhône-Alpes	13.2
Limburg, BL	25.5	Gelderland	17.2	Vienna	13.0
Lincolnshire	25.0	Madeira	17.0	Franche-Comté	12.7
Namur	24.7	Upper Normandy	17.0	Île de France	12.5
West Wales	24.6	Lancashire	16.9	Bedfordshire/Herts.	12.5
Lower Saxony	24.4	Veneto	16.3	Cornwall/Devon	12.3
Brittany	24.0	Piedmont and Aosta	16.2	Ostrobothnia	12.2
Flemish Brabant	23.7	Limousin	16.2	Styria	12.2
Luxembourg, BL	23.2	Languedoc	16.1	Leicestershire	12.1
Merseyside	22.9	Provence-Alpes	16.1	Umbria	12.0
East Wales	22.8	Auvergne	16.0	Carinthia	11.9
Liège	22.0	North Yorkshire	15.9	South Holland	11.8
Baden-Württemb.	21.9	North Brabant	15.8	South Yorksh.	11.7

Central Macedonia	11.6	West Midlands	9.2	Kymenlaakso	6.6
Lombardy	11.6	Lorraine	9.0	Pirkanmaa	6.5
Kent	11.6	Aragón	8.9	Paijat-Häme	6.5
East Anglia	11.6	Picardy	8.7	Essex	6.4
Eastern Macedonia	11.5	Central Finland	8.6	Estremadura	6.4
Alentejo	11.3	Herefordshire	8.5	Lapland	6.3
Campania	11.3	Champagne	8.4	Norte, POR	6.2
Apulia	11.1	Basilicata	8.3	South Savonia	6.1
Greater Manchester	10.9	Centro, POR	8.2	Peloponnese	5.8
Shropshire	10.7	Sussex/Surrey	8.2	Murcia	5.7
Berkshire/Bucks.	10.5	Humberside	8.1	Cantabria	5.5
Lazio	10.5	South Karelia	8.0	Satakunta	4.9
Utrecht	10.4	Thessaly	7.6	Castile and León	4.9
Lower Normandy	10.1	Calabria	7.5	Castile-La Mancha	4.1
Algarve	9.9	Crete	7.4	Attika/Centr. Greece	4.1
North Ostrobothnia	9.9	Asturias	7.1	Madrid	4.0
Lisbon	9.9	South Ostrobothnia	7.1	Tavastia	3.7
North Karelia	9.7	Burgenland	6.9	Epirus	3.4
Avon/Gloucestersh.	9.6	Thrace	6.9	North Savonia	3.3
Lower Austria	9.5	Finland Proper	6.8		
Uusimaa	9.4	Aegean Islands	6.6		

Note
Average scores across the four surveys (weighted), for regions with three or more scores.

Notes

1 Regions and regionalism

1 Eurobarometer 36.0: Regional Identity and Perceptions of the Third World.
2 In some of these cases, the agreement on the definition of a region is probably due to the fact that the sub-national administrative units are called 'regions' in the country in question.
3 NUTS is the *Nomenclature des Unités Territoriales Statistiques*, a uniform classification system introduced by the European Commission to make it easier to compare sub-state authorities across European countries. The NUTS system classifies regions as belonging to the NUTS 1, 2 or 3 levels according to their size, with NUTS 1 being the largest regions.
4 There is obviously also a connection between levels of regionalism and the extent to which people agree on what region they live in. To some extent, people who do not know what a region is can be taken as evidence of its absence, as the region apparently does not exist to them.
5 This also means that the region is not a fixed entity. Its area has to be defined by the regionalist movement, and can be based around historical, geographical or administrative entities (Smouts 1998).

2 Causes of regionalism

1 For an alternative view, see Kuran (1998).
2 Regional parties can be distinguished between those who accept the legitimacy of the larger nation-state, and those who 'deny the national character of the entire state territory' (Lancaster and Lewis-Beck 1989: 33). In the case of the latter group, the link to regionalism or regional nationalism is explicit. However, those in the former group also rely on a certain level of identification with the region and a sense of a common regional political purpose.

3 Regionalism in Western Europe

1 In some cases, the survey data used group regions together in pairs, such as 'Piedmont and Aosta Valley' or 'Cornwall and Devon', and so these are also treated as one region in this analysis for the purposes of obtaining sufficient usable data while avoiding double-counting. In other cases, regions are subdivided into smaller entities. In the United Kingdom, county data were used because these correspond best to regional authorities in England. For the purposes of continuity across the United Kingdom, Wales and Scotland are similarly divided into counties/regions. In Belgium, the analysis used data for the provinces rather than the regions. This allowed for the use of more detailed data on the geographical distribution on the dependent and independent

variables within Flanders and Wallonia. Respondents are still asked to state their attachment to the region as they themselves define it, regardless of how the data are grouped.

2 Although the set that is used here does not include Northern Ireland, Corsica and the French overseas departments, for which no data were available.

3 Examining the indices with reference to state-wide figures allows the estimates to be based on a large number of respondents – around 1,000 for each state – thus making them substantially more accurate than if regional figures were used as the basis for comparison.

4 This would be equivalent to answering either 'Catalan, not Spanish' or 'more Catalan than Spanish' on the Moreno question example above. Although the results for individual regions cannot be easily compared to responses to the actual Moreno question, they should not be distorted in any systematic way across regions and will therefore retain the validity of the original question.

5 Cronbach's alpha is a function of the number of test items and the average inter-correlation among them. It can be regarded as an expression of how similar the four distributions are to each other. An alpha score of 1 would mean that all four distributions are perfectly correlated.

6 It is worth noting that the definition of the relevant *demos* often depends on the policy area under discussion. However, levels of regional identity will affect opinions on which policy areas the regional demos should govern.

7 Construct validity tests are used to examine the validity of formative measurement models. The validity of the indicator is tested by examining its correlation with a variable that is known to be closely correlated with the theoretical variable at stake.

8 Hooghe *et al.* (2008) have more recently provided an updated 'regional authority index'. Here, they divide the regional self-rule section into four dimensions. The resulting index has a 15-point scale for measuring regional self-rule and is applied to individual regions. The Pearson's R statistic for the correlation between the regional authority index and the regionalism index is 0.45, which is also significant at the 99 per cent level.

9 As regionalism is hypothesized to influence regional institutions in the model, it seems reasonable to measure institutions at a later time-point than when most of the regionalism indices are measured. The equivalent Pearson's R coefficients for the institutions index measured in 1990 and 1995 are 0.60 and 0.59, respectively, and both of these correlations are also significant at the 99 per cent level.

10 The sources for these data are Eurobarometer (1998), European Opinion Research Group (2003, 2004) and Reif and Melich (1998).

4 Why some regions are more regionalist than others

1 The data on regional languages are mainly based on Mackenzie (1994). See Fitjar (2007: 92) for further details on the procedure.

2 This indicator distinguishes between languages that are embodied in a neighbouring state (for instance Swedish in Finland) and exclusively minority languages (for instance Catalan in Spain). This reflects a need for institutional protection to ensure the very survival of these languages, whereas languages that already enjoy such protection by other states are comparatively less dependent on such protection for their survival.

3 These indicators are based on Parker (1993).

4 Although the establishment of Great Britain in 1707 may be considered the formation of a new state, this classification considers the British state an expansion of the already existing Kingdom of England, of which Scotland did not form part at its formation.

5 The data are not available at the regional level for France, the United Kingdom,

Norway and Finland. For all regions in these countries, the scores on the index are set as equal to the national average for the relevant country.

6 Another possibility would obviously be looking at survey questions where people rate their attachment to the EU. However, these questions face the same methodological problems as did Marks's (1999) index in Chapter 3 in that the quantification of attachment is subjective and determined by cultural norms that vary across different regions.

7 See Fitjar (2007: 84ff.) for an outline of the policy areas covered and the technical procedures for transforming the responses into a standardized measure of Europeanization that covers three Eurobarometer surveys (1991, 2000 and 2002). As Eurobarometer produced data on the Swedish regions only in the 1995 study, the Europeanization measures for Sweden will be taken as being equal to the series mean for the average of the other three studies. In this way, they will not affect the parameter estimates in the regression analysis.

8 The index measures the extent to which the election results in a particular region are different from the results in the country as a whole through summing the absolute differences between the state and regional level for the vote shares of each individual party. The data are based on the parliamentary election that falls closest to 1995 in each country. Because of the strong connection between votes cast in elections for regional and national parliaments in most Western European regions, only data on national elections are used. See Fitjar (2007: 87f.) for a complete outline of the technicalities of this operationalization.

9 See Fitjar (2007: 90f.) for further details.

10 See Chapter 3 for a discussion of the merits of this argument.

11 For details on the regression analysis design and related diagnostics, see Fitjar (2007). Owing to the small sample size of 212 units, a confidence level of 90 per cent is taken as the benchmark.

5 Territorial mobilization in Scotland and Rogaland

1 The mobilization of the regional level in Scotland is regarded as a nationalist movement by most researchers, as well as by the Scottish public. Therefore, the term 'Scottish nationalism' will be used throughout this book to refer to regionalism in Scotland. The term 'regionalism' will still be used when referring to regionalism as a general phenomenon. The discussion will assume that the same theoretical framework can be used to explain both regionalism and Scottish nationalism, given that both movements are expressions of the politicization of a sub-state identity and share the aim of increasing regional autonomy.

2 All GDPR data in this section are drawn from the Office for National Statistics (ONS 1996 and the ONS website). It is worth noting that Scotland's GDPR excludes the production on the continental shelf, and hence any direct revenues from petroleum production are not credited to Scotland's GDPR. The same is true in the case of Rogaland, thus underestimating the extent of the economic boom in both regions post-1970. Offshore production has risen sharply across the period in both countries. In the case of Norway, the 'unallocated' share of GDP made up 24.7 per cent in 2000, against 14.2 per cent in 1965 (Statistisk Sentralbyrå 1970, 2003). Most of this can be attributed to offshore petroleum production in the North Sea, which is controlled from Stavanger, takes place off the west coast and uses a large amount of labour from Rogaland. Hjellum (2000) picks up this point when he questions the rationale behind leaving out the offshore production. Even though the continental shelf is regarded as national territory, the resources as well as the labour are mainly Western Norwegian, according to him. The Scottish government has worked on producing GDPR figures that include offshore production, but the methodology is still experimental and the figures are therefore uncertain (Stewart 2008).

3 From 1983 to 1991, the comparison between Scottish and British opinions refers to respondents agreeing that Britain should withdraw from the EEC (a choice of two response options). From 1993 onwards, it refers to respondents agreeing that Britain's long-term policy should be to leave the EU (a choice of five response options).

4 The petrolization processes have obviously had a greater impact on the city of Stavanger than on the rest of the region. However, the region as a whole has certainly also been affected by the developments. Approximately 75 per cent of the population of Rogaland live within one hour's travel from Stavanger, and another 20 per cent live near Haugesund, where there has also been a considerable growth in petroleum-related employment. According to Smith-Solbakken (1997), most of the offshore workers were recruited from rural areas in Rogaland, mainly from fishing and farming communities.

5 It is worth noting that the *Sun* became a strong competitor for the *Daily Record* only after heavily increasing the focus on Scotland in its Scottish edition (Hutchison 2002).

6 Although the *Daily Record* is more popular in and around Glasgow, it aims to be a national Scottish newspaper and does not focus on any particular sub-region.

7 All translations are those of the author.

8 For Finnmark, the high levels of regional attachment can possibly be explained in terms of the county's geographical position in the extreme periphery, with large distances to the centre of the Norwegian state. Vestfold is the smallest Norwegian county in terms of area (aside from Oslo), with an area of only 2,200 km^2, and it could therefore be affected by the high levels of local attachment in Norway.

9 Fitjar (2005) provides a more extensive outline of the study as well as the methodology on which it is based.

6 Scotland: from unionism to nationalism

1 In the literature, there is also a fair amount of confusion as to the direction of causality in many accounts of this relationship. For instance, Nairn manages to label the opposition to the Conservatives as both cause and consequence of nationalism within the space of a few sentences, where he first quotes the poll tax as the crucial cause of devolution, before acknowledging the 'national element in the aversion to Thatcherism' (2000: 220).

2 This graph uses the same data as Figures 5.1 and 5.7.

3 The data compared Scotland to sovereign states, rather than to sub-state regions.

7 Rogaland: petrolization and region-building

1 The language dispute has historically been one of the most important sources of conflict between centre and periphery in Norway. During the nation-building era of the nineteenth century, the Norwegian elites recognized the need for a national language to replace Danish, which remained the written language in the country even though Norway was transferred from Danish to Swedish rule in 1814. *Riksmål* evolved as the Danish language was modified to resemble the spoken tongue among the educated central elite. This later evolved into *bokmål*, which is used by 88 per cent of the population today (Grendstad and Rommetvedt 1997: 195). However, opposition to the supposedly foreign central culture from the peripheral West took on a linguistic hue, and *landsmål* was created as a competing form of written Norwegian. This language form was based on the spoken tongue in remote Norwegian villages where foreign influence had been minimal, as it sought to capture the 'natural' evolution of the Old Norse language spoken by the Vikings (Rokkan 1967: 373ff.). This later became *nynorsk*, which is used by 12 per cent of the population, mainly in rural parts of Western Norway (Grendstad and Rommetvedt 1997: 195).

2 Although neither Melberg (1997) nor Grendstad and Rommetvedt (1997) present any data for the entire region, it is reasonable to believe that the same trends are present,

albeit to a lesser extent, in rural parts of Rogaland as well. The economic and social transformation relating to the oil industry has affected the entire region, distances are small, and a large part of the population lives in or around Stavanger. The only major counter-culture that affected rural parts of Rogaland without having much influence in Stavanger was the *nynorsk* movement, but it is now declining across the region. In 2001, only 16.9 per cent of the population lived in a municipality that used *nynorsk* in the administration (however, this included twelve out of the twenty-six municipalities), and 28.3 per cent of pupils in primary and lower secondary schools used *nynorsk* (Statistisk Sentralbyrå 2002: 175, 461).

3 The FrP is categorized as a right-wing party in this context as this is how the party sees itself and also how most voters perceive the party. Ideologically, the FrP is difficult to place on a left–right scale, as the party wants both to cut taxes and to increase public expenditure.

4 Although two ministers from Rogaland – Magnhild Meltveit Kleppa of Sp and Tora Aasland of SV – were appointed to join the government by Ap's coalition partners during a reshuffle in 2007.

5 The heritage of several of these movements can be traced back to the preacher Hans Nielsen Hauge, who opposed the monopoly of priests to preach the Gospel. Again, this movement represented an expression of direct opposition to the powers of the central elites. Hauge was from Eastern Norway, but he gained a large support base in Rogaland.

6 For instance, the regional Ap branch was vocal in its demands for regionalization of power, even though the party is among the most centralist at the national level. Rogaland Høyre played a lead role in the integration of Western Norway, with one of the most prominent regionalists, the county mayor Roald Bergsaker, heading the Council of Western Norway (however, several local Høyre mayors, including Stavanger's Leif Johan Sevland, were sceptical of the plans). At the national level, Høyre wants to scrap the meso level altogether. Finally, the regional KrF branch wanted the party to make regionalization a key issue in the 2005 campaign, even though the national party did not even have an official opinion on the matter at the time.

8 Petro-regions and other prosperous peripheries

1 The myth has it that whereas one used to say 'eg e fra Stavanger, gjørr det någe?' before the discovery of petroleum, one would now say 'eg e fra Stavanger, va det någe?' The sayings roughly translate into English as 'I'm sorry, I'm from Stavanger' and 'I'm from Stavanger, just so you know', respectively.

2 However, Savoy, the eastern part of the region, is a historic region with an active regionalist movement of its own.

References

Aardal, B. (2003) 'Kritiske velgere', in B. Aardal (ed.) *Velgere i villrede...: En analyse av stortingsvalget 2001*. Oslo: N.W. Damm.

Alesina, A. and Spolaore, E. (1997) 'On the Number and Size of Nations', *Quarterly Journal of Economics*, 112 (4): 1027–56.

Alesina, A., Spolaore, E. and Wacziarg, R. (2000) 'Economic Integration and Political Disintegration', *American Economic Review*, 90 (5): 1276–96.

Almond, G. and Powell, B. (1966) *Comparative Politics: A developmental approach*. Boston: Little, Brown.

Amdam, J. (2008) 'Region Building and Economic Change in Western Norway', in O. Bukve, H. Halkier and P. de Souza (eds) *Towards New Nordic Regions: Politics, administration and regional development*. Aalborg: Aalborg University Press.

Anderson, B. (1991) *Imagined Communities: Reflections on the origin and spread of nationalism*, 2nd edn. London: Verso.

Ashford, D.E. (1982) *British Dogmatism and French Pragmatism: Central–local policymaking in the welfare state*. London: George Allen & Unwin.

Audit Bureau of Circulation (2006) 'Average Net Circulation (Scotland)'. Online, available at: www.abc.org.uk/cgi-bin/gen5?runprog=nav/abc&noc=y (accessed 13 July 2006).

Baldersheim, H. (2003) 'Det regionpolitiske regimet i omforming – retrett frå periferien; landsdelen i sikte!', *Norsk Statsvitenskapelig Tidsskrift*, 19 (3): 276–307.

Baldersheim, H. and Fimreite, A.L. (2005) 'Norwegian Centre–Periphery Relations in Flux: Abolition or reconstruction of regional governance?', *West European Politics*, 28 (4): 764–80.

Bauer, M.W. (2000) 'Classical Content Analysis: A review', in M.W. Bauer and G. Gaskell (eds) *Qualitative Researching with Text, Image and Sound*. London: Sage.

BBC (27 January 2004) 'Scots MPs Attacked over Fees Vote'. Online, available at: http://news.bbc.co.uk/1/hi/scotland/3432767.stm (accessed 16 January 2009).

—— (7 September 2005) 'Born Abroad: An immigration map of Britain'. Online, available at: http://news.bbc.co.uk/1/shared/spl/hi/uk/05/born_abroad/html/overview.stm (accessed 16 January 2009).

—— (7 June 2006) 'Mayor Provokes Anti-Scottish Row'. Online, available at: http://news.bbc.co.uk/1/hi/england/london/5056798.stm (accessed 16 January 2009).

Belgostat (2008) 'Gross Domestic Product per Resident (at Current Prices) – Absolute figures'. Online, available at: www.nbb.be/belgostat/PublicatieSelectieLinker?LinkID=946000099|910000082&Lang=E (accessed 17 December 2008).

Berg, L. (2007) 'Multi-level Europeans: The influence of territorial attachments on political trust and welfare attitudes', PhD thesis, Göteborg University.

Billig, M. (1995) *Banal Nationalism*. London: Sage.

Bolton, P. and Roland, G. (1997) 'The Breakup of Nations: A political economy analysis', *Quarterly Journal of Economics*, 112 (4): 1057–90.

Bond, R., McCrone, D. and Brown, A. (2003) 'National Identity and Economic Development: Reiteration, recapture, reinterpretation and repudiation', *Nations and Nationalism*, 9 (3): 371–91.

Bookman, M.Z. (1993) *The Economics of Secession*. Basingstoke, UK: Macmillan.

Brancati, D. (2006) 'Decentralization: Fueling the fire or dampening the flames of ethnic conflict and secessionism?', *International Organization*, 60 (3): 651–85.

—— (2008) 'The Origins and Strength of Regional Parties', *British Journal of Political Science*, 38 (1): 135–59.

Brenner, N. (1999a) 'Globalisation as Reterritorialisation: The re-scaling of urban governance in the European Union', *Urban Studies*, 36 (3): 431–51.

—— (1999b) 'Beyond State-Centrism? Space, territoriality, and geographical scale in globalization studies', *Theory and Society*, 28 (1): 39–78.

—— (2002) 'Decoding the Newest "Metropolitan Regionalism" in the USA: A critical overview', *Cities*, 19 (1): 3–21.

Brown, A., McCrone, D. and Paterson, L. (1998) *Politics and Society in Scotland*, 2nd edn. Basingstoke, UK: Macmillan.

Brown, A., McCrone, D., Paterson, L. and Surridge P. (1999) *The Scottish Electorate: The 1997 general election and beyond*. Basingstoke, UK: Macmillan.

Bruter, M. (2001) 'Understanding Identity Realignment: The emergence of a mass European identity', PhD thesis, University of Houston, Texas.

—— (2004) 'On What Citizens Mean by Feeling "European": Perceptions of news, symbols and borderless-ness', *Journal of Ethnic and Migration Studies*, 30 (1): 21–39.

—— (2005) *Citizens of Europe? The emergence of a mass European identity*. Basingstoke, UK: Palgrave Macmillan.

Bukve, O. (2008) 'Nordic Regionalisation in a Comparative Perspective', in O. Bukve, H. Halkier and P. de Souza (eds) *Towards New Nordic Regions: Politics, administration and regional development*. Aalborg: Aalborg University Press.

Bull, A.C. and Gilbert, M. (2001) *The Lega Nord and the Northern Question in Italian Politics*. Basingstoke, UK: Palgrave Macmillan.

Bullmann, U. (1997) 'The Politics of the Third Level', in C. Jeffery (ed.) *The Regional Dimension of the European Union: Towards a third level in Europe?* London: Frank Cass.

Caramani, D. (1999) *Elections in Western Europe since 1815: Electoral results by constituencies* [CD-ROM]. London: Macmillan.

—— (2002) *The Measurement of Territorial Homogeneity: A test on comparative electoral data since 1832*. EUI Working Paper RSC No. 2002/26. San Domenico: European University Institute.

Castells, M. (1997) *The Power of Identity*. Oxford: Blackwell.

Cohen, L.J. (1993) *Broken Bonds: The disintegration of Yugoslavia*. Boulder, CO: Westview Press.

Cole, A. and Loughlin, J. (2003) 'Beyond the Unitary State? Public opinion, political institutions and public policy in Brittany', *Regional Studies*, 37 (3): 265–76.

Craig, C. (1999) *The Modern Scottish Novel: Narrative and the national imagination*. Edinburgh: Edinburgh University Press.

Curtice, J. (1992) 'The North–South Divide', in R. Jowell, L. Brook, G. Prior and B. Taylor (eds) *British Social Attitudes Survey: The 9th Report*. Aldershot, UK: Gower.

Dag og Tid (6 March 2008) 'Vestlandet er farleg'.

—— (4 July 2008) 'Omkamp i Hafrsfjord'.

Dagbladet (10 March 2000) 'I "Mongoland" går alle ting an'.

Danson, M., Lloyd, G. and Newlands, D. (1989) ' "Scottish Enterprise": The creation of a more effective development agency or the pursuit of ideology?', *Quarterly Economic Commentary*, 14 (3): 70–5.

Dardanelli, P. (2002) 'The Connection between European Integration and Demand for Regional Self-Government: A rational-institutionalist, comparative analysis of Scotland, 1979 and 1997', PhD thesis, University of London.

—— (2005a) *Between Two Unions: Europeanisation and Scottish devolution.* Manchester: Manchester University Press.

—— (2005b) 'Democratic Deficit or the Europeanisation of Secession? Explaining the devolution referendums in Scotland', *Political Studies*, 53 (2): 320–42.

de la Granja, J.L. (1995) *El nacionalismo vasco: Un siglo de historia.* Madrid: Tecnos.

De Winter, L. and Frognier, A.-P. (1999) 'Les identités ethno-territoriales: Exploration dans un champ de mines politique et méthodologique', in A.-P. Frognier and A.-M. Aish (eds) *Des élections en trompe-l'œil: Enquête sur le comportement électoral des Wallons et des Francophones.* Brussels: De Boeck Université.

Deutsch, K. (1966) *Nationalism and Social Communication: An inquiry into the foundations of nationality*, 2nd edn. Cambridge, MA: MIT Press.

Dion, S. (1996) 'Why Is Secession Difficult in Well-Established Democracies? Lessons from Quebec', *British Journal of Political Science*, 26 (2): 269–83.

Driffield, N. and Hughes, D. (2003) 'Foreign and Domestic Investment: Regional development or crowding out?', *Regional Studies*, 37 (3): 277–88.

Dybendal, K. (2006) 'Innvandrerbefolkningen, etter kjønn, alder og vestlig/ikke-vestlig landbakgrunn (F) (1970–2006)' in *Innvandrerbefolkningen.* Statistisk Sentralbyrå. Online, available at: http://statbank.ssb.no/statistikkbanken/Default_FR.asp?PXSid=0&nvl=true&PLanguage=0&tilside=selecttable/hovedtabellHjem.asp&KortnavnWeb=innvbef (accessed 16 January 2009).

Economist, The (8 July 2006) 'A question that can no longer be avoided'.

Economist Intelligence Unit (2002) *Norway: Country Profile 2002.* London: Economist Intelligence Unit.

Erk, J. (2008) *Explaining Federalism: State, society and congruence in Austria, Belgium, Canada, Germany and Switzerland.* London: Routledge.

Etzioni-Halevy, E. (1993) *The Elite Connection: Problems and potential of Western democracy.* Cambridge: Polity Press.

Eurobarometer (1998) *Eurobarometer 43.1: Regional development and consumer and environmental issues, May–June, 1995* [computer file], 2nd edn. Colchester: The Data Archive [distributor], 11 May 1998.

European Commission (2000) *The Structural Funds in 1999: Eleventh annual report.* Luxembourg: Office for Official Publications of the European Communities.

European Opinion Research Group (2003) *Eurobarometer 54.1: Building Europe and the European Union, the European Parliament, public safety, and defence policy, November–December 2000* [computer file]. Luxembourg: Office for Official Publications of the European Communities.

—— (2004) *Eurobarometer 58.1: European enlargement and financial services, October–November 2002* [computer file]. Luxembourg: Office for Official Publications of the European Communities.

Eurostat (2004) *New Cronos* [data CD]. Luxembourg: Eurostat.

—— (2008) 'Regional Gross Domestic Product (PPS per inhabitant)'. Online, available

at: http://epp.eurostat.ec.europa.eu/tgm/table.do?tab=table&init=1&plugin=0&languag
e=en&pcode=tgs00005 (accessed 16 January 2009).

Farsund, A.A., Hidle, K. and Lysgård, H.K. (2008) 'The Development of City-Regions in
Norway: The importance of everyday regional interaction and economic development
policy', in O. Bukve, H. Halkier and P. de Souza (eds) *Towards New Nordic Regions:
Politics, administration and regional development*. Aalborg: Aalborg University Press.

Fichte, J.G. (1845) *Samtliche Werke*. Berlin: Veit Franklin.

Fitjar, R.D. (2005) 'Measuring Regionalism: Content analysis and the case of Rogaland
in Norway', *Regional and Federal Studies*, 15 (1): 59–73.

—— (2007) 'Prosperous Peripheries: Cross-sectional and longitudinal explorations of the
determinants of regionalism in Western Europe', PhD thesis, London School of Economics and Political Science.

Fossåskaret, E. (1987) 'Nye tema i nye fora: Kulturskifte 1860–1940', in E. Hovland and
H.E. Næss (eds) *Fra Vistehola til Ekofisk: Rogaland gjennom tidene*, vol. 2. Oslo: Universitetsforlaget.

Fox, J. (1999) 'The Influence of Religious Legitimacy on Grievance Formation by Ethno-
religious Minorities', *Journal of Peace Research*, 36 (3): 289–307.

—— (2001) 'Clash of Civilizations or Clash of Religions: Which is a more important
determinant of ethnic conflict?', *Ethnicities*, 1 (3): 295–320.

Frank, A.G. (1967) *Capitalism and Underdevelopment in Latin America: Historical
studies of Chile and Brazil*. New York: Monthly Review.

Friedman, T.L. (2000) *The Lexus and the Olive Tree*, 2nd edn. New York: Anchor Books.

Furre, B. (1987) 'Rogaland – noko for seg?', in E. Fossåskaret and B. Furre (eds) *Roga-
landskulturen mellom religion og politikk: Ei tverrfagleg vandring gjennom 120 år*.
Stavanger: Høgskolesenteret i Rogaland.

—— (1992) *Norsk historie 1905–1990: Vårt hundreår*. Oslo: Det Norske Samlaget.

Futsæter, K.-A. (2005) 'Avislesing 2004/2005: Rapportering fra 05/2 Forbruker &
Media'. Online, available at: www.mediebedriftene.no/novus/upload/file/statistikk/
Avisbarometeret%202004-05.pdf (accessed 16 January 2009).

Garrett, G. (2001) 'Globalization and Government Spending around the World', *Studies
in Comparative International Development*, 35 (4): 3–29.

Geertz, C. (1963) *Old Societies and New States: The quest for modernity in Asia and
Africa*. New York: Collier-Macmillan.

Gellner, E. (1983) *Nations and Nationalism*. Oxford: Blackwell.

Gold, T.W. (2003) *The Lega Nord and Contemporary Politics in Italy*. Basingstoke, UK:
Palgrave Macmillan.

Gordin, J.P. (2001) 'The Electoral Fate of Ethnoregionalist Parties in Western Europe: A
Boolean test of extant explanations', *Scandinavian Political Studies*, 24 (2): 149–70.

Gourevitch, P.A. (1979) 'The Reemergence of "Peripheral Nationalisms": Some comparative speculations on the spatial distribution of political leadership and economic
growth', *Comparative Studies in Society and History*, 21 (3): 303–22.

Grendstad, G. and Rommetvedt, H. (1997) 'Oljehovedstadens politiske kulturlandskap.
En sammenligning av holdninger og verdier i Stavanger-området og Norge', in H.
Rommetvedt (ed.) *Verdier og valg: Oljehovedstadens politiske kulturlandskap*. Oslo:
Norges forskningsråd.

Grindheim, J.E. (2004) 'Norway', in S. Dosenrode and H. Halkier (eds) *The Nordic
Regions and the European Union*. Aldershot, UK: Ashgate.

Gurr, T.R. (1993) 'Why Minorities Rebel: A global analysis of communal mobilization
and conflict since 1945', *International Political Science Review*, 14 (2): 161–201.

Hargreaves, J. (2000) *Freedom for Catalonia? Catalan nationalism, Spanish identity and the Barcelona Olympic Games*. Cambridge: Cambridge University Press.

Harvie, C. (1994) *The Rise of Regional Europe*. London: Routledge.

—— (2001) 'Scotland after 1978: From referendum to millennium', in R.A. Houston and W.W.J. Knox (eds) *The New Penguin History of Scotland: From the earliest times to the present day*. London: Penguin Books.

—— (2004) *Scotland and Nationalism: Scottish society and politics 1707 to the present*, 4th edn. London: Routledge.

Hassan, G. and Lynch, P. (2001) *The Almanac of Scottish Politics*. London: Politico's.

Hearl, D.J., Budge, I. and Pearson, B. (1996) 'Distinctiveness of Regional Voting: A comparative analysis across the European Community (1979–1993)', *Electoral Studies*, 15 (2): 167–82.

Hechter, M. (1975) *Internal Colonialism: The Celtic fringe in British national development, 1536–1966*. London: Routledge & Kegan Paul.

Helle, K. (ed.) (2006) *Vestlandets historie*, vols 1–3. Bergen: Vigmostad og Bjørke.

Henderson, A. (2007) *Hierarchies of Belonging: National identity and political culture in Scotland and Quebec*. Montreal: McGill-Queen's University Press.

Hix, S. (1999) *The Political System of the European Union*. Basingstoke, UK: Palgrave.

Hjellum, T. (2000) 'Kven skal styra Vestlandet?', *Stavanger Aftenblad*, 20 June.

Hodne, F. (1975) *An Economic History of Norway 1815–1970*. Trondheim: Tapir.

Hooghe, L. (2004) 'Belgium: Hollowing the center', in U.M. Amoretti and N. Bermeo (eds) *Federalism and Territorial Cleavages*. Baltimore: Johns Hopkins University Press.

Hooghe, L. and Marks, G. (2001) *Multi-level Governance and European Integration*. Lanham, MD: Rowman & Littlefield.

Hooghe, L., Marks, G. and Schakel, A.H. (2008) 'Regional Authority in 42 Countries, 1950–2006: A measure and five hypotheses', *Regional and Federal Studies*, 18 (2–3): 111–302.

Hopkin, J. (2003) 'Political Decentralization, Electoral Change and Party Organizational Adaptation: A framework for analysis', *European Urban and Regional Studies*, 10 (3): 227–37.

Hopkin, J. and Bradbury, J. (2006) 'British Statewide Parties and Multilevel Politics', *Publius: The Journal of Federalism*, 36 (1): 135–52.

Hutchinson, R. (2005) *A Waxing Moon: The modern Gaelic revival*. Edinburgh: Mainstream.

Hutchison, I.G.C. (2002) 'Scottish Newspapers and Scottish National Identity in the Nineteenth and Twentieth Centuries'. Paper presented at the IFLA Council and General Conference, Glasgow, 18–24 August.

Jolly, S.K. (2008) 'Strange Bedfellows: Public support for the EU among sub-state nationalists'. Paper presented at the MPSA Annual Conference, Chicago, 4 April.

Karl, T.L. (1997) *The Paradox of Plenty: Oil booms and petro-states*. Berkeley: University of California Press.

Keating, M. (1988) *State and Regional Nationalism: Territorial politics and the European state*. Hemel Hempstead, UK: Harvester Wheatsheaf.

—— (1998) *The New Regionalism in Western Europe: Territorial restructuring and political change*. Cheltenham, UK: Edward Elgar.

—— (1999a) 'Asymmetrical Government: Multinational states in an integrating Europe', *Publius: The Journal of Federalism*, 29 (1): 71–86.

—— (1999b) 'Regions and International Affairs: Motives, opportunities and strategies', *Regional and Federal Studies*, 9 (1): 1–16.

Kerremans, B. and Beyers, J. (1997) 'The Belgian Sub-national Entities in the European Union: Second or third level players?', in C. Jeffery (ed.) *The Regional Dimension of the European Union: Towards a third level in Europe?* London: Frank Cass.

Khaldûn, I. (1967) *The Muqadimmah: An introduction to history*, abridged edn, trans. F. Rosenthal, ed. N.J. Dawood. Princeton, NJ: Princeton University Press. First published 1377.

Kuran, T. (1998) 'Ethnic Norms and Their Transformation through Reputational Cascades', *Journal of Legal Studies*, 27 (2, part 2): 623–59.

Kyambi, S. (2005) *Beyond Black and White: Mapping new immigrant communities.* London: Institute for Public Policy Research.

Lafont, R. (1967) *La Révolution régionaliste*. Paris: Gallimard.

Laitin, D.D. (1991) 'The National Uprisings in the Soviet Union', *World Politics*, 44 (1): 139–77.

Lancaster, T.D. and Lewis-Beck, M.S. (1989) 'Regional Vote Support: The Spanish case', *International Studies Quarterly*, 33 (1): 29–43.

Lane, J.-E. and Ersson, S.O. (1994) *Politics and Society in Western Europe*, 3rd edn. London: Sage.

Lane, J.-E., McKay, D. and Newton, K. (1997) *Political Data Handbook: OECD countries*, 2nd edn. Oxford: Oxford University Press.

Law, A. (2001) 'Near and Far: Banal national identity and the press in Scotland', *Media, Culture and Society*, 23 (3): 299–317.

Le Gales, P. and Harding, A. (1998) 'Cities and States in Europe', *West European Politics*, 21 (3): 120–45.

Lecomte, P. (1994) 'Rhône-Alpes Citizens in the Political System: An emerging regional identity', *Regional Politics and Policy*, 4 (2): 132–43.

Leamer, E.E. and Storper, M. (2001) 'The Economic Geography of the Internet Age', *Journal of International Business Studies*, 32 (4): 641–65.

Leeke, M. (2003) 'UK Election Statistics: 1945–2003'. House of Commons Library research paper 03/59.

Leknes, E., Bergsgard, N.A. and Fitjar, R.D. (2008) *I hierarkiets skygge: Samhandling mellom staten og fylkeskommunene.* IRIS report no. 239.

Lie, B. (2002) *Innvandring og innvandrere 2002*. Oslo: Statistisk Sentralbyrå.

Lieberman, E.S. (2005) 'Nested Analysis as a Mixed-Method Strategy for Comparative Research', *American Political Science Review*, 99 (3): 435–52.

Lijphart, A. (1977) *Democracy in Plural Societies: A comparative exploration.* New Haven, CT: Yale University Press.

Lipset, S.M. and Rokkan, S. (1967) 'Cleavage Structures, Party Systems, and Voter Alignments: An introduction', in S.M. Lipset and S. Rokkan (eds) *Party Systems and Voter Alignments.* New York: The Free Press.

Linz, J.J. (1973) 'Early State-Building and the Late Peripheral Nationalisms against the State: The case of Spain', in S.N. Eisenstadt and S. Rokkan (eds) *Building States and Nations: Models, analyses and data across three worlds.* Beverly Hills, CA: Sage.

Linz, J.J. and Stepan, A. (1996) *Problems of Democratic Transition and Consolidation: Southern Europe, South America and post-communist Europe.* Baltimore: Johns Hopkins University Press.

Loughlin, J. (1996) ' "Europe of the Regions" and the Federalization of Europe', *Publius: The Journal of Federalism*, 26 (4): 141–62.

—— (1997) 'Representing Regions in Europe: The Committee of the Regions', in C. Jeffery (ed.) *The Regional Dimension of the European Union: Towards a third level in Europe?* London: Frank Cass.

Lynch, P. (2001) *Scottish Government and Politics: An introduction*. Edinburgh: Edinburgh University Press.

—— (2002) *SNP: The History of the Scottish National Party*. Cardiff: Welsh Academic Press.

McAllister, I. and Studlar, D.T. (1992) 'Region and Voting in Britain, 1979–87: Territorial polarisation or artefact?', *American Journal of Political Science*, 36 (1): 168–99.

McCrone, D. (1999) 'Opinion Polls in Scotland: July 1998 – June 1999', *Scottish Affairs*, 28: 32–43.

—— (2001) *Understanding Scotland: The sociology of a nation*, 2nd edn. London: Routledge.

McCrone, G. (1993) 'The Scottish Economy and European Integration', *Scottish Affairs*, 4: 5–22.

McGraw, K. (1990) 'Avoiding Blame: An experimental investigation of political excuses and justifications', *British Journal of Political Science*, 20 (1): 119–31.

MacInnes, J., Rosie, M., Petersoo, P., Condor, S. and Kennedy, J. (2007) 'Where Is the British National Press?', *British Journal of Sociology*, 58 (2): 185–205.

Mackenzie, J.L. (1994) 'Western Europe', in C. Moseley and R.E. Asher (eds) *Atlas of the World's Languages*. London: Routledge.

MacLeod, M. (1996) 'Folk Revival in Gaelic Song', in A. Munro, *The Democratic Muse: Folk music revival in Scotland*, 2nd edn. Aberdeen: Scottish Cultural Press.

McRoberts, K. (2001) *Catalonia: Nation building without a state*. Oxford: Oxford University Press.

Máiz, R. and Losada, A. (2000) 'Institutions, Policies and Nation Building: The Galician case', *Regional and Federal Studies*, 10 (1): 62–91.

Marks, G. (1997) 'An Actor-Centred Approach to Multi-level Governance', in C. Jeffery (ed.) *The Regional Dimension of the European Union: Towards a third level in Europe?* London: Frank Cass.

—— (1999) 'Territorial Identities in the European Union', in J. Anderson (ed.) *Regional Integration and Democracy: Expanding on the European experience*. Lanham, MD: Rowman & Littlefield.

Marks, G., Nielsen, F., Ray, L. and Salk, J.E. (1996) 'Competencies, Cracks, and Conflicts: Regional mobilization in the European Union', *Comparative Political Studies*, 29 (2): 164–92.

Martínez-Herrera, E. (2005) 'The Effects of Political Decentralisation on Support for Political Communities: A multivariate, longitudinal and cross-sectional comparison of the Basque Country, Catalonia, Galicia, Quebec and Scotland', PhD thesis, European University Institute.

Melberg, K. (1997) 'Fra bedehus til plattform? Politisk preferansedannelse i en oljehovedstad', in H. Rommetvedt (ed.) *Verdier og valg: Oljehovedstadens politiske kulturlandskap*. Oslo: Norges forskningsråd.

Mény, Y. (1986) 'The Political Dynamics of Regionalism: Italy, France, Spain', in R. Morgan (ed.) *Regionalism in European Politics*. London: Policy Studies Institute.

Ministero dell'Interno (1996) 'Camprop.xls' from *21aprile1996.zip* [computer file]. Online, available at: http://politiche.interno.it/dati/camera/21aprile1996.zip (accessed 20 January 2009).

Mitchell, J. (1997) 'Scotland, the Union State and the International Environment', in M. Keating and J. Loughlin (eds) *The Political Economy of Regionalism*. London: Frank Cass.

Moreno, L. (1986) 'Decentralisation in Britain and Spain: The cases of Scotland and Catalonia', PhD thesis, University of Edinburgh.

—— (2001) *The Federalization of Spain*. London: Frank Cass.

—— (2002) 'Decentralization in Spain', *Regional Studies*, 36 (4): 399–408.

—— (2006) 'Scotland, Catalonia, Europeanization and the "Moreno Question"', *Scottish Affairs*, 54 (1): 1–21.

Moreno, L., Arriba, A. and Serrano, A. (1998) 'Multiple Identities in Decentralised Spain: The case of Catalonia', *Regional and Federal Studies*, 8 (3): 65–88.

Munro, A. (1996) *The Democratic Muse: Folk music revival in Scotland*, 2nd edn. Aberdeen: Scottish Cultural Press.

Nairn, T. (1977) *The Break-up of Britain: Crisis and neo-nationalism*. London: New Left Books.

—— (2000) *After Britain: New Labour and the return of Scotland*. London: Granta.

National Readership Survey (2006) 'Newspapers & Supplements'. Online, available at: www.nrs.co.uk/open_access/open_topline/newspapers/index.cfm (accessed 22 August 2006).

Nordvik, H.W. (1987) 'Fra plog til platform: Rogalands næringsliv 1880–1980', in E. Hovland and H.E. Næss (eds) *Fra Vistehola til Ekofisk: Rogaland gjennom tidene*, vol. 2. Oslo: Universitetsforlaget.

OECD (2002) *Economic Surveys: Norway*, vol. 2002/15. Paris: Organisation for Economic Co-operation and Development.

Office for National Statistics (1996) *Regional Trends 1965–1995*. [CD-ROM].

Ohmae, K. (1995) *The End of the Nation State: The rise of regional economies*. London: HarperCollins.

Olivesi, C. (1998) 'The Failure of Regionalist Party Formation in Corsica', in De Winter, L. and Tursan, H. (eds) *Regionalist Parties in Western Europe*. London: Routledge.

Oswald, F. (2004) 'Negotiating Identities: The Party of Democratic Socialism between East German regionalism, German national identity and European integration', *Australian Journal of Politics and History*, 50 (1): 75–85.

Parker, G. (ed.) (1993) *The Times Atlas of World History*, 4th edn. London: Times Books.

Pattie, C. and Johnston, R. (1995) '"It's Not Like That Round Here": Region, economic evaluations and voting at the 1992 British general election', *European Journal of Political Research*, 28 (1): 1–32.

Persson, T. and Tabellini, G. (2000) *Political Economics: Explaining economic policy*. Cambridge, MA: MIT Press.

Pettersen, P.A., Todal Jenssen, A.T. and Listhaug, O. (1996) 'The 1994 EU Referendum in Norway: Continuity and change', *Scandinavian Political Studies*, 19 (3): 257–81.

Pettersen, S.V. (2003) *Bosettingsmønster og segregasjon i storbyregionene: Ikke-vestlige innvandrere og grupper med høy og lav utdanning*. Oslo: Statistisk Sentralbyrå.

Pierson, P. (1996) 'The New Politics of the Welfare State', *World Politics*, 48 (2): 143–79.

Pittock, M.G.H. (2001) *Scottish Nationality*. Basingstoke, UK: Palgrave.

Randall, V. and Theobald, R. (1998) *Political Change and Underdevelopment*, 2nd edn. Basingstoke, UK: Palgrave.

Reif, K. and Melich, A. (1998) *Eurobarometer 36.0: Regional identity and perceptions of the Third World, Fall 1991* [Computer file]. Conducted by INRA (Europe), Brussels. ICSPR ed. Ann Arbor: Inter-university Consortium for Political and Social Research, and Cologne: Zentralarchiv für Empirische Sozialforschung.

Renan, E. (1882) *Qu'est-ce qu'une nation?* Paris: Calmann-Levy.

Reve, T. (2003) 'Først kommer Rogaland...', *Rogaland i utvikling*, 8 (4): 46–7.

Riffe, D., Lacy, S.R. and Fico, F.G. (1998) *Analyzing Media Messages: Using quantitative content analysis in research*. Mahwah, NJ: Lawrence Erlbaum.

Rogaland i utvikling (2004) 'E39 Rogfast: Regional utvikling på sitt beste!', *Rogaland i utvikling*, 9 (1): 28–32.

Rokkan, S. (1967) 'Geography, Religion, and Social Class: Crosscutting cleavages in Norwegian politics', in S.M. Lipset and S. Rokkan (eds) *Party Systems and Voter Alignments*. New York: Free Press.

—— (1970) 'Nation-Building, Cleavage Formation and the Structuring of Mass Politics', in *Citizens, Elections, Parties: Approaches to the comparative study of the processes of development*. Oslo: Universitetsforlaget.

—— (1975) 'Dimensions of State Formation and Nation-Building: A possible paradigm for research on variations within Europe', in C. Tilly (ed.) *The Formation of National States in Western Europe*. Princeton, NJ: Princeton University Press.

Rokkan, S. and Urwin, D.W. (1982) 'Introduction: Centres and peripheries in Western Europe', in S. Rokkan and D.W. Urwin (eds) *The Politics of Territorial Identity: Studies in European regionalism*. London: Sage.

—— (1983) *Economy, Territory, Identity: Politics of West European peripheries*. London: Sage.

Roksvold, T. (1998) 'Norsk mediespråk', *Språknytt*, 26 (1).

Rosenkilden (2003) 'Vestlandspresidenten', 10 (1): 6–7.

Saxton, G.D. and Benson, M.A. (2006) 'Structure, Politics, and Action: An integrated model of nationalist protest and rebellion', *Nationalism and Ethnic Politics*, 12 (2): 137–75.

Schrijver, F. (2005) 'Regionalism in Galicia after Regionalisation', *Tijdschrift voor Economische en Sociale Geografie*, 96 (3): 275–86.

Schumpeter, J.A. (1961) *Capitalism, Socialism and Democracy*, 4th edn. London: George Allen & Unwin.

Scotsman, The (24 June 2006) 'Backlash fear as spending gap grows'.

Scott, A.J. (1998) *Regions and the World Economy: The coming shape of global production, competition, and political order*. Oxford: Oxford University Press.

Scott, A.J. and Storper, M. (2003) 'Regions, Globalization, Development', *Regional Studies*, 37 (6 and 7): 579–93.

Scottish National Party (1971) *Research Bulletin*, no. 6, June.

—— (1992) *Independence in Europe: Change now for a better life. The case for national status for Scotland as an independent member of the European Community*. Edinburgh: SNP.

—— (2001) *Heart of the Manifesto 2001*.

—— (2005) *If Scotland Matters to You Make It Matter in May*.

—— (2006) The True Wealth of the Nation: Taking a new look at Scotland's financial position.

Seip, J.A. (1974) *Fra embetsmannsstat til ettpartistat*. Oslo: Universitetsforlaget.

Smith, A. D. (1986) *The Ethnic Origins of Nations*. Oxford: Basil Blackwell.

Smith-Solbakken, M. (1997) 'Oljearbeiderkulturen: Historien om cowboyer og rebeller', PhD thesis, Norwegian University of Science and Technology.

Smouts, M.-C. (1998) 'The Region as the New Imagined Community', in P. Le Galés and C. Lequesne (eds) *Regions in Europe*. London: Routledge.

Sorens, J. (2004) 'Globalization, Secessionism, and Autonomy', *Electoral Studies*, 23 (4): 727–52.

—— (2005) 'The Cross-sectional Determinants of Secessionism in Advanced Democracies', *Comparative Political Studies*, 38 (3): 304–26.

Statistische Ämter (2008) *Volkswirtschaftliche Gesamtrechnungen der Länder*. Stuttgart:

Statistiches Landesamt Baden-Württemberg. Online, available at: www.statistik-bw.de/Arbeitskreis_VGR/tbls/tab01.asp (accessed 17 December 2008).

Statistisk Sentralbyrå (1970) *Regionalt nasjonalregnskap, 1965.* NOS A376. Oslo: Statistisk Sentralbyrå.

—— (1978a–2005) *Fylkesfordelt nasjonalregnskap.* Various issues. Oslo: Statistisk Sentralbyrå.

—— (1978b) *Historisk statistikk, 1978.* Oslo: Statistisk Sentralbyrå.

—— (1995) *The 1994 Referendum on Norwegian Membership of the EU.* NOS C235. Oslo: Statistisk Sentralbyrå.

—— (2002) *Statistical Yearbook of Norway 2002.* NOS C714. Oslo: Statistisk Sentralbyrå.

Stavanger Aftenblad, 1960–2008. Various issues.

Stavanger2008 (2003) *European Capital of Culture: The application.*

Stewart, S. (2008) 'Producing Current Price GDP Estimates for Scotland', *Scottish Economic Statistics*. Edinburgh: The Scottish Government.

Süssner, J. (2002) 'Culture, Identity and Regional Development in the European Union', *Informationen zur Raumentwicklung*, heft 4/5: 199–206.

Swenden, W. (2006) *Federalism and Regionalism in Western Europe: A comparative and thematic analysis.* Basingstoke, UK: Palgrave Macmillan.

Thatcher, M. (1993) *The Downing Street Years.* London: HarperCollins.

Torpey, J. (1994) 'Affluent Secessionists: Italy's Northern League', *Dissent*, Summer, 311–15.

Treisman, D.S. (1997) 'Russia's "Ethnic Revival": The separatist activism of regional leaders in a postcommunist order', *World Politics*, 49 (2): 212–49.

TV2 (Norway) (15 September 2004) 'Høybråten skremmer velgerne'. Online, Available at: http://pub.tv2.no/TV2/nyhetene/article278802.ece (accessed 29 March 2006).

Urwin, D. (1982): 'Conclusion: Perspectives on conditions of regional protest and accommodation', in S. Rokkan and D. Urwin (eds) *The Politics of Territorial Identity: Studies in European regionalism.* London: Sage.

Valen, H. and Aardal, B.O. (1995) *Konflikt og opinion.* Oslo: NKS.

Van Houten, P. (2003) 'Globalization and Demands for Regional Autonomy in Europe', in M. Kahler and D.A. Lake (eds) *Governance in a Global Economy: Political authority in transition.* Princeton, NJ: Princeton University Press.

Venås, K. (1998) 'Dialekt og normaltalemål', *Apollon*, 8 (1). Online, available at: www.apollon.uio.no/apollon01-98/dialekt.html (accessed 16 January 2009).

Vilar, P. (1963) *Historia de España.* Paris: Libraire Espagnole.

Wodak, R., de Cillia, R., Reisigl, M. and Liebhart, K. (1999) *The Discursive Construction of National Identity.* Edinburgh: Edinburgh University Press.

Wolczuk, K. (2002) 'Conclusion: Identities, regions and Europe', *Regional and Federal Studies*, 12 (2): 203–13.

Wold, K. (2002) 'Splitter naken var saken', *Stavanger Aftenblad*, 13 June.

YouGov (2008) 'Scotland Trackers'. Online, available at: www.yougov.com/uk/archives/pdf/Scotland%20trackers.pdf (accessed 19 December 2008).

Zürn, M. and Lange, P. (1999) 'Regionalism in the Age of Globalization'. InIIS-Arbeitspapier nr. 16/99, Universität Bremen.

Index